The Tsars

Ronald Hingley

THE TSARS

1533–1917

The Macmillan Company

New York

Library of Congress Catalog Card Number 68–24114

First American edition 1968

Originally published in Great Britain, 1968, by
   Weidenfeld and Nicolson, Ltd., London

The Macmillan Company, New York

Collier-Macmillan Canada Ltd., Toronto, Ontario

PRINTED IN ENGLAND

To my wife

Contents

CONTENTS

Illustrations

ILLUSTRATIONS

The murder of Tsarevich Dmitry. Contemporary painting. Bibliothèque Slave, Paris (photo: Foliot)

An audience given in the Kremlin by False Dmitry I. Contemporary painting in the State Historical Museum, Moscow. From a facsimile in the British Museum

The wedding by proxy of False Dmitry I and Maryna Mniszech. Contemporary painting in the State Historical Museum, Moscow. From a facsimile in the British Museum

Tsar Vasily Shuysky. British Museum

The reception of a foreign embassy in Moscow in the sixteenth century. Engraving from J. Ulefeld, Hodoeporicon Ruthenicum, 1608

False Dmitry II. Contemporary print. British Museum

Fighting at Kitay-Gorod in Moscow, 1612. Water-colour by G. Lissner. Museum of the History and Reconstruction of Moscow (Novosti)

Between pages 84 and 93

Michael, the first Tsar of the Romanov dynasty. Equestrian portrait by an unknown seventeenth-century artist. State Historical Museum, Moscow (Novosti)

The proclamation of Tsar Michael's election to the throne. Miniature from the seventeenth-century Book of the Election of Michael Fyodorovich as Tsar. State Historical Museum, Moscow (Novosti)

The orb of the Great Order of Tsar Michael. Kremlin Museum. From Lord Twining, The Crown Jewels of Europe, Batsford, 1960

The Patriarch Philaret. Anonymous seventeenth-century portrait. State Historical Museum, Moscow (Novosti)

The consecration of Philaret as Patriarch. Miniature from the Book of the Election of Michael Fyodorovich as Tsar. State Historical Museum, Moscow (Novosti)

Tsar Alexis. Portrait from the Titulyarnik of 1672. State Historical Museum, Moscow (Novosti)

Tsar Alexis and the Patriarch Nikon. Nineteenth-century lithograph. British Museum

The Patriarch Nikon instructing the clergy. Portrait, probably by Daniel Wuchters, 1667. State Museum, Istra

Plan of the Kremlin during the reign of Tsar Alexis. British Museum

View of Moscow in the seventeenth century, from Olearius's Journey to Muscovy, 1660

Plan of Moscow, mid-seventeenth century. Engraving by Pieter van der Aa, 1717. British Museum

Between pages 106 and 115

The reception of foreign ambassadors by Tsar Alexis. From Olearius's Journey to Muscovy, 1660

Three sketches by A. von Mayerberg, ambassador of the Holy Roman Empire, 1661–2. British Museum

The Palm Sunday procession, 23 March 1662. A sketch by A. von Mayerberg. British Museum

Stenka Razin being driven to execution in 1671. Contemporary English engraving. British Museum

State drive by the Tsaritsa, 1674. From Palmkvist's Album. State Historical Museum, Moscow (Novosti)

The boyar Afanasy Ordin-Nashchokin. Anonymous seventeenth-century portrait. State Historical Museum, Moscow (Novosti)

A boyar. Seventeenth-century German impression. British Museum

Theodore III. Seventeenth-century portrait by Saltanov. State Historical Museum, Moscow (Novosti)

An archbishop. Seventeenth-century German impression. British Museum

Theodore III, Ivan V, and Peter I as a child. Early eighteenth-century print. British Museum

Between pages 128 and 137

The Streltsy carrying stones for their commemorative pillar in Red Square. Miniature from Krekshin's *History of Peter the Great*. State Historical Museum, Moscow *(Novosti)*

The diamond crown of Ivan v. Kremlin Museum. From Lord Twining, *The Crown Jewels of Europe*, Batsford, 1960

The Regent Sophia. Anonymous early eighteenth-century portrait. State Historical Museum, Moscow *(Novosti)*

Prince Vasily Golitsyn. Anonymous late seventeenth-century portrait. State Historical Museum, Moscow *(Novosti)*

The boyar Leo Naryshkin. Seventeenth-century portrait. State Historical Museum, Moscow *(Novosti)*

The siege of Azov. Engraving, *c.*1699. State Hermitage Museum, Leningrad *(Novosti)*

A cartoon from Peter the Great's reign showing the compulsory clipping of beards *(Radio Times Hulton Picture Library)*

Knouting, a traditional form of beating suspects. Engraving by J. B. Tilliard from Chappe d'Auteroche, *Voyage en Sibérie*

The morning of Streltsy's execution. Nineteenth-century impression by V. Surikov. Tretyakov Gallery *(Novosti)*

Two etchings of the Streltsy by Le Prince, 1765. British Museum

The execution of the Streltsy in Moscow in September 1698. Engraving from J. C. Korb, *Diarium Itineris in Moscoviam*, 1700

The Battle of Poltava (1709). Painting by Nattier. State Hermitage Museum, Leningrad *(Novosti)*

Between pages 144 and 153

Marble bust of Peter the Great by Carlo Rastrelli. Lomonosov Museum, Leningrad *(photo: Victor Kennett)*

Anonymous caricature of Peter the Great. Musée Conde

Contemporary French print of Catherine i. British Museum

Catherine i. Late eighteenth-century engraving by D. Chodowiecki. British Museum

The wedding banquet of Peter the Great and Catherine (1712). Engraving by A. Zubov. State Hermitage Museum, Leningrad *(Novosti)*

Wedding of Volkov. Painting by A. Zubov. Pushkin Fine Arts Museum, Moscow *(Novosti)*

Peter the Great's fleet at Archangel. Engraving from J. C. Korb, *Diarium Itineris in Moscoviam*, 1700

Captured Swedish frigates entering St Petersburg. Engraving by Zubov, 1720. British Museum

The Tsarevich Alexis, son of Peter the Great. Contemporary engraving. British Museum

Peter the Great on his deathbed in 1725. Engraving by D. Chodowiecki. British Museum

Catherine i. Painting by Nattier. State Historical Museum, Leningrad *(Novosti)*

Alexander Menshikov. Marble bust by Rastrelli. Russian Museum, Leningrad *(Photo: Victor Kennett)*

Between pages 170 and 179

Coronation procession of the Empress Anne, 28 April 1730. Contemporary engraving. British Museum

Scene at the coronation inside the Uspensky Cathedral. Engraving of 1730. British Museum

Scene from a masquerade at the court of the Empress Anne. British Museum

Bronze statue of the Empress Anne by Rastrelli. Russian Museum, Leningrad *(photo: Victor Kennett)*

The celebration of the birth of Ivan vi. Contemporary German engraving. British Museum

The coronation of the Empress Elizabeth. Contemporary engraving. Bibliothèque Nationale (*photo: Foliot*)

The Empress Elizabeth. Painting by L. Tocque. Razumovsky Collection (*Photo: Giraudon*)

The *coup* of 26 November 1741 which brought the Empress Elizabeth to power. Contemporary German print. British Museum

Peter III, Catherine II and Paul. Painting of 1756 by R. M. Lisiewska. Gripsholm Castle (*Svenska Porträttarkivet, Stockholm*)

Stanislaus Augustus, King of Poland 1764-95. Painting by Bacciarelli. Gripsholm Castle (*Svenska Porträttarkivet, Stockholm*)

Gregory Potemkin, Prince of Tauris. Portrait by H. Löschenkohl. Historisches Museum der Stadt Wien

Platon Zubov, the last of Catherine the Great's favourites. Portrait by Lampi. Bibliothèque Nationale (*photo: Foliot*)

Peter III. A mosaic portrait after an original of 1758, probably by Antropov. Russian Museum, Leningrad (*photo: Victor Kennett*)

Countess Elizabeth Vorontsov, mistress of Peter III. Bibliothèque Nationale (*photo: Foliot*)

Between pages 204 and 213

· Scenes from the life of Catherine II. Three engravings by D. Chodowiecki. British Museum

Peterhof, the Tsars' residence on the Gulf of Finland. Contemporary engraving. British Museum

Catherine II. Mosaic portrait of 1763. Russian Museum, Leningrad (*photo: Victor Kennett*)

Catherine the Great and Joseph II of Austria. Water-colour by H. Löschenkohl. Historisches Museum der Stadt Wien

The coronation of Catherine II in 1762. Painting by S. Torelli. Academy of Arts, Leningrad (*Photo: Alinari*)

Catherine II taking communion. Bibliothèque Nationale (*photo: Foliot*)

Allegorical portrayal of Catherine the Great travelling through her Empire. Bibliothèque Nationale (*photo: Foliot*)

Russian victory over the Turks in 1770. Contemporary engraving by D. Chodowiecki. British Museum

Workmen moving the granite block for Peter the Great's statue in St Petersburg. Engraving of 1770. British Museum

The Bronze Horseman, equestrian statue by Falconet of Peter the Great (*photo: Camera Press*)

Scene from the play *Oleg* by Catherine the Great. Contemporary engraving. British Museum

Catherine the Great playing with her grandsons, Alexander and Constantine. Contemporary engraving. British Museum

Catherine the Great. Portrait by Lampi. Winter Palace, Leningrad (*photo: Alinari*)

Two scenes from Russian life at the end of the eighteenth century. Engravings from J. C. G. Geissler, *Tableaux Pittoresques de l'Empire Russe*, 1798

Between pages 230 and 239

The Emperor Paul. Portrait by Lampi. Gripsholm Castle (*Svenska Porträttarkivet, Stockholm*)

Caricature of the Emperor Paul. Engraving of 1804. British Museum

The Emperor Paul with his wife. Water-colour by H. Löschenkohl. Historisches Museum der Stadt Wien

Alexander I. Contemporary French print. British Museum

The Empress Elizabeth, wife of Alexander I. After a painting by Monier. British Museum

English cartoon showing Alexander I, Napoleon and the King of Prussia at Tilsit in 1807. Bibliothèque Nationale (*photo: Foliot*)

Contemporary French cartoon of the Napleonic wars. British Museum

A Russian soldier disposing of a French invader. From a Russian folk-print. British Museum

The meeting of Alexander I, Francis II of Austria and King Frederick William III of Prussia in Prague in 1813. Contemporary print. British Museum

Alexander riding in triumph into Paris on 19 March 1814. Engraving after J. Wolf. British Museum

The Russians in Paris. Contemporary French caricature. British Museum

The Moscow Kremlin in 1815. British Museum

General Count Alexis Arakcheyev. Etching from a portrait of 1818. State Historical Museum, Moscow *(Novosti)*

Between pages 246 and 255

The Grand Duke Constantine. English caricature of 1826. British Museum

The Emperor Nicholas I, the Grand Duchess Alexandra and the future Emperor Alexander II. Contemporary print. British Museum

Nicholas I driving along the embankment of the River Neva. After a painting by Sverchkov. British Museum

Four scenes from the coronation of Nicholas I in Moscow in 1826. Lithograph of 1828. Pushkin Fine Arts Museum, Moscow *(Novosti)*

The signing of the Peace of Turkmanchay on 10 February 1828. After a painting by Mashkov. British Museum

Russian officers of the reign of Nicholas I. From M. A. Demidoff, *Voyage dans la Russie méridionale*, 1840

The five Decembrists hanged on 13 July 1826. British Museum

Nicholas I on his visit to England, 1844. From *The Illustrated London News*

Russian landowners and their serfs. French caricature from G. Doré, *Histoire de la sainte Russie*, 1854

Nicholas I. From a contemporary print. British Museum

Between pages 262 and 271

Alexander II. Portrait from *The Illustrated London News*, 1881

The successful bomb attack by revolutionaries on Alexander II on 1 March 1881. British Museum

The explosion of the second bomb on the Catherine Quay. British Museum

Alexander II after death. From *The Illustrated London News*, 1881

Lieutenant Nicholas Sukhanov, nihilist and naval officer *(Staatsbibliothek Berlin)*

A scene from the Kiev pogrom of 1881 *(Radio Times Hulton Picture Library)*

Russian peasants in the second half of the nineteenth century. British Museum

Alexander III with his wife, the former Princess of Denmark, and son *(Radio Times Hulton Picture Library)*

Alexander III. British Museum

The Empress Mary, wife of Alexander III. British Museum

Constantine Pobedonostsev, tutor to Alexander III and Nicholas II. From *Leipziger Illustrierte Zeitung*, 1888

Between pages 278 and 287

Nicholas II as Tsarevich. British Museum

Nicholas II and the Tsaritsa Alexandra in full coronation regalia *(Radio Times Hulton Picture Library)*

Coronation procession of Nicholas II in the streets of Moscow *(Radio Times Hulton Picture Library)*

Nicholas II with his wife, the future Empress Alexandra. British Museum

ILLUSTRATIONS

Picture-research by Georgina Bruckner

Layout of illustrations by Jane McKay

MAPS

The maps were drawn by Arthur Banks, based on Allen F. Chew, 'An Atlas of Russian History' (Yale University Press, 1967)

GENEALOGY TABLES

Preface

The present volume offers studies of all the Russian autocrats from Ivan IV to Nicholas II, but without attempting to provide, except incidentally, a general history of Russia during the years of their rule. Despite many outstanding individual contributions on aspects of the Russian autocracy, no adequate general review of all the Tsars, Tsar-Emperors and Empresses appears to exist in any language – it has seldom even been attempted. There are, by contrast, many admirable general histories of Russia, no other field of Russian studies (certainly not literature) being so well endowed. On these general histories, beginning with those of the classic native historians of Russia – Karamzin, Solovyov, Kostomarov, Klyuchevsky and Platonov – the present study leans heavily, as also on more recent general historians of Russia writing in languages other than Russian – including Stählin, Florinsky and Stökl. Besides these works, more detailed studies of aspects of the problem have also been extensively quarried, as has the material left by the monarchs themselves in the shape of memoirs, correspondence and so on. These and other sources are listed in the bibliography.

So rich is the subject and so varied and numerous are the sources that an attempt to compass the material within a single volume has involved an unusually rigorous process of selection. The main aim has always been to give an account of what the Tsars did (as a clue to their nature and inclinations), and also of what was done to them. As this reminds one, there was a tendency for individual autocrats to be active or passive, and in either case to excess. Of this the first two Tsars provide outstanding examples, the egregiously active Ivan IV (the Terrible) being followed by his son Theodore, in whose character the element of personal initiative appears to have been entirely lacking. Among later Tsars, Peter the Great was the most creatively potent of all. Another remarkable leader, Nicholas I, devoted his considerable enterprise to crushing the enterprise of others, while his great-grandson

Nicholas II, the last ruler of the Romanov dynasty, tended to leave initiative to others, though without proceeding as far in this direction as certain of his sixteenth- and seventeenth-century predecessors. This polarizing trend affected the ladies too, among whom Catherine the Great was the outstanding trail-blazer while Catherine I, Anne and to some extent Elizabeth belonged rather to the quiescent order of rulers.

In stressing this tendency of Russian rulers to be active or passive, and in either case to excess, one is reminded that the characters in Dostoyevsky's fiction exhibit the same trend, being frequently divided by critics into strong and meek types. Dostoyevsky's characters, his adults perhaps more than his children, also have a marked tendency to manifest infantile characteristics in behaviour – which again reminds one of the Tsars. The point here is not so much that these rulers were necessarily immature in their psychological development as that many of them were exempt, or became exempt on accession to the throne, from the normal educative discipline whereby more humble individuals find their will curbed on every hand by the claims and demands of others. Since an entire country hung on the whim of a Russian autocrat, he was in a position to ignore such claims and demands, though it was often very imprudent of him to do so. Hence Russian autocrats often present the spectacle of apparently childish caprice operating unchecked at the apex of a great empire. For this reason the autocracy provides a kind of laboratory, as do Dostoyevsky's novels, in which adult human behaviour can be studied under specialized conditions.

The history of the Russian autocracy further resembles the novels of Dostoyevsky in providing a sequence of grandiose scandals (*skandaly*), as if the Ryurikids and Romanovs were a Karamazov family writ even larger. Alexander I played Ivan Karamazov to his father Paul's Fyodor Pavlovich, while Ivan the Terrible and Peter the Great each maintained an opposite tradition by killing an eldest son and heir. On a more anecdotal level, one Tsar had an elephant cut to pieces for failing to bow to him, an Empress immured two of her court buffoons in a palace of ice, and a Tsar-Emperor reputedly settled arguments about the proposed route of the railway line between Moscow and St Petersburg with a ruler and pen. To stories of this kind the Tsars have given rise on such a scale as to impose a further discipline on their historian, who will be unwise to eschew anecdote altogether – but must somehow strike a proper balance between anecdote and more solid fare.

To a large extent Russian history is characterized by the rhythm of the *skandal* (the 'time of troubles' in the early seventeenth century providing the most violent sequence of such eruptions) and what may be called the 'counter-*skandal*' – a sort of 'hushing up' operation, in which many Russian historians have co-operated from understandable motives of national pride, seeking to cover the more out-

Nicholas I with his younger brother, the Grand Duke Michael, and his eldest son, the Tsarevich Alexander (the future Alexander II). Colour print after Kruger.

rageous events with a veneer of decorum. As the alternation of *skandal* and counter-*skandal* reminds one, and as is further emphasized below, Russians have tended in their collective manifestations to oscillate between the extremes of total anarchy and total regimentation on a scale to which few other peoples have aspired. But it is beyond our scope to determine whether this oscillatory process derives from climate, Tatar-Mongol occupation in the Middle Ages, the swaddling of infants up to the present day, or to some mysterious property enshrined in the Russian character. In any case the Romanov Tsars during the last century and a half of the dynasty were German rather than Russian by origin, for which reason their notable contribution to the rhythm of *skandal* and counter-*skandal* certainly cannot be explained as the emanation of a Russian national ethos.

To the scandalous nature of the story outlined on these pages the absence (before 1797) of any proper law of succession to the throne made a large contribution. Was the Russian crown before the nineteenth century hereditary, devolving on the eldest son? Or was it awarded by appointment in the sense that a reigning sovereign could designate his own successor? The throne was both these things in various degrees at various times, but during much of the eighteenth century it was neither – being occupied by candidates of the guards regiments in St Petersburg, including the Empresses Elizabeth and Catherine II. During this great century of the *skandal*, Russia flourished or groaned under autocratic rule usurped or tempered by assassination. It was the more legitimate eighteenth-century rulers (Peter III, Ivan VI) who suffered assassination, while the usurpers escaped this fate. This trend continued after the establishment by the Emperor Paul of the law of succession of 1797 – which spared Russia much in the way of dynastic crisis, but saved neither its author nor two of his crowned descendants from death by violence.

The present study is an attempt to show the Tsars as they were without any desire to whitewash them, but it is perhaps worth pointing out in this preface that they have been painted unduly black in general repute. This is partly due to strenuous efforts by official spokesmen of the USSR to tutor non-Russians in the attitudes to be adopted to Russian affairs. That the Tsars had many defects is undeniable, but it does not follow that they deserve the reputation of cruel monsters. Inheriting a system based on widespread use of torture and execution, most of them did at least leave it marginally less inhumane than they found it on taking over – with the notable exceptions of Ivan IV and Paul, who increased the element of cruelty and oppression during their tenure of supreme office. Modern students of the Tsars may naturally wish to condemn them for being unduly dilatory in demolishing the apparatus of oppression; but most of the Tsars at least belong to the tradition of a Khrushchev (with all his defects, a dismantler of terror) among their Soviet successors rather than to that of a Lenin or Stalin, who manufactured terror where none existed before. One Tsar in particular –

B

Alexander II – has a record for humane legislation unequalled by any other ruler of Russia, imperial or Soviet, and this despite his militantly reactionary outlook.

The Tsars were in general remarkable for their conscientiousness and industry in discharging their difficult task, which immeasurably increased in difficulty as the nineteenth and twentieth centuries proceeded. Few if any of them can properly be regarded as embodiments of evil, and they managed their cumbrous empire in a fashion probably less incompetent than their noisier critics would have contrived if elevated to a similar position.

The following terms for members of a Tsar's family perhaps require explanation: Tsaritsa=a Tsar's wife, Tsarevich=a Tsar's son, Tsarevna=a Tsar's daughter. The terms Tsesarevich and Tsesarevna were also used on occasion to designate the heir to the throne and his wife.

In the text below dates are given according to the system generally followed by historians of Russia, which differs from the calendar used in western Europe in certain respects. Russian names are transliterated or otherwise rendered along the lines laid down at some length in the prefaces to volumes i, ii, iii, and viii of *The Oxford Chekhov*, edited and translated by myself and published by the Oxford University Press.

I am deeply grateful to my colleagues Paul Foote, Alban Krailsheimer and Harry Willetts for their kindness in advising and encouraging me.

Frilford, Abingdon, 1968   RONALD HINGLEY

Genealogy of the Last Ryurikids and their Successors, with Dates of Rule

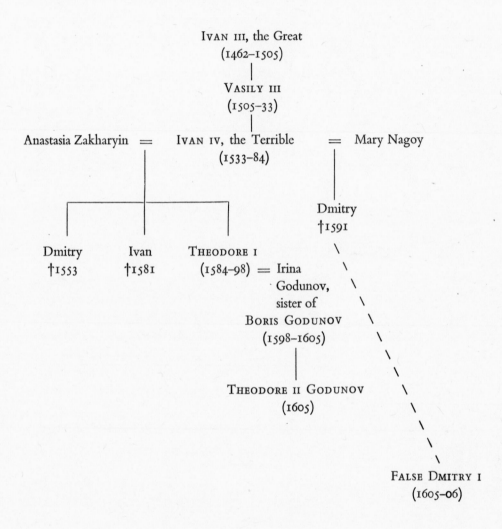

IVAN III, the Great
(1462–1505)

VASILY III
(1505–33)

Anastasia Zakharyin = IVAN IV, the Terrible = Mary Nagoy
(1533–84)

Dmitry
†1591

Dmitry   Ivan   THEODORE I
†1553   †1581   (1584–98) = Irina
                                       Godunov,
                                       sister of
                              BORIS GODUNOV
                                (1598–1605)

THEODORE II GODUNOV
(1605)

FALSE DMITRY I
(1605–06)

Part I   Before the Romanovs

1 Heir to Muscovy: Ivan IV, 'the Terrible'
1533-47

Ivan IV, better known in English as Ivan the Terrible, was the first Russian sovereign to be crowned Tsar and to hold Tsar as his fully official title in addition to the traditional title of grand duke. His coronation took place in Moscow on 16 January 1547 in the Uspensky Cathedral – where successive Tsars, Tsar-Emperors and Empresses were to be crowned in their turn during the next three and a half centuries until the monarchy itself collapsed. After outlasting all the Tsars, the cathedral still stands in a secularized Kremlin: onion-domed, many times restored and richly ornate with a profusion of icons, beaten gold and frescoes – some dating from the sixteenth century. It has witnessed its share of ritual splendours over the years, as also of unseemly outrages such as are part of the history of every nation, but in Russia seem particularly apt to erupt where the setting is most overwhelmingly decorous.

Though only sixteen years of age at the time of his coronation, Ivan himself was already a seasoned provoker of outrage. But no improprieties were permitted to mar the ceremony as he entered the cathedral resplendent in heavy robes and heading a procession of princes, boyars and other courtiers. A thunderous anthem greeted him as he solemnly took his place on a dais in the centre, sitting on a throne draped with cloth of gold while the Metropolitan of Moscow and All Russia took his place on another throne beside him. They rose together and the Metropolitan placed a richly decorated tippet on the Tsar's shoulders. Setting the crown on Ivan's head, he prayed that the Almighty should grant the youth a gracious eye towards his obedient subjects, but also make him the terror of the recalcitrant – the second of which hopes, at least, was to be fully realized in course of time. When the elaborate ceremony was completed, Ivan passed through the cathedral doorway, to be showered with gold coins by his feeble-minded younger brother Prince Yury and welcomed with great uproar by a throng of onlookers who were waiting to rush inside. The precious fabrics used during the ceremony were torn to pieces, more as relics than as souvenirs; for the common people revered their monarch as a semi-divine being, though it is also true that these pickings had a cash value.

By his devotion to pomp and ritual, by his close association with the church and by the august status accorded to him as one placed immeasurably high above his subjects, the first Tsar set the tone for his successors, on whom many contemporaries in western Europe came to look as oriental despots.

At the time of his coronation Ivan had already been nominal ruler of Muscovy, as the Russian state of the period is commonly known, for over thirteen years. Born on 25 August 1530, he had succeeded his father, Vasily III, as Grand Duke of Moscow in December 1533 at the age of three. His mother, the Grand Duchess Helen, became regent. She was aided by a lover with political interests, and contrived to keep Tatar and Lithuanian enemies at bay on Russia's frontiers, while also checking the many ambitions and intrigues which swirled around her son's throne. Ivan presumably enjoyed a comparatively stable childhood so long as she was alive, but found himself alone in the world when she suddenly died in April 1538 – reputedly by poison.

There was now no force capable of restraining the ambitious Muscovite aristocracy, which consisted of princes and boyars (the latter forming in principle a council of state to advise the ruler, though the term boyar was often used rather loosely). The years 1538–47 became notorious as a period of boyar rule. Misrule would be a better term, but there is no point in following here the twists and turns whereby members of the Shuysky, Belsky, Glinsky and other princely families outwitted, supplanted and murdered each other – inspired largely by motives of greed. It may be suggested in passing that this, if ever, was a time when more public-spirited and united noblemen might have asserted themselves by imposing limits on the triumphant march of Russian autocratic absolutism. But so far as Ivan's personal evolution is concerned, the important point is the disastrous effect which a background so lurid and menacing had on him as a sensitive and intelligent boy between the ages of seven and sixteen.

He must have felt himself in constant danger of assassination or imprisonment, for these things were happening on all sides. Yet he remained unscathed – perhaps the boyars, disorderly as they were, never quite lost their sense of the divinity which hedged a grand duke. But while deferring to the child Ivan on ceremonial occasions, they neglected and humiliated him in private – little suspecting that they were rearing an outstanding nurser of grudges. When Prince Ivan Shuysky, one of the many successive temporary masters of Russia (and apparently something of a contortionist), dared to lounge about in the boy's presence 'sitting on a bench, leaning his elbow on our father's bed and with his foot on a chair' (as Ivan later recorded),[1] he cannot have realized that he was offering an insult which would rankle throughout a lifetime and be avenged on countless others. It was this same prince's minions who once burst noisily into the young monarch's bedroom in the middle of the night. They were in hot pursuit of the Metropolitan of Moscow, an escapade typical of the period; but it was small consolation for Ivan to realize that armed hoodlums could hunt the chief Russian pontiff through the royal palace with impunity, and he was badly frightened. From such early fears the terror which he imposed in later life certainly derived in some degree.

Increasing self-assertion accompanied by a streak of viciousness is the theme of Ivan's adolescence. One favourite pastime was the tormenting of animals which he would toss to their death from high buildings, and he formed the habit of robbing and beating the people of his capital, galloping through streets and market-places at the head of a posse of high-born delinquents.[2] At the age of thirteen he chose a more formidable victim in Prince Andrew Shuysky, reigning warlord of the hour and most powerful man in Muscovy. He had the prince murdered by royal kennelmen, from which time onwards the 'boyars began to fear the sovereign', according to one early record.[3] For the slaughter of Prince Andrew, Ivan did not necessarily provide the main initiative, which may have come from the Metropolitan Macarius or from the Glinskys (his maternal grandmother and uncles), who now appear to have taken the Shuyskys' position as power behind the throne.

It was not until a little later ('when we reached the fifteenth year of our life', according to the Tsar's own testimony) that 'we took it upon ourselves to put our kingdom in order' – a claim which receives some confirmation from the fact that the same year, 1545, reportedly coincided with a wave of executions and mutilations.[4] It is tempting to describe the assumption of the title Tsar – and the decision to be crowned with that title in 1547 – as Ivan's outstanding act of self-assertion in youth. But unfortunately lack of evidence makes it hard to assess the degree of his personal initiative. Though the chief impulse may indeed have come from him – especially as he was to reveal himself in later life as master of such grand and simple gestures – it is also likely, once again, that the prime movers may have been the Glinskys or the Metropolitan.

Wherever the impulse arose, it is clear that Ivan greatly promoted the prestige of the Russian crown by adding the dignity of Tsar to the traditional title of grand duke. In Russian ears there were few words more vibrant with ancient grandeur, legend and fear than 'Tsar' – by ultimate origin a form of the Latin *Caesar*. A legend had gained currency whereby the ruling house of Muscovy was ultimately descended from a brother of Augustus Caesar named Prus, ancestor of the Prussians, and hence, by a curious twist, of the Russians. Less obviously ludicrous were the Old Testament echoes of the word. The early nineteenth-century Russian historian Karamzin calls Tsar a Biblical term which 'with its reminders of Assyrian, Egyptian, Jewish and ... Orthodox Greek monarchs raised the prestige of their sovereigns in Russian eyes'.[5] Of the associations listed by Karamzin the most recent – that with the Orthodox Greek (or Byzantine) Emperors – was especially potent. Their capital, Constantinople, was known to Russians as Tsartown (*Tsargrad*). By calling himself Tsar, the Russian sovereign was therefore posing as heir to a chain of defunct empires of which the latest had fallen to the Turks less than a hundred years previously. Finally, a more parochial association linked the word with the Tatars, Russia's deadly enemies and occasional allies for more than three centuries, whose rulers, or khans, the Russians were accustomed to call Tsars. This association added a dash of contemporary terror to ancient historical links.

Though the title of Tsar was new in Russia, its assumption was only an episode in the long history of Russian sovereignty which stretches back to the days of the Viking or Varangian Ryurik – said to have died in AD 879 and sometimes described as semi-legendary, but regarded in the days of the monarchy as official founder of the first Russian ruling house. Beginning in the ninth century, when Kiev became the centre of the first Russian state, the Ryurikid age includes the disintegration of Kievan Russia from the mid-eleventh century onwards; as also the conquest of Russia by the Tatars in the early thirteenth century and the Tatar yoke which lasted for over two hundred years, during which time the princes of Moscow raised themselves to the dignity of grand princes (or grand dukes, as *velikiye knyazya* is here translated) under Tatar overlordship, and their seat from obscurity to the capital of the Muscovite grand dukedom and core of the future Russian Empire.

At the time of Ivan's coronation the dynasty had, accordingly, spanned nearly seven centuries. The first Tsar represented the twentieth generation of Ryurik's line.[6]

Before Ivan's record as Tsar is examined, it is necessary to glance briefly at the Muscovy which he inherited.

An important development during the half century and more preceding the first Tsar's accession lay in the field of growing contact with the West, as Russia entered into diplomatic and cultural relations with European countries which had forgotten her existence or been barely aware of it previously. During the sixteenth century western Europeans – craftsmen, merchants, diplomats, doctors, mercenary soldiers, adventurers and charlatans – increasingly came to ply their trades in Moscow. Muscovy is thus found forging Russian links with Europe – or rather reforging them, since Kievan Russia had been part of the European community

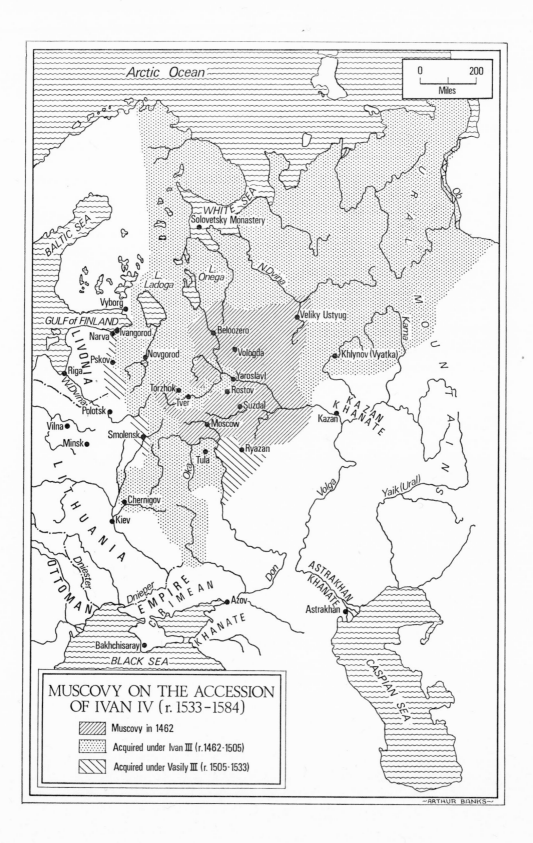

Arctic Ocean

0   200
Miles

BALTIC SEA

WHITE SEA

Solovetsky Monastery

L. Onega

L. Ladoga

N.Dvina

Kama

URAL MOUNTAINS

Ob

Vyborg

GULF of FINLAND

Narva • Ivangorod

Beloozero

Vologda

Veliky Ustyug

Khlynov (Vyatka)

LIVONIA

Pskov

Riga

W.Dvina

Novgorod

Yaroslavl

Torzhok • Rostov

Tver

Suzdal

KAZAN KHANATE

Polotsk

Moscow

Kazan

Vilna

Minsk

Smolensk

Ryazan

Oka

Tula

Volga

Yaik (Ural)

L I T H U A N I A

Chernigov

Kiev

Don

ASTRAKHAN KHANATE

OTTOMAN

Dniester

Dnieper

EMPIRE

CRIMEAN

Azov

Astrakhan

KHANATE

Bakhchisaray

BLACK SEA

CASPIAN SEA

MUSCOVY ON THE ACCESSION
OF IVAN IV (r. 1533–1584)

Muscovy in 1462

Acquired under Ivan III (r. 1462-1505)

Acquired under Vasily III (r. 1505-1533)

~ARTHUR BANKS~

before the arrival of the Tatars. On the western Europeans who penetrated Muscovy in the sixteenth century, Russians commonly made a strange and even barbarous impression. The very sight of them was startling. Here was a Christian people wearing clothes of eastern style, and practising the kowtow – an obeisance which consisted of banging the forehead on the ground and which they had acquired from their former Tatar masters. They kept their womenfolk secluded, but not so rigorously as to prevent them alarming visitors by their appearance, for Russian females went about daubed with extravagant cosmetics. Nor were the rigours of Muscovite purdah such as to save these ladies from a reputation for extreme wantonness. Besides sexual promiscuity the practices of wife-beating and drunkenness seemed characteristic of the country. The latter topic figures, for example, in the three remarkable verse epistles of the Elizabethan English poet George Turberville, who visited Moscow in 1568. He calls the Russians:

> A people passing rude, to vices vile inclinde,
> Folke fit to be of Bacchus traine, so quaffing in their kinde.
> Drinke is their whole desire, the pot is all their pride,
> The sobrest head doth once a day stand needfull of a guide.

Turberville's general impressions are that:

> Wilde Irish are as civil as the Russies in theyr kinde.
> Hard choice which is the best of both, ech bloudy, rude and blinde.[7]

These uncharitable comments well illustrate the impression which Muscovy made on most western observers in the sixteenth and seventeenth centuries. It was not yet the vast size of the country which struck visitors, for the first Tsar was heir to a land small indeed by comparison with the far-flung territory over which later Russian Tsar-Emperors and Communist dictators were to hold sway. The area of Muscovy was, in fact, about the same as that of England and Wales combined – roughly sixty thousand square miles. Only in the north of European Russia did the bounds of Ivan's realm coincide with those of the later Russian Empire and USSR in the sense of reaching the Arctic Ocean. The number of inhabitants fell somewhere between five or six million at the end of the fifteenth century and nine million odd fifty years later.[8] As these figures show, Muscovy's population was rapidly increasing. So was her territory – from the tiny nucleus of some three hundred square miles ruled from Moscow two centuries earlier to the area about two hundred times greater over which the first Tsar's fiat ran at his accession. This tradition of territorial expansion owed something to Ivan the Terrible's father, Grand Duke Vasily III, who ruled from 1505 to 1533. But the main architect of Muscovite expansion had been Ivan III, the Great (Ivan the Terrible's grandfather), who extended his domain in all directions except the south-east, multiplying the area under his rule about fourfold during his long reign from 1462 to 1505.

Having inherited or carved out a realm consisting to a large extent of Russian principalities recently independent, Ivan III set about fusing this amalgam into a centralized state with patience, cunning and brutality – qualities by now thoroughly bred into the Muscovite ruling house and later inherited in full by his grandson. Ivan III also made a point of adding the outer trappings of prestige to the realities of power. Besides such potent symbols as his marriage to a niece of the last Byzantine Emperor, his adoption of the double-headed eagle of Byzantium as his emblem, and the introduction of a more stylized court ceremonial on Byzantine lines, he also showed himself sensitive to the value of new titles. These included that of 'Tsar' itself (which he occasionally used in diplomatic dealings), besides 'autocrat' and 'sovereign'; he also made a practice of calling himself ruler 'of all Russia'.

The Russian church gave ideological support to Ivan III's grand designs. Even before the fall of Constantinople in 1453, Russian churchmen had already begun to think of Moscow as the centre of true Orthodoxy. And barely had the Greeks of Constantinople become vassals of the Turks before Moscow had moved decisively in the opposite direction by finally throwing off the Tatar yoke, the year 1480 being traditionally regarded as marking the formal end of Muscovite dependence on the disintegrating Tatar Golden Horde. Thus in the early sixteenth century Muscovite grand duke and Muscovite church could both exult in a sense of growing power, and they tended to work together in an alliance from which both parties gained added lustre. An example of such co-operation was the celebrated doctrine put forward in the reign of Vasily III, flattering to secular and ecclesiastical Muscovy alike – that Moscow was the Third Rome, successor for all time to Rome itself and Constantinople. Besides being allies, church and grand duke were also to some extent competitors for power. But the grand duke was acknowledged senior partner, especially as he had come to determine appointment to the chief church office of Metropolitan of Moscow.

Muscovy's social composition was complex, and at its apex stood two competing privileged groups. The higher of these consisted of princes and boyars, and owed its privileges to hereditary position, while the lower was that of gentry and officials who received land and office on the basis of service to the sovereign. Since, as already indicated, it was the princes and boyars who formed the chief secular rival to the monarchic power, a grand duke tended to look to the lower privileged stratum as his natural ally against the higher. It is possible, however, to exaggerate the extent to which sixteenth-century and later Russian history reduces itself to the grinding of an aristocracy of boyars and princes between the upper and nether millstone of Tsar and gentry. Successful as this combination was to prove in destroying aristocratic pretensions, it was against the peasants that it chiefly operated – forcing them into progressively stricter conditions of enserfment. Peasants of various categories formed the overwhelming majority of the Russian population in the sixteenth, as in succeeding centuries; but had little impact on high policy. Nor did merchants and townsfolk of the lower orders exercise much political influence, though they came to alarm the authorities by occasional riots.

Despite many elements of disharmony it was a powerful, flourishing and expanding state, with dawning international status and a semblance of cohesion conferred by many years of strong rule, that Ivan the Terrible inherited on his accession as grand duke in 1533, and one which even the violent fluctuations of boyar rule had not entirely shaken to pieces at the time when he had himself crowned as Tsar in 1547.

2 The Young Tsar: Ivan IV   1547-64

Shortly before his coronation Ivan proclaimed his intention of marrying and set in motion the elaborate procedure whereby the grand dukes of Muscovy had taken to choosing a bride – one of their many borrowings from the practice of the Byzantine emperors. Throughout the realm fathers of socially eligible nubile virgins received orders backed by threat of disgrace and execution to parade their daughters for inspection by the monarch's representatives in local centres. The winners of these regional heats then proceeded, several hundred strong, to Moscow, where they lived in special quarters. Further research by a panel of experts into their piety, chastity, health, beauty and general desirability would help to narrow the sovereign's choice until it finally settled on a single girl.

On the present occasion the successful contender was Anastasia Zakharyin, member of an old and well-known boyar family. The choice justified the care of her selectors, giving the young Tsar thirteen years of happy married life . . . with the result that when his biographers divide the reign into a mild and harsh period, the former is often taken as coinciding with his marriage to Anastasia and the latter as lasting from her death in 1560 to his own death in 1584. It is certainly true that during Anastasia's lifetime Ivan's subjects could feel less likely to suffer decapitation, impalement, burning, exile or the order to become monks than was the case after the Tsaritsa's death.

Not that Ivan's streak of viciousness disappeared immediately after marriage. In the spring of 1547 seventy men of Pskov accosted the young bridegroom in a village near Moscow, and sought to lay complaint against a provincial official. But Ivan would not listen. Shouting and stamping with rage, he poured burning spirits on the hapless petitioners, singed their hair and beards with a candle, and gave orders to strip them and lay them on the ground. Worse might have befallen had not a messenger suddenly ridden up to report that a great bell in Moscow had crashed to the ground, news which distracted the Tsar's attention. In the same spring a series of fires broke out in Moscow, leading to a vast conflagration on 21 June. This catastrophe, in which several thousand people died, gave rise to rumours that Ivan's grandmother and uncles had started the fires . . . and by a bizarre form of arson. The story was that they had steeped human hearts in water, thereby obtaining a combustible fluid which they had sprinkled about the streets. Rioters inflamed by this tale caught Prince Yury Glinsky (Ivan's uncle) and stoned him to death in or near the Uspensky Cathedral where he had sought sanctuary. Three days later Ivan found himself facing an armed mob in a near-by village to which he had withdrawn from his burning capital and rioting citizens. The rabble demanded that he should hand over his grandmother and another uncle, who were not on the premises. Ivan ordered his troops to fire, and some of the rioters fled; others sought pardon on bended knee, and the Tsar had several of them seized and killed.

If Ivan indeed suffered a temporary transformation, a conversion almost, in 1547 from delinquent grand duke to statesmanlike Tsar, the change was due, according to his own testimony, to the Moscow fires. He spoke of these incidents as follows in his address to a church assembly: 'The Lord punished me for my sins. ... God sent great fires and fear entered my soul and trembling entered my bones. My spirit was humbled. I was deeply moved and acknowledged my transgressions.'[9]

One important effect of this change of heart was the end of boyar rule as Russia had known it since the death of the Regent Helen in 1538, for the riots following the fires of Moscow destroyed the Glinskys' influence without bringing any similar clan to power. Advisers of different calibre now rose to prominence, chief among them being Sylvester and Adashev – both men of low rank. Sylvester was a priest in one of the Kremlin cathedrals who managed to gain ascendancy over the young Tsar by threatening him with hell-fire or something of the kind;[10] his influence was all-powerful according to early evidence.[11] Alexis Adashev was a member of the minor gentry, not a boyar; but his sway was such that a modern authority calls him 'de facto head of government' from 1549.[12] The Tsar himself has confirmed the ascendancy of Sylvester and Adashev, and it is not hard to credit since he was so young when he first came under their influence shortly after his coronation. There emerges the picture of a cruel, wayward youth soothed by the gentle Anastasia, the eloquent Sylvester and the saintly Adashev – the last-mentioned being 'like unto the angels', according to Kurbsky.[13] It sounds a little unreal, and the young Tsar may well have exercised more initiative at the time than he would later admit. At least his new advisers were men of his own choice, unlike the usurpers of his childhood.

Whatever the exact relationships within the administration, it marked a change from boyar rule, being thoroughly dedicated to reform in many important areas under the Tsar's direct control. He was head of the armed forces, and it was now that the corps of Streltsy musketeers was founded as part of a new military establishment and nucleus of a regular army. Military reforms also included the erosion of precedence, the traditional basis for promotion which had sometimes deprived Russia of her best generals because mediocrities could claim command on genealogical grounds. The Tsar was also supreme judge, and the reforms included the new legal code of 1550 – besides taking in church organization, land tenure, local government and other material.

During most of Ivan's reign Russia was at war, simultaneously or by turns, with all her immediate neighbours – with the Tatar khanates on the eastern and southern marches of Muscovy; and with countries to the west – Livonia, Poland-Lithuania and Sweden.

Though Muscovy had long ceased to be formally dependent on the Tatars, she was still subject to raids by Tatar armies – enemies who were fortunately no longer united, being now separated into the three khanates of Kazan, Astrakhan and the Crimea. Of these Kazan was most accessible, and it was Kazan that Ivan first resolved to attack. In 1552 a Russian army about one hundred and fifty thousand strong, led by the Tsar in person, launched a victorious assault. After the stronghold had fallen, its walls breached by gunpowder, Ivan returned to Moscow to celebrate this triumph – and also the birth of a son in his absence. In 1556 the khanate of Astrakhan also fell, putting the entire Volga in Ivan's hands. By acquiring Tatar lands and those of minor peoples in the area, he became the first Muscovite sovereign to rule a multi-national state, besides which the way to Siberia now lay open.

Meanwhile an event of March 1553 had begun to change the glorious conqueror of Kazan into the grim figure of later years by undermining his chief advisers' influence. He fell ill, so seriously that he seemed on the point of death. Knowing that his wife and family would be in great danger if he should die, he tried to ensure from his sickbed that his newly-born son, the Tsarevich Dmitry, should not be prevented from succeeding – for though the principle of succession by eldest son had the sanction of custom among the grand dukes of Muscovy, it was not established in law. Ivan therefore willed the throne to his son by testament, and further insisted that his boyars and high officials should then and there kiss the cross in allegiance to the child. Though it is unlikely that any of his subjects would have dared to defy even a dying Ivan later in his reign, such a hitch now did occur. His first cousin, Prince Vladimir of Staritsa, stepped forward (or was pushed forward by his ambitious mother) to assert his own claims to the throne. They were not entirely without basis – and he had the advantage of being more or less adult, though barely seventeen years of age.[14] The prince also turned out to have some influential supporters, and to the Tsar's fury his own closest allies seemed to be among them as an unseemly dispute developed around his sickbed. Sylvester was supporting Prince Vladimir outright and Adashev seemed compromised by the hesitant attitude of his father. In the end the quarrel was smoothed over. Prince Vladimir swore allegiance to the Tsarevich, and Ivan recovered – but added this

33

attempt to put his cousin on the throne to his growing stock of grudges. Unhappily these efforts on behalf of his heir proved futile when the baby died later in the same year during a pilgrimage made by the Tsar to express thanks for his own recovery. But another heir, the Tsarevich Ivan, was born in 1554.

In the late 1550s a disagreement over foreign policy contributed to turning Ivan against Sylvester and Adashev. After annexing Kazan, the Tsar began to look for fresh conquests. He might strike southwards at the Crimean Khan – or to the west. There were arguments in favour of both courses. Sylvester and Adashev were for the southern solution, which offered a crusade against the infidel and the opportunity to end the raids from the Crimea. But Ivan rejected their advice in favour of an aggressive policy in the west, where he coveted an outlet to the Baltic. An outlet of sorts he already had – the coast of Ingermanland on the Gulf of Finland, including the site of the future St Petersburg. But if only he could now capture ports on the Baltic proper, he might improve trade with many European countries less hostile than his immediate western neighbours – who already feared Russia and did everything in their power to prevent her from importing the foreign specialists and weapons which she badly needed.

It was Livonia, weakest of Ivan's western neighbours, which chiefly blocked his path to the Baltic. Ruled for centuries by Germans of the Teutonic Order of Knights (now in some disarray), the country seemed ripe for attack, and in 1558 the Tsar launched his armies – beginning what a modern German historian has called an 'unprovoked war of aggression with purely imperialist aims'.[15] In the first three years of the war, Narva and Dorpat fell to Russia among other towns, Russian forces laid waste Livonian territory, and the military power of the Order was broken. A firm hold on the Baltic seemed within Ivan's grasp. Undertaken against the advice of Sylvester and Adashev, this attack on Livonia ushered in their disgrace, though neither adviser became one of Ivan's more spectacular victims. Adashev was honourably banished by posting to a military command in Livonia, but died soon afterwards, probably under arrest. Sylvester voluntarily withdrew from affairs to become a monk and was afterwards imprisoned in a monastery in the far north. Ivan viciously denounced them after they had disappeared from the scene. Amongst other misdemeanours they had been on bad terms with the Tsaritsa Anastasia; the details of the quarrel are unknown, but it was very much alive in Ivan's mind.

The extension of the war to Poland–Lithuania took place in 1561 when the defeated Teutonic Knights handed over part of their realm to Sigismund II Augustus (King of Poland and Grand Duke of Lithuania) – an enemy far more dangerous to Russia than Livonia. First success in this extended conflict went to the Tsar, who captured the Lithuanian stronghold of Polotsk in 1563. The seizure

34

Ivan IV, who succeeded to the throne in 1533 at the age of three. In 1547 he became the first Muscovite sovereign to be crowned as Tsar, and he ruled until his death in 1584. An anonymous contemporary portrait.

of this strategic point was a major feat of Russian arms, and earned the Tsar a triumphal reception in Moscow on his return.

Ivan's transformation into the 'classic Russian tyrant',[16] and a 'torturer whose like we may scarce find in the very chronicles of Tacitus',[17] made progress within a year or two after the disgrace of Sylvester and Adashev. He staged a minor wave of terror in the early 1560s, among those executed being many associates of Adashev. They also included an otherwise unimportant prince who had accused Ivan of homosexual relations with one of his new favourites.[18] Another victim, Prince Michael Repnin, died for being the spectre at one of the Tsar's more unsavoury feasts. When the tipsy monarch put on a mask and began dancing with his roistering cronies, the prince tearfully protested against such frivolity . . . only to have a mask clapped on his own face by the royal hooligan. The prince angrily threw it off and trampled it underfoot. But it is always risky to shun a despot's frolics, and a few days later Ivan's agents stabbed Prince Repnin to death as he was worshipping in church on a Sunday.[19] These years also saw milder punishments imposed, including exile and compulsion to enter a religious house. The Tsar's precautions further included the system whereby a suspect took a solemn oath – backed by a host of guarantors sometimes running into several hundreds – not to commit certain offences among which desertion to Lithuania was prominent. But despite all counter-measures peasants and princes still contrived to flee from the centre of the kingdom.

Prince Andrew Kurbsky – boyar, Muscovite general and former member of the circle of Sylvester and Adashev – was most prominent among the runaways. He deserted his army to attack the Tsar from Lithuania by sword and by pen, and in July 1564 Ivan replied at length to a letter from the traitor denouncing him as a bloody tyrant. The reply is a self-justifying screed in which – as in his shorter letter to Kurbsky written thirteen years later – Ivan has unintentionally drawn a vivid portrait of himself. Among its features is a towering ego to which Muscovy and its works are a mere appendage. This consciousness of his own superiority was not effortless, for Ivan was a painstaking scorer of debating points. He was also a man of learning. Besides knowing much of the Scriptures by heart (to judge from the errors in his many quotations), he was steeped in the history of the early church and of Russia itself, as of the medieval and ancient world in general. This fund of erudition underlies his simple theory of government whereby a society is doomed to perish from internal strife unless held down by a strong ruler dispensing rewards and punishments. As some of his diplomatic missives show, Ivan scorned rival monarchs whose powers seemed incomplete. He pointed out to the Polish king Stephen Batory that the Polish throne (being elective) was bestowed by 'the unruly will of many people' [20] – in contrast to his own throne, granted by God. As for Queen Elizabeth of England, she had yielded power to 'clodhopping tradesmen' (he told her), being no true sovereign but just an 'ordinary spinster'.[21] Clearly the Tsar would have approved of the dispensation whereby Russia has been largely denied constitutional rule since his death – a heritage for which he might surely claim some credit.

Ivan's epistle to Kurbsky of 1564 is a clinical document and a fine quarry for amateurs of abnormal psychology, illustrating as it does the Tsar's tendency to descend from peaks of manic self-glorification to depths of self-abasement. It shows him harrowed by a gnawing sense of insecurity – haunted by phantom images of plots, spies and evil machinations; and by suspicions of treachery exaggerated in his mind . . . but not wholly unfounded. The repetitive, incoherent, sarcastic, ungrammatical and abusive harangue makes a compelling impression. It is not hard to believe that its author stood poised, even as he wrote it, to plunge his subjects into a persecution bloodier than any other inflicted on Russians by a Tsar.

3 The Oprichnina: Ivan IV 1564-72

On 3 December 1564 the Tsar opened his major reign of terror, and in strange fashion. He abandoned Moscow in a convoy of hundreds of sledges loaded with icons and other holy objects seized from churches in the city as well as the entire royal treasury, including numerous gold vessels. A large retinue escorted him. Among them were boyars and other notables who paraded in military array, but also had their wives and children with them – as did Ivan himself, having remarried after Anastasia's death. Did the Tsar intend to set up another capital elsewhere? He had no definite plan, it seemed, for he first moved south, and then spent nearly a month in apparently aimless wandering before establishing himself about seventy miles north-east of Moscow at Aleksandrovskaya Sloboda. Panic seized the capital, and did not subside when messengers at last appeared on 3 January bearing two missives from the Tsar. In one, addressed to the Metropolitan, Ivan declared that 'we have abandoned our realm and set off for wherever God may direct us'.[22] To this oracular threat to abdicate were added long familiar denunciations of boyar greed and treachery, and Ivan also rebuked the clergy for trying to shield such traitors. In his second letter he addressed the common people, adopting a milder tone, and assuring them that they were not the target of his rage. He thus sought to drive a wedge between patricians and plebeians – only to alarm both, since many thought strong rule on any terms preferable to anarchy. A deputation led by the Archbishop of Novgorod accordingly hastened to Aleksandrovskaya Sloboda and implored the Tsar to return and rule again.

Ivan agreed, provided that he should be free to rule as he pleased and punish traitors. He returned in February 1565 after over two months' absence, and seemed a completely different man. Only thirty-four years old and remembered as a tall, strongly built, handsome figure with small but piercing grey eyes, he now looked almost senile. For whatever reason – prolonged rage, perhaps – he had become nearly bald and had lost most of his beard, while his gaze, now dulled, seemed to exhale a fury smouldering ... but far from impotent, for within a day or two of his return he had half a dozen princes and dignitaries publicly beheaded or otherwise executed on charges which included plotting against his life with Kurbsky. He had one victim impaled, and he banished others or forced them to become monks.

The Tsar next proceeded to set up the puzzling institution known as the Oprichnina – a specially recruited corps of violent men personally loyal to him. This might be described as his private army or personal bodyguard had it not more resembled a large-scale criminal organization. As head of this disreputable array of cut-throats, the Tsar became in effect chief gangster of the realm – besides which the Oprichniks also functioned to some extent as a political security force. An Oprichnik was easily recognized by his black garb, his black horse and the emblems of a dog's head and broom carried on his saddle. Members were enrolled only after careful individual inquiry (often conducted in the presence of the Tsar himself) into their political reliability, and many were recruited from the ranks of the lower gentry. But princes and boyars were not rejected if they seemed to be of the right type. Nor were foreigners, among whom the semi-literate German adventurer Heinrich von Staden has provided valuable memoirs of his experiences in the corps. The Oprichnina was, in short, a demeritocracy open to all talents.

Once recruited, Oprichniks received the right to murder, rob and ill-use non-Oprichniks with impunity – a privilege of which they made free use until their name was feared throughout Muscovy. They formed a state outside the state. Being above the law, they were responsible only to the Tsar, had their own separate administration and lived apart from the rest of the population on lands specially allotted to them. From these they summarily evicted the previous occupants, who were treated like a defeated enemy and turned out to fend for themselves in the middle of winter. These lands gradually took in whole provinces, to the distress of a peasantry handed over to Oprichnik landlords. Oprichnik territory also came to embrace towns or parts of towns and included a sizeable portion of Moscow itself, where the Tsar abandoned his ancestral royal palace to build a new, fortified Oprichnik palace outside the Kremlin. Eventually the area assigned to the Oprichnina comprised about half the realm, and the total number of the Oprichniks reached six thousand.

Although there is no need to dwell upon individual acts of Oprichnik violence in harrowing detail, certain especially important episodes call for attention. It was in 1569 that Ivan's vengeance at last overtook Prince Vladimir of Staritsa, who had put himself forward as successor to the throne in 1553. After toying with the prince's fate for a decade and a half, and gradually removing his supporters, Ivan had him murdered – by poison according to one of several conflicting accounts. The outrage occurred at Aleksandrovskaya Sloboda – the Tsar's reserve headquarters, where he was now spending much of his time. Showing increasing signs of mental instability, he had turned this fortress, surrounded by a moat and ramparts, into a kind of militarized abbey by setting up a brotherhood of three hundred false friars: Oprichniks who paraded as members of a mock monastic order. An elaborate parody of a religious institution was combined with carousing in the

refectory and visits to the torture chambers. However, the Tsar's devotions were
by no means facetiously intended, being performed in such deadly earnestness
that bruises appeared on his forehead from beating it on the ground with excessive
zeal.

As these exercises confirm, the pious sovereign was now devoting increasing
attention to church affairs. The scope of his theological activity was wide, ranging
as it did from abstruse theoretical dispute to the wholesale murder of priests.
Foremost among these was Philip – appointed Metropolitan of Moscow in 1566,
though a known opponent of the Oprichnina. It is to the Metropolitan Philip that
the credit belongs of challenging the terrible Tsar as boldly as anyone on record.
On at least one occasion the Uspensky Cathedral, witness of so many scandals of
the age, saw a spectacular public clash between monarch and high priest when
Philip dared to refuse Ivan his blessing and rebuked him for robbing and murdering his subjects. Even Ivan did not venture to deal with his head churchman as
summarily as if he were a mere boyar, but had the victim framed at an elaborately
rigged trial. Then a gang of Oprichniks under Alexis Basmanov seized the metropolitan while he was conducting a service, again in the Uspensky Cathedral. They
tore off his rich vestments, wrapped him in a monk's robe and hustled him away –
to a monastery at Tver where he was subsequently strangled in his cell by Malyuta
('Babe') Skuratov, most notorious Oprichnik of all.

This was only one among many outrages against the church. The Tsar liqui-
dated two successive Archbishops of Novgorod – Pimen and Leonid. He had the
latter sewn up inside a bearskin and hunted with a pack of hounds, according to
the Pskov Chronicle. But before slaughtering these archbishops, Ivan had already
presided over the sacking of their diocese. This massive punitive expedition took
place in early 1570, and saw the Tsar terrorizing his subjects on a scale which out-
stripped all his other atrocities, besides being the largest repressive operation in
which the Oprichniks took part. Situated some three hundred miles north-west of
Moscow and rivalling it in historical and commercial importance, Novgorod had
now been under Muscovite rule for less than a century. Despite the forcible removal in the past of many leading local families (replaced by transplanted Muscovites), the inhabitants still retained memories of former independence; which is
far from saying that they were entertaining treasonable relations with Lithuania,
as Ivan allowed himself to think. That such an intention existed is unlikely.[23] In
any case the Tsar had long nursed a grudge against Novgorod, and his festering
suspicions reputedly came to a head when an otherwise insignificant mischief-
maker laid information against the city, claiming it to be on the point of deserting
to the Polish–Lithuanian ruler.

The Tsar moved against Novgorod in December 1569 with an army fifteen
thousand strong, including Oprichnik troops. Plunder, torture and murder began

long before his men reached the doomed city – at Klin, about fifty miles north-west of Moscow – and continued along the road. They killed chance wayfarers and slaughtered thousands in Tver and at other points on the route. The monas-teries formed a major target for Ivan's spite and a prime object for looting by Oprichniks during the entire expedition, not least in Novgorod itself. Throwing a cordon round the city, the Tsar's advance troops seized hundreds of monks from whom they sought to extort money by beating. Then the Tsar arrived in Novgorod on 6 January with the Tsarevich Ivan, now aged fifteen, set up his head-quarters in the merchant quarter and gave orders to finish off the captive abbots and monks. On the following Sunday, the Tsar advanced across the River Volkhov, and Archbishop Pimen greeted him on the bridge according to custom. Always at his most picturesque when facing a prince of the church, Ivan refused Pimen's blessing – cursing him as a wolf, traitor and beast of prey, but permit-ting the archbishop to conduct a cathedral service and to stage a banquet. This ill-starred feast was barely under way when the Tsar suddenly uttered a piercing yell, at which signal his minions seized the archbishop and set about looting his palace and cathedral.

The prolonged massacre of the populace began, burning being prominent among the many methods of torture employed. Oprichniks trussed living, dead or half-dead bodies and tossed them into the river, which had not frozen in the area by the bridge despite the winter cold. Nor was the Tsar on this or any other occasion chivalrously inclined to spare women and children; his henchmen hauled their bodies too, sometimes tied together, over the bloody snow on sledges and threw them into the river, while men armed with pikes, axes, spears and boat-hooks patrolled in small craft to finish off those struggling in the icy water. For some five weeks these massacres were a daily occurrence, and when the Tsar at last called a halt the tally of dead had probably reached several tens of thousands. After his men had destroyed food supplies for many miles around he abandoned the mutilated city to famine and plague – and all this at a time when he was involved in a major war with Poland.

Ivan next made for Pskov, where he seems to have schemed similar atrocities. But whether weary of blood-letting or swayed by humble demonstrations of loyalty, he relented and confined himself more strictly to the plunder of monas-teries and churches. Legend has it that a local hermit, protected by his status as a holy fool (*yurodivy*), cowed the superstitious Tsar and bundled him out of town in terror with bodings of doom for battening on human flesh and blood – in Lent of all seasons.[24]

The sack of Novgorod preceded the public torture and execution of over a hundred people in Moscow after investigation into the supposed Novgorod con-spiracy had implicated some of the highest in the land through denunciations extorted by torture. This horror, one of the most repellent episodes in Russian history and Ivan's foulest hour, occurred on 25 July 1570 in an open place no longer identifiable. A huge wooden scaffold stood there, while eighteen gallows and a vast cauldron of boiling water were among the devices of death publicly displayed. Fearing Novgorod's fate, the citizens of the capital gave the grim arena a wide berth, but Oprichniks forced them to attend. The Tsar rode up, armed and escorted by fifteen hundred troops, and his victims were paraded already broken by previous tortures. Accused of traitorous relations with Poland, Turkey and the Crimean Khan, the head of the diplomatic chancery, Ivan Viskovaty, was dispatched first, strung up by the feet while the Tsar's intimates took turns to hack off parts of his body; Malyuta Skuratov opened proceedings by slicing off the Chancellor's ear. The second victim was the state treasurer, Nikita Funikov, who was scalded to death. The smaller fry included, according to one version, a victim of especial interest in the chef who had poisoned Prince Vladimir of Staritsa in the previous year – and on the Tsar's own orders; the charge against him had a certain piquant symmetry ... intention to poison Ivan on Prince Vladimir's orders. It was typical of the Tsar that he personally chose the fate of individuals (according to contemporary account), and he himself slaughtered some with pike and sabre.[25]

Though the victims of 25 July were not Oprichniks, their star was now on the wane, for with a ruler of Ivan's temperament it was only a question of time before he would turn and rend any close associate. At about the period of the Moscow massacre he accordingly began to liquidate leading Oprichniks. The victims included Alexis Basmanov and his son Theodore, the son being forced to kill his father before being executed in turn.[26] The Tsar summoned another leading henchman, Prince Afanasy Vyazemsky, for interview, and addressed this intimate with his usual cordiality, at the very time when his men were murdering the prince's servants by previous arrangement. Confronted by the corpses on his return home, Vyazemsky tried to behave as if nothing untoward had occurred; but this display of *sang-froid* did not spare him imprisonment from which he never emerged.

The Oprichnina ceased to have any open existence in about 1572, though opinions differ as to when if ever the Tsar effectively disbanded it, while speculation has also continued on his motives for establishing it in the first place. Scholars have examined the lists of Oprichniks and victims, have analysed their social composition and have propounded ingenious theories – but without reaching any generally accepted conclusion. All attempts to interpret Ivan's character fall somewhere between two extreme conceptions – of a maniac whose actions defy explanation, and of a wise statesman stooping reluctantly to the brutal methods of his age. According to the latter view, his chief aim in deploying terror was the establishment of a strong centralized state, to which the crushing of church, princes and boyars (main rivals to the central power) formed a regrettably essential preliminary, while the looting of monasteries was merely a novel way of collecting taxes. It is true that Oprichniks did kill many boyars and clerics. It is also true that Ivan's treasury was depleted. But it does not follow that his prime motive in instituting the Oprichnina was something as impersonal as a concern for centralization, absolutism and fiscal probity, important though these issues may have been as secondary considerations. Still less does it follow that the blessings of authoritarian rule by an unchallenged autocrat were so bountiful as to recompense Russia for the associated sufferings. Nor, if one studies the sequel to Ivan's rule, is it even clear that the Oprichnik terror necessarily advanced the cause of authoritarianism.

Far more persuasive is the suggestion that Ivan's overriding motive in establishing the Oprichnina was a sense of personal insecurity. It was, perhaps, a terrified man's way of saving his skin from dangers exaggerated in his mind, at no matter what cost to his subjects. 'The first and main purpose of the Oprichnina [one of its more convincing interpreters states] was to ensure the Tsar's personal security.'[27] The Oprichnina may also represent a desperate attempt to take a firm grip, such as had previously eluded Ivan, on the administration of his country.

Ivan III, the Great, Grand Duke of
Moscow, ruled from 1462 to 1505. He increased
the area of Muscovy about fourfold
during his reign and sometimes called
himself Tsar in diplomatic dealings.
He was the father of Vasily III and
grandfather of Ivan IV, the Terrible.
From A. Thevet's *Cosmographie Universelle*,
1555.

(*opposite*) The emblem of the double eagle, first adopted by Ivan III. From the *Titulyarnik* (list of titles of the Russian rulers) of 1672.

Vasily III. Grand Duke of Moscow (1505–33), he was the son of Ivan III and father of Ivan IV. Woodcut, 1560.

Russian ambassadors at the court of Maximilian I. Woodcut, 1516.

A Russian embassy at Regensburg in 1576.
A contemporary engraving by G. Peterle.

Gold coins are showered
on Ivan IV, the Terrible,
after his coronation in
the Uspensky Cathedral on
16 January 1547.
A miniature from
the sixteenth-century
Book of the Tsar.

The young Tsar Ivan IV makes a public
appearance in the Red Square.
A nineteenth-century drawing by Sarleman.

IOVAN
BASILLI
GRÃ DVCA
DI MOSCOVIA
stampato nouamente.

Ivan IV, a contemporary
Italian woodcut.

Ivan IV clutching the body
of his dying son whom he
had struck in a fit of rage in
November 1581.
The well-known painting
by Repin (1844–1930).

Contemporary impressions by German travellers
of Russians in the sixteenth century:
(*above*) Russian cavalry; (*top*) a Russian soldier;
(*centre*) a Tatar soldier;
(*bottom*) a Russian merchant.

4 Ivan IV: Last Years   To 1584

Foreign affairs had not ceased to claim the Tsar's attention during the period of the Oprichnina. His war with Poland continued while he was waging war on his own subjects, and shortly after the sack of Novgorod the Crimean Tatars showed themselves as well able to destroy a Russian city as any Russian Tsar.

It had been Ivan's hope to appease the Crimean Khan, thus securing Muscovy's southern flank and leaving her free to fight Poland. But the Khan was otherwise minded and presented himself on the outskirts of Moscow with a huge army. On 24 May 1571 – a fine, blustery day – his men set fire to the suburbs, and within four hours the whole wooden city was ablaze. Trapped between the Tatars outside and the stone-built Kremlin barred to them from the inside, multitudes of citizens, soldiers and refugees from the surrounding countryside perished in the flames or trampled each other to death. The marauders withdrew to the steppes with a large haul of Russian slaves, leaving the Moscow River choked with corpses, though an English chronicler of these horrors certainly exaggerated when he put the casualties at eight hundred thousand.[28] The Tsar himself had prudently withdrawn from his capital – by no means the first Grand Duke of Moscow to take evasive action when menaced by Tatars. Expecting the victors to attack again, he tried to gain time by diplomatic argument, and even offered to give up Astrakhan – tactics which did not prevent the Tatars from returning to the assault in the following year. But on this occasion Russian forces under Prince Michael Vorotynsky routed them about thirty miles from Moscow and threw them back on the steppes.

Meanwhile the Tsar's war over Livonia with Poland (as it is convenient to term Poland–Lithuania after 1569) had already lasted for more than a decade, and was to continue for as long again. Interrupted by lulls and negotiations, the hostilities brought out many contradictions in Ivan – showing him imperious and patient, arrogant and tactful, stubborn and flexible by turns. Among his less successful devices was the appointment of a puppet King of Livonia, the Danish Prince Magnus, to whom the Tsar married the Prince of Staritsa's daughter Euphemia shortly after having her father murdered. But despite such evidence of good will, Magnus several times betrayed Ivan's trust. The Tsar pardoned him, relieved perhaps to be confronted with real treachery rather than with the terrors of his imagination.

He also launched political moves more directly against Poland herself. When the childless King Sigismund died in 1572, Ivan became a candidate for election to his throne, though Russia and Poland were still at war. Discussing his candidature with an envoy from Poland, the Tsar seemed well aware that he was no ideal monarch. He pleaded guilty to bad temper, but added the consoling rider that his spite was directed only against those who were spiteful to him; he also promised to preserve or increase the rights of his future Polish subjects, an election pledge which was luckily never put to the test.[29]

It was not Ivan, but Stephen Batory who eventually became King of Poland in 1576 and inherited King Sigismund's war. An able general, he struck hard against Muscovy, and within five years had recaptured Polotsk, taken Velikiye Luki and laid siege to Pskov. Driven back on Russian soil, the defeated Tsar appealed to Pope Gregory XIII, who responded by sending a Jesuit envoy, Antonio Possevino, to mediate between Russia and Poland. The hope was to win Russia for Roman Catholicism. But Ivan, himself something of a Jesuit in the vulgar sense of the word, adroitly left this prospect open only so long as Possevino's offices were useful to him, allowing the matter to lapse when peace was made in 1582. This took the form of a ten-year armistice by which Ivan gave up all claim on Livonian and Lithuanian territory. More shamefully still, he was forced to yield to Sweden even the section of coast on the Gulf of Finland which had originally been gained for Muscovy by his grandfather. Far from achieving a footing on the Baltic, he had thus lost even his toehold on the Gulf – and that after a quarter of a century's campaigning now revealed as a disastrous failure.

Faced by enemies on his frontiers, Ivan cultivated England, being so fascinated by this distant kingdom that his subjects nicknamed him the English Tsar. It was in his reign that close contact between the two countries was first established – pioneered by the sea-captain Richard Chancellor who set sail from Gravesend in May 1553 seeking a north-east passage to China by the Arctic Ocean. Anchoring near the mouth of a river unknown to him (in fact the Northern Dvina), and learning from friendly natives that he was in the realm of Muscovy, Chancellor went to Moscow where he was graciously received by the Tsar: 'in a chaire gilt, and in a long garment of beaten golde, with an empirial crowne upon his head, and a staffe of Cristall and golde in his right hand.'[30]

The meeting led to close commercial relations. Ivan granted certain privileges to English merchants, and trade developed over the years – but on terms less satisfactory to the Tsar than to Queen Elizabeth, who succeeded in 1558. Whereas Elizabeth was concerned chiefly with commerce, Ivan sought a full political and military alliance, wanting her to fight Poland or at least to supply him with more shipwrights, sailors, guns and military stores. She replied evasively, and when it dawned on the autocrat of all Russia that he was being fobbed off by the queen of a nation of shopkeepers he was moved to scornful protest. It was in a missive of 1570 that he called the English sovereign the puppet of tradesmen and no true ruler. Well equipped to deal with such impertinence, the Virgin Queen gave a suitably frigid rebuff – which, however, did not end warm diplomatic relations between two monarchs who were never to meet. They might have done so if Ivan's fears had been realized, for he insisted (and this is the most revealing feature in his English dealings) that political asylum in England should be available to himself and his family; on which matter he extracted from Elizabeth a secret oath. The Tsar's urgent concern to keep this escape route open confirms that he was far from joking when he spoke of the perils which beset his throne.

The Tsar had remarried in 1561 (a year after the death of his first wife), choosing as his bride a Circassian princess of fabled beauty who died eight years later. After that his marital career became a more chequered affair.

Widowed for the second time, Ivan reverted to the procedure now traditional among Muscovite grand dukes by selecting his next wife from a concourse of eligible Russian virgins. He had over two thousand girls brought to Aleksand-rovskaya Sloboda and took pains to inspect them all individually. Scrutinized, short-listed and re-scrutinized by Tsar, leeches and midwives, they eventually yielded up a third royal bride in Martha Sobakin, daughter of a Novgorod merchant; but she unfortunately died after only two weeks of wedlock and with the union still unconsummated according to the bridegroom's own evidence. Her death is especially mysterious since she had so recently passed as medically fit; but, though only speculation, Stephen Graham's suggestion – that the dread Tsar somehow made away with her in an orgy of unbridled sexual perversion – is consistent with many reports of his habits.[31]

Ivan's fourth wife was Anna Koltovsky, whom he married without any parade of damsels or other ostentation, well knowing that he was doing wrong since his church permitted three marriages and no more. For thus exceeding his quota he sought the forgiveness of an assembly of prelates specially summoned to the Uspensky Cathedral. He pointed out in a typical self-pitying harangue that his three previous Tsaritsas had all perished by poison or witchcraft, and secured – at the expense of some trifling details of penance – the church's blessing for his fourth marriage, only to tire of his new wife after a few years. She entered a convent, thus being effectively divorced. Ivan's fifth Tsaritsa (or seventh if two intervening ladies of disputed status are included in the series) was Mary Nagoy, who bore him a son – the second Tsarevich of his reign to be christened Dmitry; the first Dmitry, Anastasia's son, had died in 1553.

Additional light on Ivan's character is shed by his relations with two foreign noblewomen, one Polish and one English, whom he pursued for years without ever setting eyes on either. On the threshold of war with Poland, he attempted to avert hostilities by marrying whichever of the Polish King's sisters should impress a Russian envoy as the more sexually attractive. The choice settled on Princess Catherine, but Ivan's suit miscarried and she became the wife of Duke John of Finland, brother and rebellious subject of King Eric XIV of Sweden. The curious point is that Ivan was still vainly trying to gain possession of the Polish princess long after she had become Duchess of Finland, and made a pact with the deranged King Eric providing for her to be handed over to Moscow. Not that the Tsar wanted to make her his mistress (he explained), but she might prove useful as a means of blackmailing her brother, the King of Poland.[32] Fortunately for the duchess, nothing came of this nefarious scheme to kidnap her and obtain Livonia as ransom.

Ivan was equally stubborn in seeking the hand of Lady Mary Hastings, cousin of Queen Elizabeth of England, whom he also pursued through diplomatic channels. But the suitor's reputation as the cruel monarch of a distant, barbarous land was not a recommendation. Nor was a kinswoman of the late Henry VIII of England likely to overlook one by no means minor detail bearing on the Tsar's proposal – he was married already, and to his fifth or seventh wife at that; although she (as he instructed his envoy) could easily be removed if necessary. After much delay the unwilling Lady Mary submitted to scrutiny by Ivan's envoy in the English Lord Chancellor's garden; but events developed in such a way that she escaped the ordeal of becoming Ivan's sixth or eighth bride without offending the Tsar by a direct refusal.

The Tsar reputedly maintained a unit of fifty staff concubines whom he took with him everywhere.[33] He certainly impressed his contemporaries as a very monster of potency, profligacy and lust. Similar rumours surround the lives of many later Russian sovereigns, both male and female, and to discount them all would be a grave error. But it must be noted that exact truth is often harder to obtain about a supreme ruler's sexual life than about any other aspect of his biography, for the subject is a hothouse in which tropical weeds run riot. So far as Ivan is concerned, many accounts of his erotic exploits contain a marked sadistic element – for instance, those collected from various sources by Yevreinov.[34] These stories show him as a confirmed rapist drawing freely on a reservoir of several million potential victims and combining their violation with torture and murder, whether by strangling, stabbing, exposing naked to the Russian winter, hanging (sometimes in the presence of a husband), burying alive or mauling by the bears which often figure in anecdotes about the dread Tsar.

The winding up of the Oprichnina attributed to 1572 did not see the end of Ivan's use of terror as an instrument of internal policy. Among the victims of the ensuing wave of atrocities – the sixth and last in the reign according to Karamzin's reckoning – one particularly outrageous example stands out. Prince Michael Vorotynsky had held high command during the victorious assault on Kazan in 1552; twenty years later, after an intervening period of disgrace, he once more led Russian troops to a decisive victory over the Tatars. But now, shortly after his second triumph, he was denounced for practising witchcraft and put in chains. He was lashed to a stake between two fires which, according to Kurbsky, the Tsar personally stoked with his staff.[35] Not long afterwards the cruelly tortured general died, only one among a number of reported victims in the early 1570s.

The last seven years of Ivan's reign are free from creditable reports of executions, whether because the evidence has not survived or because the grim Tsar's blood lust was at last sated. It was perhaps weariness of high office and its cares which caused him to stage in the middle 1570s a mock abdication by handing over the trappings of power for some two years to a Tatar prince who had embraced Orthodoxy, Simeon Bekbulatovich. While the real Tsar lived privately with the style of Ivan of Moscow, 'Tsar' Simeon was signing official documents and presiding over ceremonies in the royal palace, until the true Tsar tired of obscurity and resumed his original status.

A keen concern for the future of his dynasty and an urgent desire to maintain the principle of absolute rule after his death inspired Ivan's testament of 1572, which he composed with his sons Ivan and Theodore in mind. It was remarkable for the particularly strict terms in which the Tsar enjoined the younger son to obey the elder. Ivan also considerably reduced (by comparison with earlier grand-ducal practice) the size of the lands willed to the junior offspring – but to no avail. In November 1581 there suddenly occurred an appalling tragedy at Aleksandrovskaya Sloboda when the elder Ivan lashed out savagely in a fit of rage and struck the younger on the head with his iron-pointed staff. He might almost have struck himself. In tastes and temperament the Tsarevich – aged twenty-seven at his untimely death – seemed like a copy of the Tsar. The two Ivans regularly appeared together on official occasions, besides presiding jointly over mass executions at Novgorod and Moscow and sharing an appetite for debauchery, for they reputedly went out together on raping expeditions. The Tsar therefore had ample reason to look on his son as his 'second self'.[36]

The cause of their tragic quarrel is not known with certainty. One version is that given by Possevino, who claims that the young man provoked his father by remonstrating with him for striking his (the Tsarevich's) pregnant wife; in which case Ivan may well have deprived his kingdom of more than one heir in the course of this unhappy affair. Be that as it may, no sooner had he felled his son than he rushed to his side and took the young man in his arms, kissing him, weeping, praying and calling for doctors. The Tsarevich died a few days later after protesting his love and forgiveness. But Ivan could not forgive himself. For several days he kept vigil over his son's body without eating or sleeping, and when the time came to convey it in solemn cortège to Moscow he followed behind. The burial took place in the Church of St Michael the Archangel; and as attendants lowered the Tsarevich into the tomb, his father flung himself on the coffin with a great cry. Distraught with grief, he could not sleep, and took to wandering about his palace at night, brooding on his bereavement and sins. He conceived the idea of retiring to a monastery and proclaimed to his boyars a wish to abdicate, asking them to choose a successor. But they urged him to continue as sovereign with the Tsarevich Theodore as his heir.

In early 1584 portents of death came to obsess Ivan. A comet terrified him, seeming to presage his end, and he summoned astrologers to Moscow. Ill, his body swollen and afflicted with a disorder described as internal putrefaction, he died on 18 March as he was just about to begin a game of chess. In a final testament he willed his kingdom to Theodore, his elder surviving son, appointing a special regency council; to his younger son, the infant Tsarevich Dmitry, he bequeathed only the town of Uglich and its surroundings.

Shortly before expiring, the Tsar was 'shorn', in accordance with grand ducal tradition, and it was as the monk Jonas that Ivan the Terrible went to meet his Maker.

Ivan was not the only ruler of his period with a reputation for cruelty, nor was Russia the only scene of atrocities in a century which also witnessed the massacre of St Bartholemew and the Spanish Inquisition. But though it is not proposed to arraign the Russian Tsar 'at the bar of history', as Waliszewski has done,[37] it may be profitable to compare him with later rulers of Russia – among whom the most striking comparisons are with Peter the Great and Joseph Stalin. His affinities with Peter will be left to a later chapter, but some points of resemblance with Stalin may be considered now.

In Stalin's own day parallels between the Soviet dictator and his sixteenth-century predecessor as autocrat became part of an official cult in which both were idealized as benevolent masters, the expression of this best known outside Russia being the first part (1944) of Sergey Eisenstein's film *Ivan the Terrible*. But the true parallels hardly come within the area of philanthropy, for Ivan and Stalin more resemble each other in the scale of the sufferings inflicted on their subjects, and also in the fact that the reputation of both rulers has much benefited from the curious and faulty assumption commonly made that extreme brutality tends to be closely correlated with extreme efficiency. The contribution made by Ivan and Stalin to strengthening the Russian and Soviet state has, accordingly, often been exaggerated. If the promotion of Russian power was indeed the primary aim of both autocrats, it may be argued that each chose means ill adapted to the end.

However, it is also arguable (as has already been suggested in the context of Ivan's Oprichnina) that self-preservation was an overriding motive for instituting terror in each instance. If so, the devices of both rulers in seeking to protect themselves appear on first consideration over-elaborate, fussy and counter-productive. But their tactics did after all pass the supreme functional test in the sense that each despot contrived (so far as has been established) to achieve the unlikely feat of dying a natural death. There may therefore have been more method in their seeming madness than is immediately apparent.

Stalin and Ivan also resemble each other in that each felt himself to be persecuted; in the credit which both gave to malicious denunciations; and in the use of labels as brand marks set on those marked for liquidation. Thus, to Ivan's 'evil men' and 'traitors' corresponds Stalin's more sophisticated 'enemies of the people'; but it seems likely that Ivan was less cynical than the later dictator and that he was not simply making use of a convenient formula, but passionately believed in the malice and treachery of his victims.

As is illustrated by certain incidents related above, Ivan often showed a deviousness similar to Stalin's. For the Tsar to receive the Oprichnik Prince Vyazemsky cordially – and at the very time when the prince's downfall had secretly been set in motion – was a typical Stalinist device. Even more so (if the story is to be credited) were the charges quoted above against the chef who had been induced to poison Prince Vladimir on Ivan's orders. By requiring his underlings to indulge in horseplay to order (as in the episode of Prince Repnin and the mask), Ivan foreshadowed the Stalin who once ordered Nikita Khrushchev to dance the *gopak* – though in that particular case without a fatal sequel. Wholesale slaughter of the highest as well as the lowest in the land was also a marked feature of both autocrats' policies, though it is probable that Stalin brought death to members of his central committee on an even greater scale than that of the liquidations meted out by Ivan within his boyar council. A tendency to suspect their closest associates of being in league with foreign powers was another feature in common; leading, for example, in 1570 to the execution in Moscow of Viskovaty, Funikov and others – the Trotskyite or Bukharinist bloc of their period. Above all, both autocrats created a gangster-state within a state in their Oprichnina and NKVD, and both also turned in the end to the slaughter of some of their chief gangster-policemen.

However, Stalin was a Georgian whereas Ivan was a Russian, and it is also arguable that the similarities between the two were less than the differences. The contrast is most marked in those traits of Ivan's character which call to mind certain key preoccupations of Dostoyevsky – in particular, the Tsar's much advertised sense of sin, and his constant need to communicate his innermost thoughts. No taciturn tyrant, Ivan often wore his heart on his sleeve, and several times took the opportunity to confess his sins at some public gathering. Nothing could have been less Stalinist than that. Un-Stalinist too was Ivan's habit of commemorating his victims by having lists of them kept at monasteries and allotting sums of money for prayers to be said for their souls. Then again, there was the acute concern for individuals revealed by the Tsar's practice of torturing his victims with his own sacred hands – a chore which the more squeamish Georgian was inclined to delegate to specialists.

Perhaps because some of his characteristics are so 'Russian', Ivan enjoyed a degree of popularity in his own age and country which seems otherwise difficult to explain in view of his excesses, and which contrasts with the comparative unpopularity of Peter the Great and the silent loathing in which Stalin was held. Ivan has accordingly passed into folk lore to a greater extent than any other Russian sovereign – also, perhaps, because he had the art of being so arrestingly picturesque. There was always a certain grandeur about him. A man who could have an elephant hacked to pieces for refusing to bow to him[38] is somehow above the criticism of ordinary mortals.

Boris Godunov. Before ruling as Tsar (1598–
1605), he acted as regent to the saintly and
inactive Tsar Theodore I; Godunov was an able,
but increasingly unpopular, ruler.

(*opposite*) The Tsarevich Dmitry, Ivan the Terrible's younger surviving son, for whose death at Uglich in 1591 Boris Godunov was held responsible in popular gossip. Silver head from a reliquary in the Kremlin.

False Dmitry I. Posing as the Tsarevich Dmitry, son of Ivan the Terrible, he usurped the throne of Muscovy in 1605, but was deposed and murdered in the following year.

Maryna Mniszech. Daughter of a Polish squire, she became Tsaritsa to False Dmitry I shortly before his downfall, and afterwards the consort of False Dmitry II and mother of a third pretender.

The murder of the Tsarevich Dmitry on 15 May
1591. Aged nine at the time of his death, the
cause of which remains obscure, Dmitry was the
younger surviving son of Ivan IV, and half-
brother of Theodore I. A contemporary painting.

The wedding by proxy of False Dmitry I
and Maryna Mniszech at Cracow in 1605.
A contemporary painting.
(*top*) An audience given in the Kremlin
by False Dmitry I. A contemporary painting.

ВАСИЛІИ ІОАННОВИЧЬ ШУЙСКОЙ

Царь и Самодержецъ всероссійскій

Wassili Ioannowicz Schuiskoi

Tzaar et Autocrator totius Russiae

The reception of a foreign embassy in Moscow
at the beginning of the sixteenth century.
A contemporary engraving.

(*opposite*) Tsar Vasily Shuysky plotted the *coup*
which overthrew False Dmitry I in 1606. He
ruled until 1610, when he was deposed, forcibly
'shorn' as a monk, captured by Poles and
exhibited in Warsaw as a trophy of war.

False Dmitry II. The second of two pretenders
who posed as Ivan the Terrible's son Dmitry,
he maintained a rival administration to that
of Tsar Vasily Shuysky in the years 1608–10
at the village of Tushino near Moscow.
A contemporary print.

Fighting at Kitay-Gorod in Moscow, 1612,
part of the operations which freed the Russian
capital from occupation by the Poles and ended
the Time of Troubles. A watercolour by
G. Lissner.

5 Theodore I
Boris Godunov as Regent

The immediate effect of Ivan the Terrible's death was a relaxation of tension such as Russia was later to feel after the death of Peter the Great and other masterful Tsars or dictators. Decades of severity had left the community exhausted, and there was a general sensation of relief over which Ivan's successor seemed well qualified to preside.

Aged twenty-seven at the time of his father's death, Tsar Theodore I is well described by his contemporary, the English diplomat Giles Fletcher:

The Emperour . . . is for his person of a meane stature, somewhat lowe and grosse, of a sallowe complexion, and inclining to the dropsie, hawk nosed, unsteady in his pase by reason of some weakness of his lims, heavie and inactive, yet commonly smiling almost to a laughter . . . simple and slowe witted, but verie gentle, and of an easie nature, quiet, mercifull, of no martiall disposition.[39]

Here was a monarch with the mentality of a gentle child, whose chief interests were attending divine service, ringing church bells and observing the antics of dwarfs and jesters. His angelic simplemindedness went to the hearts of a people always indulgent to half-wits, and helped to create the impression of a 'holy fool' on the throne. But Theodore was not so saintly that he neglected a popular blood sport of the period – the fights in which a man armed with a spear would face a bear in a specially constructed pit. The use of wild animals for the entertainment of sovereign and populace was already well developed in Moscow, and there is even a report of one contest witnessed by Tsar Theodore in which a bear fresh from the forests fought another trained to defend itself with bow and arrows.[40] The outcome of this duel is not recorded.

Theodore was temperamentally incapable of taking initiative, and soon after his accession Russia had a new master in all but name – Boris Godunov. About seven years older than the Tsar and supposedly of Tatar descent, Godunov owed his rise to ambition, ability and powerful connexions. He had been a favourite of Ivan the Terrible for many years, and was linked with the Oprichnina by his marriage to the daughter of Malyuta Skuratov. But he was not a notorious man of violence, being better known for his role as would-be peacemaker in the tragic

D

scene which had led to the Tsarevich Ivan's death. Godunov had placed himself between the young man and his father, and though failing to save the Tsarevich, he had received wounds helpful to his own career. It was, however, the marriage of his sister Irina to Tsar Theodore which chiefly enabled Godunov to thrust his rivals aside and emerge as regent to his brother-in-law.

Among these rivals were the Shuyskys, a family with a long tradition of public intrigue. They tried to undermine Godunov's position by persuading Tsar Theodore to send the childless Tsaritsa Irina to a convent and remarry. They also provoked a riot on the Moscow streets against the Godunovs – a sign of the times, for the mob of the capital was soon to play a role in palace revolutions. But on this occasion the Shuyskys failed and were banished from Moscow. To outwit a Shuysky was to obtain a master's diploma in political guile, and by now Godunov (who could not read or write) seemed well versed in the grammar of power – including its irregular declensions. He was also a successful accumulator of wealth and symbols of prestige, piling up an imposing array of titles, keeping separate court of his own and dealing directly with foreign powers. The English found an apt name for his position: Lord Protector of Russia.

Godunov did not seek to rival Ivan IV as a promoter of atrocities. He employed terror, but sparingly and with discretion – functionally, as it were, and less as a means of self-expression. Not for him were great public holocausts such as those staged by the terrible Tsar in Novgorod and Moscow, for he preferred to work in the background through the network of spies controlled by his cousin Simon Godunov, head of police. Perhaps it was this secretive posture which helped to impress Godunov on the popular mind as a devious figure, suspected of staging crises deliberately so that he could pose as the saviour of his country. He incurred blame for setting fire to Moscow and inviting Tatar attack to distract attention from popular grievances and strengthen his own position – inevitably insecure so long as it rested solely on the good will of a Tsar notoriously feeble-minded.

As has been well said, Boris was a more modern ruler than Ivan the Terrible.[41] Professionally ingratiating as a good politician should be, he distributed largess to the poor and posed as protector of the common people. Though he was not a man of war, Russia did not suffer unduly from his lack of fighting spirit. In 1591 his troops beat off a serious Tatar threat to Moscow, the first in nearly twenty years; and on the north-west frontier Russia won back from Sweden the section of the coast on the Gulf of Finland forfeited by Ivan the Terrible in 1583. The new reign saw the further colonization of western Siberia, while Godunov also cultivated contact with western European countries and sent young Russians to study abroad. In the domestic field, his main achievement as regent was the promotion in 1589 of the Metropolitan Job to the supreme rank of patriarch, hitherto held only outside Russia. Since the Russian church had been autocephalous in all but name

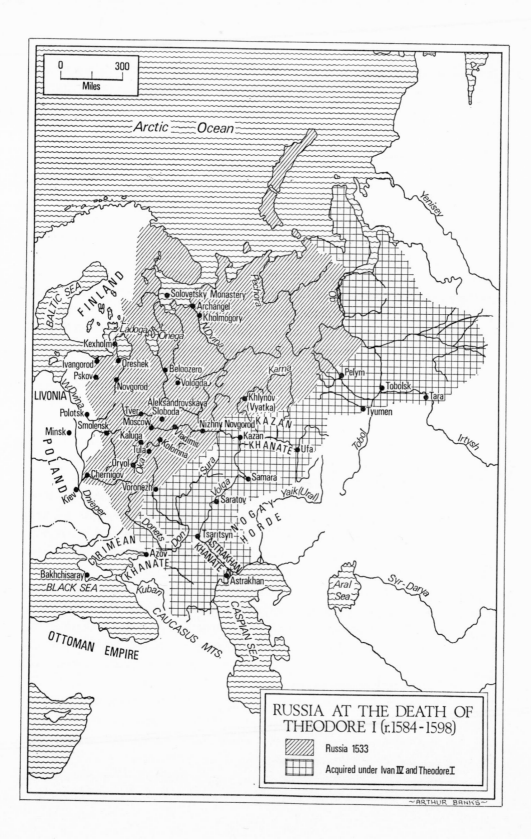

Arctic Ocean

0   300
Miles

BALTIC SEA

FINLAND

Solovetsky Monastery
Archangel
Kholmogory

Ladoga
Onega

Kexholm

Ivangorod
Pskov
Oreshek
Beloozero

Novgorod
Vologda

N.Dvina

Pechora

Kama

Pelym

Tobolsk
Tara

LIVONIA

Polotsk

Smolensk

Minsk

POLAND

Kiev

Dnieper

W.Dvina

Khlynov
(Vyatka)

Aleksandrovskaya
Tver
Sloboda
Moscow
Kaluga
Vladimir
Kolomna
Tula
Oryol
Chernigov
Voronezh

Nizhny Novgorod

KAZAN
Kazan
KHANATE
Ufa

Tyumen

Tobol

Irtysh

Yenisey

Oka

Donets

Don

Sura

Saratov

Samara

Volga

Yaik (Ural)

NOGAY HORDE

CRIMEAN
KHANATE

Azov

Bakhchisaray

BLACK SEA

Kuban

Tsaritsyn

ASTRAKHAN
KHANATE

Astrakhan

CAUCASUS MTS.

CASPIAN SEA

Aral
Sea

Syr-Darya

OTTOMAN EMPIRE

RUSSIA AT THE DEATH OF
THEODORE I (r.1584-1598)

Russia 1533

Acquired under Ivan IV and Theodore I

~ARTHUR BANKS~

for about a century and a half, the promotion was long overdue. It later proved a shrewd political move on Godunov's part, for the first Russian patriarch eventually repaid his patron by helping to make him Tsar.

An unhappier domestic event was the mysterious death of the Tsarevich Dmitry – the only surviving son of Ivan IV apart from Tsar Theodore himself. Dmitry's importance as a possible successor to the throne was steadily increasing as the years passed without Theodore siring an heir, but even at the time of Theodore's accession his infant brother had already seemed dangerous enough to be worth exiling to his patrimony at Uglich about a hundred and twenty miles north of Moscow. In this quiet backwater Dmitry, his mother and other relatives were living in honourable banishment but closely supervised by Godunov's agents when, on 15 May 1591, the nine-year-old Tsarevich was found with his throat cut in the courtyard of his residence under circumstances which remain obscure. Had he been murdered, as his mother claimed? And by Godunov's henchmen? Summoned to the scene by church bell, the outraged townsfolk of Uglich took this view immediately after the event, and they helped to confuse the evidence by lynching Godunov's agents there and then. A different view was that of the official commission from Moscow under Prince Vasily Shuysky, which visited Uglich and reported that the Tsarevich had died accidentally of a self-inflicted wound – overtaken by an epileptic fit while playing with a knife. Somehow this version does not carry the ring of truth, and Shuysky himself afterwards disavowed it to suit his own convenience – then reauthenticated it later for the same purpose. There is also the curious point that Godunov's government carried out savage repressions in Uglich after the Tsarevich's death, executing many of the townspeople or cutting out their tongues – a means of discouraging careless talk effective in an age of general illiteracy. They even removed the offending church bell, a measure which suggests that official eagerness to cover up events, whatever they may have been, had passed the bounds of reason.

Successfully as the authorities had blurred the traces, it by no means follows that the murder of the Tsarevich was Godunov's doing, although this came to be widely believed. The charge remains unproven, which is typical of his ambivalent record, for though his ability is generally conceded, his moral calibre remains a puzzle. Was he an ambitious scoundrel or a statesman devoted to the true interests of his country? The evidence is not clear. In any case the death of the Tsarevich Dmitry had removed an obstacle in the Lord Protector's path. No limit seemed set to his ambitions when, on 7 January 1598, Theodore I died – last of the line of Ryurik, which had provided first Kiev and then Moscow with grand dukes and Tsars over a period of seven centuries.

6 Boris Godunov as Tsar 1598–1605

The decade and a half following Theodore's death marks a gap between the Ryurikids and the Romanovs, and a period when increasingly disreputable Tsars belonging to neither dynasty occupied the Russian throne. In 1613 the election of the first Romanov marked the end of this 'time of troubles' – a deceptively mild name for a period of utter devastation; but it is not possible to assign such an exact date to the beginning of the troubles, for they gained momentum gradually.

At the time of Theodore's death, Boris Godunov had ruled Russia for a dozen years. There was still no law of succession, and he seemed well fitted to become Tsar by experience and ability. But no upstart, however capable, could assume so ancient a crown without a show of decent reluctance, as he himself was well aware. The weeks after Theodore's death accordingly witnessed prolonged negotiations between Boris and his protégé the Patriarch Job. Privately and publicly, alone or with attendant dignitaries and claques, the patriarch implored the Lord Protector to accept the throne. But even after a properly constituted national assembly (*zemsky sobor*) had unanimously offered Boris the crown, he still hesitated – provoking a threat by the patriarch to excommunicate him and suspend church services unless he would yield. In the end he did so – his resistance further sapped, according to one tradition, by crowds of suppliants who besieged his headquarters and wept tears of entreaty . . . ordered to do so on pain of beating by the reluctant Tsar's own agents.[42] But Platonov points out that the accession was no vulgar farce. Tsar Boris was a legitimate sovereign properly elected in the most reputable manner available.[43] And though he was the first prince of Moscow to owe his throne to election, not to birth, he acquired unlimited autocratic power like any hereditary autocrat.

The dazzling ceremonial of his coronation did not blind Tsar Boris to the dangers which beset the throne. His spies and police remained vigilant, and staged a notable *coup* by arresting his main rivals (the Romanov brothers) as sorcerers and banishing them to northern Russia. They forced Theodore Romanov, the outstanding member of the family, to become a monk, thereby apparently retiring him from active politics – though neither his change of status nor the accompanying change of name (from Theodore to Philaret) was to prove effective in removing the Romanovs from the pages of history.

Meanwhile Godunov was becoming more unpopular than ever. The people held him guilty of a growing tally of crimes from the murder of the Tsarevich Dmitry downwards. Three years of acute famine in 1601–03 further hastened his decline. Many thousands of citizens starved, reports of cannibalism being common, and though he was conspicuous in organizing food supplies, the people blamed him for the famine too. Other symptoms of disintegration began to accumulate as more and more peasants fled from the centre of Muscovy to join the Cossacks – disorderly frontiersmen barely under Moscow's control. The new Tsar's attempts to restrain them failed, mass banditry developed, and although regular troops turned out to suppress such disorders, the anarchic spirit of the age infected them too.

It was into this chaotic atmosphere that a young man styling himself the Tsarevich Dmitry injected a new element fatal to Godunov and his dynasty by invading Russian territory in 1604.

The identity of the pretender is not known. It was as Grishka Otrepyev, a runaway monk and former serf of the Romanov family, that Godunov's government officially denounced him. That this was indeed his identity is likely or probable. Another possibility – that he was no pretender, but the true Tsarevich Dmitry who had somehow escaped death at Uglich – is not universally discounted;[44] and it seems from some of the young man's actions that he believed himself genuine, as every good impostor should. He is agreed to have been a native Russian and an expert horseman, and though he was ill-favoured – with warts on his face, and arms of uneven length – his bearing was not so undistinguished that aristocrats or common people hesitated to join him. He first launched himself in 1603, and spent a year canvassing help in Poland, where his main supporter was an enterprising squire, George Mniszech. Dmitry fell in love with Mniszech's daughter Maryna, who was to become his Tsaritsa if his escapade should succeed, and he accepted Catholicism as the price of Polish support.

The pretender crossed into Muscovy in October 1604 at the head of over a thousand adventurers, chiefly Poles. He proclaimed himself rightful heir to the Russian throne and Godunov as a usurper, and it is a measure of Godunov's unpopularity that Cossacks and disaffected elements in south-west Russia rallied to the invader in large numbers. As Dmitry marched towards Moscow, many towns went over to him without a shot being fired. Demoralized or incompetently led, a powerful Muscovite army failed to move effectively against him, while Tsar Boris himself seemed paralysed in the Kremlin by a sense of impending doom. He did not take the field in person against the pretender, and on 14 April 1605 he suddenly died – presumably just in time to escape defeat and humiliation.

His son Theodore succeeded him.

7 Theodore Godunov 1605

Boris Godunov had groomed Theodore for the succession, and he seemed an ideal crown prince – robust, good-looking and well-educated. But it was for only a few weeks that the sixteen-year-old youth presided over his disintegrating realm. In the middle of May his main army went over to Dmitry about two hundred and fifty miles south of Moscow, after which the pretender's agents began to penetrate the capital. On 1 June his emissaries recited from the Place of the Skull in the Red Square a resounding manifesto which whipped up the excitement of the mob. Rioters stormed the royal palace and seized the Godunovs, mother and son. Soon afterwards a gang of assassins killed them, strangling Tsar Theodore's mother in his presence, while the youth himself struggled fiercely. They murdered him with peculiarly revolting cruelty.

8 False Dmitry I   1605–06

On 20 June 1605 False Dmitry entered the capital on a white horse, acclaimed by excited throngs and deafening peals of church bells. His supposed mother, the widow of Ivan the Terrible, came to Moscow and publicly recognized him as her son, which seemed to put his credentials as Tsar beyond doubt. He was crowned in her presence in the Uspensky Cathedral with the usual ceremony, and to a display of greater enthusiasm than the elevation of either Godunov had inspired.

In a bid for popularity Dmitry increased the pay of soldiers and officials, and held an orgy of celebrations in his capital. But his vogue did not last. His subjects disliked his Polish Catholic entourage, and frowned on his neglect of royal etiquette as understood in Moscow. What manner of Tsar was this who hob-nobbed with all and sundry, walked about unescorted and was lax in observing Orthodox practice? Spurning the traditional Russian siesta and steam bath, he surrounded himself with foreigners, ate veal, rode bareback and on unbroken stallions, and once insisted on climbing into a bear-pit with a spear and dispatching one of the beasts himself – anticipating Peter the Great in the violence of his frolics and antagonizing a people accustomed to a more stately regal pace. Maryna Mniszech made matters worse by arriving in Moscow with yet more Poles and attendant papists, a further affront to the Orthodox.

Soon after marriage to Maryna, Dmitry fell victim to a *coup* plotted by Vasily Shuysky and was murdered in the Kremlin on 17 May 1606, after ruling for less than a year. Placed on show in the Red Square, his body was burnt and the ashes fired from a cannon in the direction of Poland. Many of his Poles met their death in the accompanying pogrom, and their women were raped by Russian boyars who – according to one report – strutted through the Kremlin exposing their 'equine pudenda' and boasting: 'Behold, you whores! We are much better men than your Poles! Try us!'[45] The False Tsaritsa Maryna escaped this ordeal, to continue her career elsewhere as consort to later pretenders.

On 19 May, Vasily Shuysky became Tsar. Neither elected nor born to the throne, he owed his elevation to the shouts of the Moscow rabble and the support of a caucus of boyars.

9 Vasily Shuysky 1606-10

Though Tsar Vasily came of an ancient line, his accession did nothing to restore the monarchy to its former dignity. Known as the boyars' Tsar out of compliment to those who had helped him to power, he failed to champion anyone's interests effectively, even the boyars' or his own. Little, indeed, could be expected from any Tsar in these chaotic circumstances. The new occupant of the throne was not likely to forget that his two immediate predecessors had been murdered – one of them, so to speak, twice. Nor could the fourth Tsar to reign within fourteen months regard his tenure as secure, especially since much of the country did not accept his authority. He tried to assert himself by having the Tsarevich Dmitry of Uglich canonized (to prove that he was really dead), and the remains were traced with some difficulty and brought to Moscow. But this demonstration failed to prevent more Dmitrys from emerging. Nor did the device save Russia from further upheaval.

The new Tsar fought the first peasant war in Russian history when challenged by Ivan Bolotnikov, who appeared from the south to threaten Moscow in October 1606 at the head of what has been called a revolutionary army. Bolotnikov's programme involved no subtleties of doctrine – the poor were to kill the rich and take their wives and property. He did not pretend to be a Tsar. Nor, at first, could he even claim the support of a pretender. He later acquired a False Peter – a reputed son of Theodore I, who was hanged after the capture of Bolotnikov's last stronghold in October 1607.

Tsar Vasily next found himself faced with a second False Dmitry, whose identity is a greater mystery than his predecessor's. False False Dmitry was, moreover, an even greater fraud – partly because he pretended to be not one, but two persons (False Dmitry I and the true Tsarevich); partly because he did not, apparently, believe in his own credentials, or even inspire such belief among many of his followers. However, he became a rallying point for forces opposed to Vasily, including yet more Polish adventurers. Though he failed to take Moscow, he was able to maintain a headquarters in the near-by village of Tushino for about two years from early 1608. During this time his forces came near to blockading the capital, and he himself aped Moscow by setting up parallel institutions of his own.

While Tsar Vasily ruled Moscow, Tsar Dmitry was lording it in Tushino over the varying and at times extensive areas commanded by his supporters. Maryna Mniszech endorsed him as her husband, no doubt as thoroughly bewildered by now as were the many dignitaries who contrived to keep one foot in Tushino and another in Moscow – switching allegiance between the two or holding simultaneous appointments in both. Early in 1610 the Tsardom of Tushino collapsed, and False Dmitry II withdrew to the provinces, where he was murdered later in the same year. His death did not end the series of bogus Tsars and Tsareviches, among whom was surely the most illegitimate child on record – his own baby son by Maryna Mniszech, the product, that is, of False False Dmitry and his False Tsaritsa. To him further impostors were added in the shape of various Yeroshkas, Gavrilkas, Martynkas and the like, for no little local army or gang of brigands felt complete without its portable autocrat.

From 1609 onwards confusion grew worse when foreign governments began to interfere directly. The Swedes occupied Novgorod, but Poles wrought the greater havoc. They besieged Smolensk and advanced towards Moscow itself, where the mob deposed Tsar Vasily on 17 July 1610, sparing his life. 'Shorn' as a monk, he struggled desperately, having to be held down as the ceremony was performed . . . and then, as if to add further indignity, his very induction was pronounced invalid by the patriarch, with the result that this one-time Tsar – as improperly deposed as he had been improperly elected – no longer rated even as a monk. Nor had fate yet finished with Vasily Shuysky, whose further tribulations included capture by Poles. They dressed him in a white smock and drove him in an open carriage as a trophy into Warsaw, there to do homage to the Polish king, and also to serve as a visual aid at a public lecture on the mutability of human fortune delivered by his verbose captor, the Hetman Żółkiewski. Native Russian historians may be excused if they sometimes gloss over this episode, which surely represents the lowest point in their national history.

10 Interregnum 1610-13

After Vasily Shuysky's dethronement a group of seven Russian boyars claiming authority over Muscovy concluded with King Sigismund III of Poland an agreement providing for the election of Sigismund's fourteen-year-old son Władysław as Tsar of Russia. Soon afterwards, however, the Polish King decided that he himself should supersede his son as Tsar, thus uniting Poland and Russia under a single crown. Though neither father nor son was able to enforce his claim to be ruler of Russia in any effective sense, Polish forces occupied Moscow itself in September 1610 and held it for two years. Meanwhile the Russian throne lay vacant, though it is also arguable that two absentee monarchs, Władysław and Sigismund, held it in turn. The two Poles combined the disadvantages of foreign nationality and alien religion with disreputable status in the sense that their elevation to sovereignty over Russia did not even conform with such rudimentary constitutional and legal precedent as the history of Muscovy could offer.

Polish behaviour at this period might have been calculated to provoke a fiercely patriotic reaction from Muscovy, for the divided Russians would less easily have acquired a rallying cry had it not been for their loathing of Poles and the Catholic faith. A Russian national revival began to make headway, encouraged by the Russian Orthodox Church under the Patriarch Hermogenes, who refused to take the oath of allegiance to Sigismund of Poland and suffered imprisonment in the Kremlin by its Polish occupiers. Russian popular armies arose in the north and east, and on 25 October 1612 they forced the Polish garrison of the Kremlin to capitulate and made the Russians masters in their own capital once again.

As the very proliferation of bogus Tsars so eloquently demonstrates, the Russian community was as dedicated to the institution of the monarchy as it was to that of the *skandal*. It was, accordingly, the Muscovites' first thought, after recovering their capital city from the Poles, to equip themselves with a new Tsar – but one with impeccable credentials. Only election by a national assembly could confer the proper status, and in January 1613 such a body convened. It included several hundred delegates from fifty towns, pains being taken to make it regionally and socially representative. There was no lack of candidates for the throne, but the delegates simplified their task at the outset by rejecting all foreigners; among whom a Swedish and a Habsburg prince had been mooted.

Eventually, on 7 February 1613, the choice fell on Michael Romanov.

Part 2   The First Romanovs

11 Michael   1613-45

Tsar Michael's accession at the age of sixteen brought to the throne the new ruling house of Romanov, which was to govern Russia until the dynasty ended in 1917.

To the national assembly of 1613 the Romanovs had commended themselves in many ways, including links with the last Ryurikids. Actual descent from Ryurik (which Michael Romanov could claim on his mother's side) weighed less than family connexions through his father Theodore, a nephew of Ivan the Terrible's first wife. This was a stronger association than other candidates could offer, and Theodore Romanov himself might well have obtained election as Tsar in 1613 had he not lost his secular status under Boris Godunov. As the monk Philaret he had held high church office under both False Dmitrys, an association which does not seem to have cost him any of his considerable popularity. But he was unable to exercise direct influence on the election of a new Tsar in 1613, being a prisoner of the Poles at the time. That only improved Michael's chances, however, for in Russian eyes there could be little wrong with a young man whose father was suffering ill-treatment at the hands of the traditional enemy.

Michael Romanov, too, was absent from Moscow at the time of his election. Even his electors did not know his exact whereabouts – a monastery at Kostroma, about two hundred miles north-east of Moscow, where he was residing with his mother. Traced to this provincial retreat by a mission from the national assembly, the youth reacted to the offer of the crown with 'great anger and weeping'.[1] Mother and son replied to the envoys' pleas by pointing to the grim fate of many recent Russian rulers; and they had every reason to hesitate, for where was the attraction in reigning supreme over total chaos? But six hours of tearful entreaty won Michael over, and his mother blessed him as Tsar. According to a well-known patriotic Russian legend, Polish marauders attempted to capture and kill Michael Romanov before he could leave Kostroma. This kidnapping party tried to force a

Russian peasant, Ivan Susanin, to lead them to the Tsar – instead of which he lured them into the virgin forests. Realizing what had happened, they murdered the great folk hero, who lives on in Glinka's opera *A Life for the Tsar* (1836).

On 19 March the royal party left Kostroma for Moscow on a journey which lasted six weeks owing to the chaotic condition of the countryside and the sovereign's natural timidity. About forty miles from the capital he refused to go on, and informed the assembly's envoys that they had made him Tsar on false pretences – for order had not been restored in the land, as they had assured him.[2] But he eventually reached the makeshift quarters prepared for him in the ruined Kremlin, and was duly crowned on 11 July – thus formally ending the time of troubles. Troubles did, however, continue on a diminishing scale. After the new Tsar's accession several warlords remained active, and one such threatened Moscow with an army of several thousand Cossacks before his defeat and execution. Another rebel Cossack leader, Ivan Zarutsky, became the last in the series of Maryna Mniszech's protectors, but loyal forces drove him back on Astrakhan with the lady and her infant son by False Dmitry II, now deceased. Captured and brought to Moscow, Zarutsky suffered impalement; Maryna herself died in prison, and her four-year-old son was hanged at the city gates. Meanwhile a more august pretender, Prince Władysław of Poland, had not given up his claim to the Russian throne; nor did he do so even after invading Russia in 1618 and failing to capture Moscow.

These events ushered in the most featureless reign of any Tsar. Michael contrived to rule for almost a third of a century, yet barely left any imprint behind him, whether because insufficient evidence has survived or because he was indeed so pallid a figure. Contemporaries compared the youth with his distant relative and predecessor Theodore, once renowned as a 'holy fool' on the throne. Michael, however, developed along less picturesque lines. Holy he undoubtedly was, showing the traditional piety of a Tsar and making the customary pilgrimages to Russian shrines; but he was less of a fool than his saintly predecessor – and to that extent a less memorable figure. Platonov calls him intelligent,[3] and he seems to have suffered not so much from lack of wit as from a reluctance natural in a chronic invalid to assume responsibility. He had an ailment of the legs such as was to afflict later Romanovs, and it was sometimes necessary to carry him to his sledge. His predilections included such curiosities as exotic flowers and Englishmen.

During the early years of Michael's reign the national assembly continued to sit on a more or less permanent basis, advising on such matters as taxation and foreign policy. It provided the nearest approximation to rule by a representative institution exercised under any Tsar before the twentieth century. But the assembly was no parliament, even in embryo. Recalled occasionally at times of crisis later in the seventeenth century, it remained a consultative organ; its recommendations were not binding on the Tsar, nor did its existence threaten his autocratic power.

Michael's reign was not a period when the might of Russia overawed her western neighbours. The troubles had drastically reduced a Russian population of some fourteen million – perhaps by as much as a third – and it was not until the mid-seventeenth century that the number of inhabitants again stood at its former level.[4] Moreover, the country was so weak that Sweden and Poland were able to make good a claim to sizeable Russian territories – Sweden obtaining areas in the north-west (including Ingermanland), while Poland acquired Smolensk and extensive lands in the west.

Ambitious favourites so commonly filled the power vacuum left by a weak monarch that it is tempting to assume such a situation for the first years of Michael's reign, when the young Tsar's energetic mother was dominant. But though she brought certain associates to prominence, it is not clear that they were as active in exercising political influence as in pursuing personal advantage. In the seventh year of the reign, however, a real power appeared behind the throne with the release of Michael's father Philaret from Polish captivity and his return to Moscow, where the post of patriarch had been left vacant for him. He was miscast as pontiff, being more of a secular despot by inclination – but then his monkish son was also miscast as Tsar. Michael appears to have raised no objection when his father assumed the position of *de facto* monarch and almost became co-Tsar in name by taking the official title of 'great sovereign', shared with his son. Though Philaret's name appeared after Michael's on official documents, no one doubted where the main initiative lay in an administration more decisive in tone than that of the reign's earlier and later years. The arrangement also had the advantage of leaving each great sovereign to his natural bent – the son to his flowers, the father to political activity.

Philaret began his reign by shedding rival influences. He allowed the national assembly to lapse and banished the Saltykovs, relatives of Michael's mother, for intriguing against the young Tsar as follows. Before his father's return from Poland, Michael had arranged to marry a certain Mary Khlopov, but she unfortunately came to suffer from attacks of vomiting possibly caused by a Kremlin diet too heavy for her. The Saltykovs seized the opportunity to have her proclaimed a chronic invalid 'too frail for the sovereign's pleasure'.[5] Their motive was to preserve their own influence from the competition of a rival family – a stock situation in the domestic dramas of the Tsars, which is why charges of 'spoiling' a sovereign's bride by sorcery, poisoning and the like, were so common. The intriguers contrived to exile Mary to Siberia – an indication of how little Michael's wishes counted in a matter so closely concerning him, for he was devoted to his betrothed. Though Mary Khlopov's personal fortunes improved after Philaret's return to Moscow, she did not regain her status as royal bride, attempts being made to unite Michael with some western European princess.

These failed, but the quest for a Tsaritsa went on, since it was necessary to ensure the succession at all costs. All seemed settled at last with the Tsar's marriage at the age of twenty-eight to a Russian bride, Princess Mary Dolgoruky, when she suddenly died – another victim of reputed 'spoiling'.[6] In the next year, however, he at last married a suitably durable and fruitful Tsaritsa in Eudoxia Streshnev.

The years between Philaret's death in 1633 and that of Michael in 1645 witnessed several episodes discreditable to the sovereign. A Russian army surrendered to the Poles at Smolensk in 1634 after unsuccessfully besieging the city; but it was not the disaster itself which brought shame on the Tsar and his advisers so much as their decision to decapitate their own defeated commander-in-chief and second-in-command. A few years later another inglorious decision followed the seizure of the Turkish fortress of Azov near the mouth of the Don by a party of Cossacks. They offered it to the Russian crown, but met with delays and hesitations. In the end the Tsar ordered them to quit Azov, incurring criticism for his feebleness and displeasing the Cossacks concerned, who angrily dismantled the stronghold stone by stone. However, Michael's caution did at least spare Russia a clash with Turkey.

The Tsar also shared responsibility for the shabby treatment of the Danish Prince Waldemar after approving arrangements for him to marry Irina, the eldest Tsarevna. Amongst other provisions the marriage contract specifically reserved the groom's right to retain his Protestant faith. But once on Muscovite soil, Waldemar found his Russian hosts set on revoking this crucial clause. By trying to insist on the prince's conversion to Orthodoxy and detaining him against his will when he refused, the Tsar showed the stubbornness of a weak nature, and his persecutions proceeded in the maddeningly saintly style of old Moscow – well larded with professions of love for the prospective son-in-law. With such a friend as Tsar Michael, Prince Waldemar hardly needed an enemy. Nor did the charms of his fiancée keep the young man's enthusiasm at fever pitch, since he was never allowed to see her, and soon his only thought was to escape. One night he tried to fight his way out of Moscow with his personal bodyguard, but Russian troops beat off the desperate sally. Great scandal ensued and the unwilling bridegroom had to wait for Michael's death before he could leave Russia unencumbered by alliance with the house of Romanov.

Though the Tsar's actions may have been ill-judged or petty on occasion, he did not neglect the duty of providing an heir to the throne – a task complicated by the high mortality rate of Romanov infants, as of children in general during the period. Michael himself had been one of four survivors among eleven brothers and sisters, and he sired twelve offspring most of whom also perished in infancy.

Michael, the first Tsar of the Romanov dynasty,
was elected to the throne by a national assembly,
and reigned from 1613 until 1645.
An equestrian portrait by an unknown
seventeenth-century artist.

(*opposite*) The Patriarch Philaret, formerly Theodore Romanov, was the father of Tsar Michael and became the real ruler of Russia between his release from Polish captivity in 1619 and his death in 1633. Anonymous seventeenth-century portrait.

The orb of the Great Order of Tsar Michael, 1627–8.

The proclamation of Tsar Michael's election to the throne (on 7 February 1613) in the Red Square in Moscow. Miniature from the seventeenth-century *Book of the Election of Michael Fyodorovich as Tsar*.

СВЯТЫШИ КУРЪ ФИЛАРЕТЪ НИКИТИЧЬ ПАТРIАРХЪ МОСКОВСКИЙ И ВСЕЯ РОССIИ

(*opposite*) The consecration of Philaret as
Patriarch. Miniature from the seventeenth-
century *Book of the Election of Michael
Fyodorovich as Tsar*.

Tsar Alexis. Portrait from the *Titulyarnik*
of 1672.

Tsar Alexis and the Patriarch Nikon.
A protégé of the young Tsar, the Patriarch
sought to dominate him; a quarrel between them
began in 1658, ending with Nikon's trial
and condemnation eight years later.
A nineteenth-century lithograph.

(*opposite*) The Patriarch Nikon instructing the
clergy. A seventeenth-century portrait.

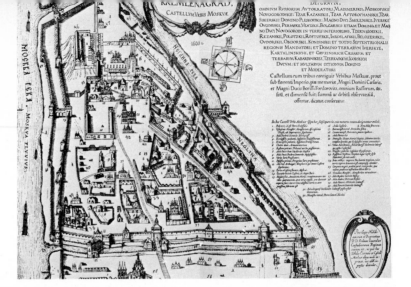

Plan of the Kremlin during the reign of Tsar Alexis.

Panoramic view of Moscow in the seventeenth century, from Olearius's *Journey to Muscovy*, 1660.

Plan of Moscow in the mid-seventeenth century. Engraving by P. van der Aa.

12 Alexis 1645-76

The Tsarevich Alexis succeeded his father in 1645, at the age of sixteen. His personal physician, the Englishman Samuel Collins, later described his royal patient as follows:

His Imperial Majesty is a goodly person, two months older than King Charles the Second, of a sanguine complexion, light brown hair, his beard uncut, he is tall and fat, of a majestical Deportment, severe in his anger, bountiful, charitable, chastly uxorious, very kind to his Sisters and Children, of a strong memory, strict in his Devotions, and a favourer of his Religion; and had he not such a cloud of Sycophants and jealous Nobility about him, who blind his good intentions, no doubt he might be numbered among the best and wisest of Princes. His Father was . . . a man of peace; but this Emperour is of a war-like spirit ingaged aginst the *Crim*, *Polacks* and *Swedes*, with what success let time declare.[7]

And, again: 'He is a goodly person, about six foot high, well set, inclin'd to fat, of a clear complexion, lightish hair, somewhat a low forehead, of a stern countenance, severe in his chastisements, but very careful of his subjects' love.'[8]

As these descriptions suggest, Alexis was more of an average man than the average Tsar, an exception to the tendency for Russian sovereigns to be forceful or feeble, and in either case to excess. The only superlative commonly applied to him was his unofficial title of 'most gentle', which apparently conflicts with certain details given by Collins. But the rougher features of Alexis's character are well attested, for he often lost his temper – and in the most unsuitable surroundings. To quarrel with the Patriarch of All Russia in church and call him a son of a bitch was by no means untypical of the gentle Tsar, since he repeated this same ill-chosen phrase when rebuking another cleric for misuse of an ecclesiastical title in the presence of the visiting Patriarch of Antioch.[9] Objecting to a bombastic speech by his own father-in-law at a meeting of the boyar council, the Tsar slapped his face, pulled his beard, kicked him out of the room and slammed the door after him. However, the jovial monarch was quick to regret these brief outbursts; they left no sting behind, for who could hold a grudge against one so obviously without malice?

Alexis devoutly performed his religious duties, remaining on his feet up to six hours on end at divine service, or executing a thousand devotional bows at a stretch. He kept the many church fasts with great strictness, taking neither food nor drink on Mondays, Wednesdays and Fridays during Lent, while confining himself to kvass and a single meal of cabbage, mushrooms and berries on other days.[10] He was also apt to require self-denial from his subjects, issuing instructions early in his reign – to be read out in market-places and churches – that devilish games were forbidden. This meant that traditional Russian clowns were not to ply their craft on pain of flogging, while secular music also came under a ban; there is a record of five wagon-loads of assorted dulcimers, rebecks and other satanic objects being taken across the Moscow River and burnt.[11]

Jesters, dwarfs and acrobats held less fascination for Alexis than for some earlier Tsars, but he maintained a large contingent of beggars and holy fools in special quarters, and loved to listen to aged men tell stories of long ago. He was also an outdoor Tsar who delighted in field sports – the pursuit of bear, wolf and elk in his forests. Above all, he adored falconry, and composed a technical manual on this fancy. No fanatic of puritanism, he would play practical jokes (innocent by the standards of a Tsar) such as ducking unpunctual courtiers in a pond, but it is also reported that: 'His Majesty will laugh to see his subjects handsomely fuddled, and sometimes he will put *Mercury* into their liquor.'[12] Gross as such a frolic may seem, Alexis was well mannered and well educated by the standards of Muscovy.

As already noted, Alexis was easily swayed by favourites. They included enlightened statesmen as well as self-seekers, and one who seemed to unite both kinds of urge – Boris Morozov, earliest favourite of the reign. While supervising the boy Alexis's education (which consisted principally of studying Church Slavonic texts and singing hymns), Morozov was gaining the ascendancy which made him the power behind the throne when the Tsarevich became the Tsar. Shortly after the accession, Morozov reputedly interfered in his pupil's marriage plans. Alexis had summoned the customary assembly of virgins to Moscow, and had selected Euphemia Vsevolozhsky as his bride, giving her the traditional kerchief and ring in token of his choice. But the young girl had the misfortune to faint at an official ceremony – perhaps because her handmaidens (primed by Morozov?) purposely bound her hair too tightly. She was pronounced an epileptic and sent to Siberia, her father reputedly suffering torture for attempting to foist a defective consort on the Tsar.[13] Much in love with Euphemia, Alexis showed himself no more effective in defending his betrothed than his father had proved under very similar circumstances, and once again a royal bride had been 'spoilt'. Soon afterwards Morozov arranged for the Tsar to marry Mary Miloslavsky, himself marrying her sister Anne and thus strengthening his own ties with the royal house.

Morozov's supremacy did not last long. The common people detested him, as they also detested certain lesser favourites – relatives of the Miloslavskys held to have exploited the populace with a rapacity beyond the accepted norm. Riots broke out, and a hostile crowd even dared to waylay the sacred person of the Tsar on the streets of Moscow, seizing the bridle of his horse and compelling him to listen to their grievances. They were not angry with Alexis himself, for he enjoyed a Tsar's immunity from popular wrath. But they forced him to sacrifice two hated associates – one being lynched, the other executed. Although the mob also sought vengeance on Morozov, the kindly young monarch would not give him up, pleading for his life with tears in his eyes according to one version of the incident.[14] Morozov suffered temporary exile, and never regained his old power in full.

Alexis came to preside over renewed Russian expansion in the tradition of earlier Muscovite monarchs. But though Samuel Collins has spoken of his 'warlike spirit', he was by no means a fighting Tsar, and it is significant that his chief territorial gain arose from the initiative of the annexed. The area concerned was the large Polish-ruled territory centred on the River Dnieper and part of the later Ukraine. Its Ukrainian Cossack inhabitants had successfully revolted against the Poles, but saw no prospect of maintaining their independence unaided. They therefore sought the Tsar's protection in an association with Muscovy the more attractive to both parties since both professed the Orthodox faith. Alexis hesitated, being unwilling to antagonize Poland, but eventually accepted the Ukrainian oath of allegiance in 1654 – only to accomplish far too thoroughly (from the Ukrainian point of view) what he had been so reluctant to embark upon in the first place. The Ukrainians had envisaged the new relationship as more of a voluntary partnership, and were dismayed to find themselves incorporated in Russia. Nor was the Muscovite habit of calling them 'Little Russians' calculated to soothe their *amour propre*. But they had to accept the situation, which the Tsar formalized in 1655 by expanding his official titles to include sovereignty over Little Russia, as also over White Russia.

Through accepting Ukrainian territory, the Tsar found himself at war with Poland. He reviewed, addressed and accompanied his troops on their victorious Polish campaigns of 1654-5. He also shared some of their hardships and dangers, being present at the hostilities which led to the Russian capture of Smolensk in 1654 and of Vilna, Kovno and Grodno in the following year. Embroiled in a war with Sweden, he joined his army on a drive against the Swedish-held southern Baltic coast in 1656, thus reviving the ambitions of Ivan the Terrible. But he suffered defeat by the Swedes after laying siege to Riga, and had to withdraw.

Alexis honourably distinguished himself by his kindliness in the field. The capture of Smolensk having led to wholesale rape and massacre by Russian soldiers – of fellow-nationals at that – he tried to discourage such atrocities by imposing the death penalty. He was also eager to stop the reckless firing of dwellings in occupied country. The Tsar's humane instincts are further illustrated by his charitable reference to a minor engagement during which Russian troops fled the battlefield. 'Our men have lost 51 killed and 35 wounded [he wrote in a letter of 1657], but I thank God that only such a number was lost out of three thousand. The rest all survived because they ran away.'[15] These were the words of an innocent, not of a natural conqueror. Nor were Alexis's wars by any means uniformly successful. But he managed to retain all the land east of the Dnieper ceded to him by union with the Ukraine. His acquisition of Kiev, the first Russian capital, was especially significant; and Smolensk also remained with Moscow after being long disputed between Russians and Poles. Such successes led to expansive moments when the Tsar paraded as champion of all Orthodox believers under foreign yoke. He also became, like Ivan the Terrible, a candidate for the Polish throne when that fell vacant. But the more effective prosecution of such designs was left to later Tsars.

Soon after Alexis had settled the boundaries of his expanded territory in the west (by the Armistice of Andrusovo with Poland in 1667), he temporarily lost control over an extensive area in south-eastern Russia through the rebellion of Stenka Razin. This was the most serious among many popular revolts of the reign, and swept along the Volga until its whole central and lower course was in Razin's hands. It ended after Cossacks loyal to Moscow had arrested the great guerrillero chieftain, who was executed by quartering in the capital in 1671. It is significant once again that the rebels showed no hostility to the Tsar's person, but proclaimed themselves loyal subjects of the crown and concentrated their hatred on gentry and landowners. A Tsar remained an object of awe to these insurgent armies of peasants, Cossacks and non-Russian peoples of the Volga.

Many lesser outbreaks of violence during Alexis's reign included an insurrection by monks of the Solovetsky Monastery on islands in the White Sea. There were also civil revolts in Pskov and Novgorod, and there was more than one outbreak in Moscow itself. The immediate impulse might be an increase in the salt tax, unpopular liturgical reform or the debasing of the currency, but one underlying cause lay in the development of an increasingly regimented society – already a totalitarian police state according to Florinsky.[16] Taxation and military service grew more burdensome, and the enserfment of the peasantry continued. Constant man-hunts against escaped bondsmen, brutal methods of extracting taxes, the corruption and greed of officials – all were factors helping to foment popular unrest to the point where a mystique of special blessedness was a necessity if the Tsar's person was to remain sacrosanct. Since Alexis was anything but a brutal dictator by temperament, the intensification of autocratic rule during his reign seems to have proceeded by momentum largely independent of the autocrat's will.

The Tsar's patience was sorely tried over the years by his conflict with the Patriarch Nikon, an awesome figure who dominated everyone within his orbit, sovereign or commoner. He was twenty-four years older than Alexis, and regarded the young Tsar as a junior officer; to him the patriarch's spiritual power was like the sun, while the Tsar in his secular office was a mere moon.[17] For such a relationship the previous reign offered a parallel in the domination of Tsar Michael by the Patriarch Philaret; but that was a family arrangement among Romanovs, whereas Nikon bid for power as an ambitious outsider. His was the most serious challenge to the state made by the church under the Tsars, though it represented a clash of personalities as much as a struggle between institutions.

Of peasant origin, Nikon rose to the rank of patriarch in 1652 – becoming, in effect, second citizen of Muscovy. But second best was not good enough for this tall, commanding personage with his huge head, loud voice and bushy eyebrows. Even before attaining the supreme church office, he had already begun to tutor his amiable Tsar in the ritual of self-abasement by arranging for the transfer to Moscow of the remains of the Metropolitan Philip (strangled under Ivan the Terrible) and compelling Alexis to make ceremonious public apology for the wrong done to this martyred head of the church nearly eighty years earlier by an autocrat of another dynasty. Alexis obligingly humbled himself, as he was to do again at Nikon's election to the patriarchate when he prostrated himself before his protégé in the Uspensky Cathedral, tearfully imploring him to accept office; as the price of compliance Nikon extorted from Alexis a solemn promise not to meddle in church affairs.

Church reform was among Nikon's main concerns. The development of printing made it essential to establish authoritative versions of the Orthodox Russian liturgical texts. Having diverged from their Greek originals, these stood in urgent need of correction by scholars, and Nikon helped to put this in hand, also sponsoring reform in such matters as the spelling of the name Jesus, the use of the exclamation Alleluia and the number of fingers which the devout should hold together as they crossed themselves. Nikon's innovations caused grave scandal in an age when trivialities of external detail often symbolized deeply held convictions on matters of principle. However, there was no conflict between Nikon and Alexis on such questions, and for this reason the great schism which the reforms provoked between Old Believers and reformed Orthodox had less immediate bearing on the history of the autocracy than did the patriarch's clash with the Tsar over the issue of power.

Installed on the patriarchal throne, Nikon surrounded himself with regal pomp. He assumed the title of great sovereign like Philaret before him, creating the impression that Moscow had two Tsars, and he functioned as sole autocrat when Alexis was absent. The patriarch's pretensions did not much trouble the common people, always fascinated – in Russia or elsewhere – by the spectacle of a megalo-maniac in high office. But they much distressed the church hierarchy, for Nikon was typically high-handed in dealing with his clergy; he degraded many, including some of the highest, threw them in irons and made them work in his palace bakery. Lay potentates also took offence at the pontiff's arrogance and interference in civil matters.

Nor did the Tsar himself remain indifferent to Nikon's egocentric quirks. His campaigns against Poland and Sweden had matured him, besides which the whis-perings of the patriarch's many enemies were constantly in his ears. The year 1658 accordingly saw the opening shots in a duel which was to last many years. The Tsar did not seek a direct confrontation. Inspired by Christian forbearance or moral cowardice, he withdrew his favours and took to avoiding his terrible adversary – whereupon the patriarch decided to call his sovereign to heel. He refused to perform his official functions, yet without fully resigning his office, and withdrew from Moscow to a near-by monastery, intending to bluff Alexis into begging for his return on bended knee. But that was asking too much, even from the most gentle Tsar. Alexis was still prepared to implore Nikon's blessing and forgiveness, and to send him presents, but would not stoop to unconditional surrender. Meanwhile Nikon varied his tactics, attempting both to intimidate the Tsar and to play on his sympathies. More than once the pontiff descended on Moscow from his retreat, but on each occasion the Tsar quickly ordered him away.

Eventually, in 1666, Nikon appeared before a court which included two of his peers – the foreign Patriarchs of Alexandria and Antioch, who had made the long journey to Moscow for the trial. Alexis pleaded his own case as plaintiff or prosecuting counsel before a superior court, the first and the last time that any Tsar ever put himself in such a position.[18] True to character, Nikon carried con-tempt of court to extreme lengths. He called the two eastern patriarchs beggarly vassals of the Turks and claimed that they were not entitled to sit in judgement on him at all, since they themselves had been dismissed from office. However, their authority prevailed and the Russian patriarch was sentenced to deposition from his office and degradation to the rank of an ordinary monk. The Patriarch of Alexan-dria personally unfrocked him, tearing off his white cowl and regalia. Nikon then proceeded to exile in a northern monastery where, though nominally a prisoner, he dominated the whole establishment. Remaining in communication with Moscow, he periodically granted or refused his blessing to the Tsar as part of tactics designed to secure his return, but the Tsar continued to keep him at a distance, while showing his usual kindness in trying to soothe the ex-patriarch's tantrums by letter.

Thus ended the main trial of strength between church and state in the history of the Tsars – a confrontation of saint and natural autocrat which saw the traditional roles reversed, for the saint represented the victorious secular power and the natural autocrat appeared in the robes of the church.

Firmly attached to old Muscovite tradition, Alexis did not much relax the stately conventions of his court which had the purpose of maintaining the Tsar's lofty status and preserving his physical security in a dangerous age. No sick person might enter the palace lest he infect the sovereign; nor might any visitor bear arms, a provision which gravely offended western European ambassadors in an age when a gentleman felt improperly dressed without his sword. Even the most exalted personage might not drive up to the palace entrance, and regulations governed the exact distance at which different classes of individual must dismount. The common people might not even enter the Kremlin compound on horseback, and would remove their hats at the mere sight of the Tsar's dwelling in the distance. Complex rules also governed access to various parts of the palace. Specially trusted officials naturally watched over a Tsar's bedchamber, and precautions against poisoning went beyond the employment of a single taster; the chef himself partook of the monarch's food under supervision, after which relays of officials sampled it, passed it on and guarded it.

Court ranks formed an elaborate hierarchy from boyar downwards through a variety of flunkeys – for it was as flunkey that every subject, high or low, rated with the autocrat. Courtiers served for ostentation as well as use, sometimes lining up as a living backcloth to ceremonial. Granted audience in the royal palace, foreign ambassadors would find the staircases and porches peopled by august personages refulgent in caftans of cloth of gold, who stood like dummies and did not move a muscle in reply to the visitor's bows. But at other times these living statues erred on the side of excessive animation by their addiction to the *skandal*, swearing at each other and fighting on the premises, though Alexis's code of laws of 1649 contained an entire chapter of measures designed to prevent dishonour to his court through such unseemly behaviour and cursing.[19]

Alexis was austere in his tastes. He ate and drank in moderation even when he was not fasting, and had no string of concubines nor even a single confirmed mistress. In public, however, he maintained full regal splendour. He would drive about with leading boyars standing on the running-boards of his carriage and other officials up in front, while high functionaries followed, the whole cortège escorted by a bodyguard of a hundred foot-soldiers who beat off the rabble with truncheons. On ceremonial occasions the Tsar had an escort of priests, officers, soldiers, officials and courtiers, and of special attendants who carried a foot-stool, a mat for him to stand on, his sunshade or umbrella, and his handkerchief. Earlier Tsars made a practice of keeping a basin of water by them when receiving a foreign ambassador, so that they could cleanse their hands from pollution by the heretic.[20] It is therefore hardly surprising if many western European envoys to Moscow felt that they had travelled more than half way to Peking.

The Tsars of Muscovy devoted much of their time to religious ritual. A typical morning began at four a.m. with worship in a private chapel before a glittering, candle-lit iconostasis. Such a ceremony also ended the Tsar's evening, and he would normally attend two or three far more lengthy church services in the course of his day. These devotions, and the three-hour siesta which he took after his main meal, left comparatively little time for domestic distractions and official business, which included consultations with boyars and the hearing of many petitions.

Hunting expeditions, military campaigns and pilgrimages provided breaks in routine – as also did the many special church festivals in Moscow itself. Such was Epiphany, when the patriarch blessed the frozen Moscow River. At midday the Tsar solemnly left his palace by the Red Staircase for the Uspensky Cathedral, his appearance signalled by deafening peals from the belfry of Ivan the Great. In the cathedral he arrayed himself in robes so heavily encrusted with gold and jewels that he could barely stand. They included a broad-sleeved caftan of cloth of gold surmounted by a particularly sumptuous mantle studded with precious stones and further surmounted by an ornate tippet. The royal crown, traditionally known merely as a cap (*shapka*) because of its edging of sable fur, scintillated with diamonds and emeralds, and his footwear of velvet or morocco sparkled with pearls and other precious stones. Round his neck was a golden chain and cross, and he carried a sceptre, also burning with gold and jewels, as he tottered to the river supported by two courtiers and flanked by a bodyguard of Streltsy in brightly coloured uniforms, some with gilded pistols and others with truncheons to beat off the crowds as the procession moved through an area packed with troops in martial array and a multitude of sightseers from all over Russia. On the river a small ornate temple of mica had been constructed beside a hole in the ice through which the patriarch immersed the cross. He thrice made the sign of the cross over the sovereign, who bent to kiss it before returning to his quarters by sledge.

The Tsar's womenfolk lived in seclusion in their quarters (the *terem*), another feature of old Muscovy to impress foreign visitors as oriental. Shielded from public gaze, they would witness ceremonial from some screened vantage-point, and even the slowest procession provided a welcome distraction from the customary needlework, alms-giving, private devotions and gossip. To be sister or daughter to a seventeenth-century Tsar was to be wedded to spinsterhood, for difference of religion rendered marriages to foreign princes impossible. Nor could the young ladies of the royal *terem* easily strike up an attachment with gallants of the Kremlin, since these were not permitted to set eyes on a Tsarevna; nor were they eligible as husbands, being mere flunkeys. The Tsaritsa's purdah was

Alexis, son of Tsar Michael, ruled from 1645 to 1676 and was known as the Most Gentle Tsar. He was a devotee of church ritual and Muscovite tradition. Anonymous portrait.

especially severe, and the penalty for catching sight of her by accident could be torture and disgrace. Even her doctor might not properly examine a sick Tsaritsa, but must attend in a specially darkened room and feel her pulse through a layer of cloth lest he defile her by contact. She kept the windows of her carriage covered to protect herself from the vulgar gaze, a practice abandoned by Natalia Naryshkin, Alexis's second wife and the mother of Peter the Great. She thereby caused scandal, for Alexis's first wife had been a Tsaritsa of the old school who would not have behaved so flightily. But Alexis compounded this licence by himself appearing in an open carriage with his handsome young second wife, and even took her hunting. Natalia also broke new ground by receiving boyars on her name-day and handing them portions of cake herself.

The Tsaritsa Natalia had been a ward of Artamon Matveyev, a favourite of the Tsar and one of those modern spirits who made no attempt to put their females in purdah – and since his wife was a Scotswoman this was no doubt just as well. Himself an advocate of European ways, he installed western pictures and furniture in his house and he set up his own domestic theatrical troupe. It was under his influence that the Tsar himself established a theatre in the Kremlin – a far cry from the beginning of his reign, when he had banned clowns and musical instruments. Alexis dealt another blow to tradition by allowing his children to study such new-fangled subjects as Latin in addition to the scriptural lore of old Russia, and he also had western European periodicals read out to him in translation.[21]

As these details show, the conservative Tsar could easily conceive an interest in foreign fashions, as in anything else which happened to catch his attention. It happens that his main favourites (Nikon excepted) all wished to see Russia take note of western European example in charting her development. The reign also saw a great increase in the number of foreigners attracted to service in Russia. These included army officers (the Russian army having been reorganized on foreign models) as well as merchants, apothecaries and doctors. For such aliens a special enclave, the German Quarter, was set up just outside Moscow.

Thus the bastions of old Muscovy were already slowly crumbling before Alexis's son Peter casually pulled them down about his subjects' ears.

13 Theodore III 1676–82

By his two marriages Alexis had sixteen children not remarkable for the general level of their suitability to succeed him. Several died in infancy. Others were girls, and thus apparently destined for seclusion in the *terem*. As for Theodore and Ivan (Alexis's only sons by his first wife to survive him), both were invalids and Ivan was feeble-witted as well. By his second wife, Alexis left Peter – a more rugged Tsarevich in potential, but only four years of age at his father's death.

At the age of fourteen the elder of Peter's two half-brothers mounted the throne as Tsar Theodore. To be more precise, his boyars hoisted him on to it. Weak in the legs, suffering from chronic scurvy and too feeble to doff his hat without help, he seemed ill-equipped to discharge even the ceremonial duties of a Tsar. During his short reign, which ended with his death at the age of twenty, favourites exercised power against a background of rivalry between the families of Alexis's two wives – the Miloslavskys and the Naryshkins. For a time Artamon Matveyev, a Naryshkin by association, maintained his position as a major influence, but he fell victim to intrigue and suffered exile for practising the black art – a charge which gained colour in the eyes of devout Russians from his addiction to western European manners. It was not the Miloslavskys who succeeded him as main policy-makers, but certain other associates of the young Tsar. Their régime coincided with a fashion for things Polish – the Polish language (which the Tsar himself knew), Polish clothes and Polish hair styles. These novelties now came into vogue, to the scandal of the more fanatical Orthodox.

Tension between old and new continued in Theodore's Muscovy. He himself was a yet more zealous champion of Orthodoxy than his father, and he led – as was natural for an invalid – a still more ascetic life. But the main feature of his reign, apart from Russia's first war with Turkey (1677–81), was a wide programme of minor domestic reform. Hard though it is to discern the ailing young Tsar's profile behind his many advisers, these innovations show a philanthropic and discreetly modernizing impulse in keeping with what may be suspected of his personal inclinations. They included the abolition of precedence – the institution whereby abstruse genealogical reckoning had for centuries influenced appointment to high civil and military rank. Progressively relaxed in various ways, the cumbrous system had continued to overshadow the conduct of affairs. It was abolished in 1682, the records concerned being burnt. To judge from his speech on that occasion,[22] the invalid Tsar could throw over tradition with a certain panache. Other reforms affected the penal code and brought the abolition or suspension of some particularly harsh penalties – the cutting off of hands and feet and the practice of burying women alive in public places where they were left to starve with only their heads protruding from the ground. Theodore's administration also abolished less brutal but no less significant traditions, among them that which required ordinary citizens to dismount from their horses and kowtow on meeting a boyar in the street. The same reasonable and humane spirit inspired the founding of certain charitable and educational establishments, and the Tsar personally intervened on behalf of the banished ex-patriarch Nikon, whose release from exile in the bleak north he eventually secured – though Nikon unfortunately died on his way back to civilization.

Among other relaxations of Theodore's reign was the virtual collapse of his own *terem*. The crowned weakling was in no position to enforce the traditional seclusion of females on six active sisters and several maiden aunts, a 'battalion of Tsarevnas'[23] commanded by the most forceful of their number, Theodore's elder sister Sophia. These emancipated young women now abandoned purdah to adopt the latest fashions in Polish dress and take lovers, while Sophia's interests also extended to political affairs.

The Tsar was briefly married to a girl of obscure and reputedly Polish origin, but she died giving birth to a son who did not long survive her. A few weeks before his death on 27 April 1682, Theodore took another wife; but this marriage too proved barren of heirs.

The first three Romanov sovereigns had given Russia a long period of comparatively undisturbed rule, while the crown twice passed from a father to an eldest son – an orderly sequence not repeated by other Romanovs until the late nineteenth century. Since Michael and Theodore were nonentities and Alexis barely rose above mediocrity, such order as obtained under these rulers owed little to the force of their personality. However, far from withering away, the institution of autocracy only flourished more vigorously than ever during these seven decades, for which reason it is tempting to deduce the presence of an overriding collective urge to submit to a supreme individual, however personally insignificant. The observation may also be risked that Russians tend to cultivate the extremes of order and disorder with astonishing singlemindedness – oscillating between the poles of total decorum and total *skandal* with an abandon beyond the attainment of more phlegmatic peoples. The time of troubles had seen the *skandal* enthroned, with Cossacks and other bandits indulging in wild lawlessness for its own sake. Then, with the accession of the first Romanov Tsar, the forces of order and decorum had gained control – which by no means ended violence, but switched the emphasis from popular upheaval to its suppression. Landowners, officials and the gentry as a whole allied themselves with the autocracy and strengthened their own positions, while the peasantry was the main loser. Thus, in the seventeenth century the institution of autocracy flourished at the expense of personal freedom, while Russia's power, territory and international self-confidence also grew – but through forces largely independent of her first three Romanov Tsars.

The reception of foreign ambassadors
by Tsar Alexis, illustrating the habit of using
boyars and court officials as a decorative
backcloth on these occasions. From
Olearius's *Journey to Muscovy*.

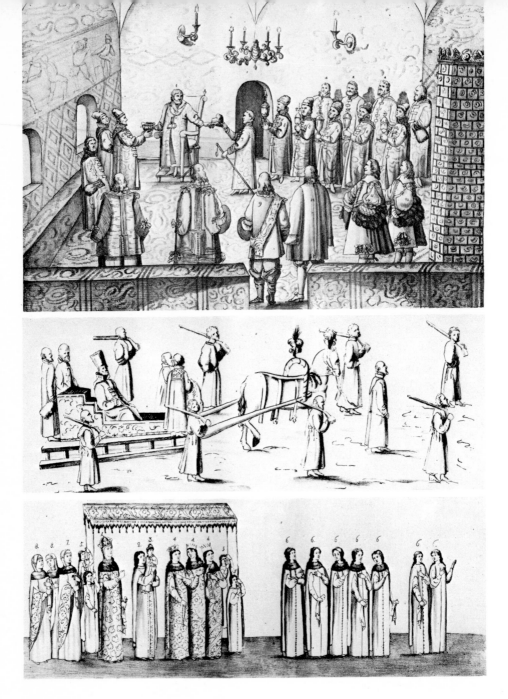

Sketches made by A. von Mayerberg, ambassador
of the Holy Roman Empire, 1661–2.
(*top*) The ambassador's reception by Tsar Alexis
on 24 April 1662. (*centre*) Tsar Alexis driving
in his crimson-upholstered sledge with two
boyars standing on the footboards behind, other
court officials in front and attended by Streltsy on
foot. (*bottom*) The solemn procession of the
Tsaritsa Mary, Tsar Alexis's first wife, to
church. The procession includes the baby
Tsarevich and the Tsar's three sisters.

The Palm Sunday procession forming up on 23 March 1662. A contemporary sketch by von Mayerberg.

Stenka Razin being driven to execution in 1671 after the failure of his great rebellion of Cossacks, peasants and non-Russian peoples along the central and lower course of the Volga. Contemporary English engraving.

(*overleaf*) The Tsaritsa Natalia drives out in state (1674). Mother of Peter the Great, she broke the Tsaritsas' traditional practice of travelling with their carriage windows covered. From Palmkvist's *Album*, 1674.

A boyar. Boyars and princes
formed an *élite* around,
but often in conflict with,
the Tsar. Seventeenth-
century German impression.

The boyar Afanasy
Ordin-Nashchokin, who was
responsible for the conduct
of foreign affairs under
Tsar Alexis and was
an admirer of western
European traditions.
Anonymous seventeenth-
century portrait.

An archbishop. The power
of the Russian Orthodox
Church was gradually
reduced by the Tsars.
Seventeenth-century
German impression.

Theodore III. An invalid,
he came to the throne on the
death of his father,
Tsar Alexis, in 1676
and died in 1682, aged
twenty. Various favourites
exercised power during his
reign. Seventeenth-century
portrait by Saltanov.

Die drey Gebrüder
Czar Theodor, Czar
Iwan, und der jetzige
Czar Peter Alexiwitz
in seiner ersten Jugend

Der letzte Rußische
Patriarche Adrian
welcher Ano. 1702. ge=
storben, und der
Metropolite.

Tsar Theodore III (*left*) and his brother (later
Tsar Ivan V) with their infant half-brother
(later Peter I, the Great) in the foreground.
On the right is the Patriarch Adrian
and a Metropolitan.
Early eighteenth-century print.

Part 3

14 The Regency of Sophia 1682–9
Peter I, 'the Great', in Childhood

A new time of troubles seemed to loom ahead when Theodore III died without leaving issue or declaring a successor. By historical precedent the task of appointing a Tsar fell to a national assembly, and an assembly with a fair claim to be representative hurriedly convened in the Kremlin. There were only two possible candidates: the surviving sons of Tsar Alexis. The sixteen-year-old Ivan, son of Mary Miloslavsky, was the elder, and would certainly have been the stronger contender had he not been feeble-minded and partially blind, whereas his half-brother Peter (son of Natalia Naryshkin and born on 30 May 1672) already had the look of an autocrat about him at the age of nine. It was to Peter that the gathering accordingly gave its choice by acclamation.

The Naryshkins thus scored a victory over the Miloslavskys, and Russia received her greatest autocrat – but came close to losing him within a month in the riots of the Streltsy, the privileged soldier-traders who held a key position as garrison of the capital. Who controlled these janizaries controlled Moscow, and they were well poised to play the role of tsar-makers later inherited by the guards regiments of St Petersburg. They happened to be in a particularly bloodthirsty mood at this time, and members of the Miloslavsky faction seized the chance to persuade them that the Naryshkins had strangled the Tsarevich Ivan. Inflamed by this lie, a mutinous rabble of Streltsy decided to call the culprits to account on 15 May 1682, when they had the alarm rung on the church bells of the capital and surged into the Kremlin in their gaudy caftans with banners flying and drums beating.

The Tsaritsa Natalia scotched the rumour of Ivan's death by leading him out with Peter to the top of the Red Staircase for the mutineers to see. But the Streltsy were in no mood for anti-climax. Sparing the young Tsar Peter and his mother, they set upon lesser Naryshkins and their supporters. Rioters rushed the staircase, seized leading members of the faction and tossed them down to be caught on waiting pikes below and hacked to pieces; among those butchered in this way was the Tsaritsa's former guardian Artamon Matveyev. For three days the riots continued. Mutineers rampaged through the royal chambers, rummaging under beds and prodding altars in the palace chapels with their pikes as they hunted for Ivan Naryshkin, most hated of Peter's uncles. In the end their threats forced the Tsaritsa to give him up, and he received the last sacraments before the mob took him – to be dragged through the Kremlin, cruelly tortured, hoisted on pikes and finally cut in pieces and trampled into the mud of the Red Square. In this way Peter's near kinsman perished, as did many of his other relatives and friends – some before his eyes and shortly before his tenth birthday. The claim that the boy-Tsar faced the shambles with unflinching courage is not confirmed; nor is another common assertion – that the nervous twitching of head and shoulders which afflicted him in adult life derived from these experiences. That the bloody scenes nourished his loathing of the Miloslavskys and the Streltsy – and of the whole city of Moscow and its works – may be taken for granted.

The boy had carefully noted these people's methods . . . as they were one day to discover.

When the worst rioting was over, the Streltsy enforced political demands. They raised Peter's half-brother Ivan to the throne as co-Tsar to Peter – and with senior status. But neither boy could be more than an ornament for the time being, and it was their elder sister, the Tsarevna Sophia, whom the mutineers in effect appointed regent at the age of twenty-four. She thus became one of the very few women – and the first unmarried girl – to have ruled Russia. To what extent she had been personally responsible for unleashing the horror of the Streltsy is not clear, but she was well equipped to exploit the massacre – ambitious, energetic, well-educated and perhaps a fine figure of a woman. Opinions differed on this last point; she was too fat for foreign taste, and thus better suited to her own country, where slim women were thought unwholesome and would lie in bed drinking vodka to gain weight.

Sophia had been closer to Tsar Theodore than any of her five sisters, and at the time of his death was already a familiar figure to the boyars. One favourite of that reign, Prince Vasily Golitsyn, became her lover and was her chief political adviser under the regency. As regent, Sophia showed her aptitude for power politics by outwitting the very Streltsy whose pikes had carried her to office, for she reduced their pretensions soon afterwards by trapping and beheading their overweening leader. Her failures included two disastrous expeditions against the Crimean Tatars – led by Vasily Golitsyn, among whose virtues military skill was not numbered. In the last year of the regency a treaty with China formalized Russian frontiers in the far east, where the penetration of Siberia had been continuing throughout the century. One feature of Sophia's domestic administration was a particularly savage persecution of Old Believers; many of them perished at the stake as heretics, while others anticipated the official inquisition by congregating in wooden buildings, setting fire to them and burning themselves alive.

A masterful woman, Sophia assumed the title of autocrat and gave other signs of hoping to graduate from regent to fully established sovereign. Had she been more unscrupulous, she might have found some means of putting her young half-brother out of the way before he became old enough to rule. As it was, she left Peter and his mother to their own devices and did not prevent him from joining his co-Tsar Ivan v in discharging ceremonial duties. A special double throne was obtained for the boys' use and the contrast between the occupants struck all observers. While Ivan sat motionless on his semi-detached seat beneath the icons, his crown pulled nearly over his downcast eyes, Peter would be fidgeting next to him in similar headgear and looking about him in his lively, confident way. It was Sophia's habit to sit below her brothers on these formal occasions.

At the beginning of her regency, Sophia had little to fear from Peter. He and his mother took to living away from the Kremlin for much of the year, at the near-by village of Preobrazhenskoye. His upbringing was a casual affair. Although he learnt the usual religious texts by heart, his Russian spelling was bizarre even by the lax conventions of the day, and he learnt all his most important lessons through play. From drilling toy soldiers at home he moved to extensive manœuvring out of doors with animate 'toy regiments' recruited in Preobrazhenskoye and district. Stable-boys and the sons of his father's falconers jostled shoulders in these ranks; young noblemen joined them, and the contingent gradually evolved into a serious military force as Peter amused himself with drums, flags, pikes, pistols, carbines, muskets and cannon supplied on request by the Kremlin armoury. If fire was his element from boyhood onwards, so too was water. As often recorded, he came upon a dilapidated English sailing-boat in a village shed, repaired it and took it to the large lake at Pereyaslavl, north of Moscow, where he practised sailing and started to build his own boats. He also practised numerous handicrafts as carpenter, stone-mason, printer, blacksmith and the like.

15 Apprentice Autocrat: Peter I 1689-99

In January 1689, in his seventeenth year, Peter married Eudoxia Lopukhin, daughter of a court official, and with his marriage he came of age according to the notions of the time. This brought his relations with the regent Sophia to a head, and he began to show impatience at her ambitions. On 8 July 1689, he objected to her presence in a religious procession, and when she refused to leave on his demand he abandoned the ceremony himself and quitted Moscow.

After this challenge each side feared violence from the other – as was shown by Peter's panic at Preobrazhenskoye on the night of 7–8 August 1689. Suddenly woken by messengers from Moscow with the news that the Streltsy were on their way to arrest him (in fact a false alarm), he did not stop to argue but jumped out of bed, ran barefoot to his stables, leapt on a horse, galloped to a near-by wood and hid himself. Servants arrived with his boots and other clothing, and his small party rode through the night to the Monastery of the Trinity some forty miles to the north-east. The Tsar arrived at 6 a.m., collapsed on a bed, burst into tears and threw himself on the mercy of the archimandrite – an unsuitable posture for an autocrat. However, Peter's instincts had led him to behave wisely. In the well-planned political campaign which followed, he and his advisers gradually syphoned power from Moscow as more and more dignitaries, officers and soldiers made their way to the monastery to join the Tsar. His mother, the patriarch and the 'toy' regiments were among the first to arrive; then the many foreign officers in Russian employ also went over, and when the very Streltsy of the capital turned against Sophia, the issue was no longer in doubt. Her supporters executed or exiled, she suffered imprisonment in the Novodevichy Convent in Moscow, but was not yet forced to become a nun. Peter made it clear that he had no designs against his fellow-Tsar Ivan, who did not endanger his own position; besides, he had the usual Russian respect for the mentally afflicted. Ivan died in 1696.

Although Peter became a young father with the birth of the Tsarevich Alexis in 1690, domestic life was not for him – least of all with such a typical product of the *terem* as the Tsaritsa Eudoxia. His thoughts were not turned inwards on family life as understood in Muscovy, but outwards on the world at large. Foreigners became increasingly important as his teachers and drinking companions. General

Peter the Great, a painting by Art de Gelden.

Patrick Gordon, a Scot in Russian service, acted as his chief military instructor. Franz Lefort, a Swiss fugitive from Calvinism, became the leading favourite of the period, receiving honours and riches, and becoming a general – and an admiral too, though he knew little of the sea. Lefort helped to introduce Peter to the German Quarter situated about a mile from Moscow. This western European city in miniature offered a new kind of social life. Its inhabitants did not practise the seclusion of women, and it was now that Anna Mons, reputedly daughter of a German wineseller or jeweller, became Peter's mistress.

Peter was soon able to indulge his passion for boats on a grander scale than allowed by the lake at Pereyaslavl. In 1693 and 1694 he visited Russia's only port at Archangel, inspecting foreign merchantmen and sailing far out into the White Sea in his own yacht. But he did not omit to attend divine services in this pious quarter of the globe; active in church as on the ocean, he would read the lesson and sing in the choir, always anxious to take a hand himself.

By now the 'toy' soldiers stationed at Preobrazhenskoye and Semyonovskoye were receiving regular pay, and had formed the nucleus of the future guards regiments named after these villages. Peter himself started as drummer-boy and rose through the ranks as his military adventures gained ever wilder momentum. Manœuvres in autumn 1694 involved many thousands of troops, and over a score fell in action from the wadding in dummy bullets and other causes. It was all great fun, especially as the participants in these affrays, from Peter down to his jesters – and even a detachment of dwarfs – were often fighting drunk. The boisterous Tsar was always active, loving risks and uproar from his own drum, or from fireworks, grenades, bombs and cannonades set off by himself. Among the many reported victims of such sport was a boyar killed by a five-pound rocket manufactured and let off by the Tsar. Peter himself was lucky enough to come through the rowdy escapades of a lifetime with no worse damage than a burn on the face caused by the explosion of an improvised grenade.

From war games Peter proceeded to real warfare with expeditions in 1695 and 1696 against the Turks of Azov – the beginning of his lifelong drive for access to more seas. He shared the troops' hardships on campaign, but did not take supreme command himself – perhaps unfortunately – because rivalry between Generals Gordon and Lefort contributed to a Russian defeat when, in 1695, the siege of Azov had to be raised after three months. However, misfortune always tended to call forth Peter's great reserves of determination, and no sooner had he returned from the first Azov campaign than he at once set about redeeming his defeat. At Voronezh, south-east of Moscow, he created a fleet of galleys and barges intended for Azov by way of the River Don. In February he went to Voronezh himself and worked on the wharves. He also mobilized some seventy thousand men, freeing serfs who volunteered for the colours, and forced Azov to yield. Returning to

Moscow, Peter staged a triumphal march through the city. The procession trooped past all day, the Tsar himself appearing in the modest role of captain of ships' crews – he wore black, western-style dress with a white feather in his cap, and carried a halberd. One exhibit at his triumph was a captured traitor, the Dutchman Janssen who had gone over from Russian service to the Turks at Azov. Peter had him driven through Moscow in a cart, dressed as a Turk and flanked by two headsmen with axes and instruments of torture prominently displayed. Later he was knouted, broken on the wheel and beheaded, his head being publicly displayed on a pike.

As another event of this period shows, Peter's rancour could reach beyond the very tomb. When a plot against his life came to light in early 1697, he interpreted it as the work of the Miloslavsky family now generally forgotten. No other members of the clan being available, Peter had the coffin of Ivan Miloslavsky (twelve years deceased) exhumed, dragged on a sleigh by a team of pigs to the scaffold, and placed where the blood of the beheaded plotters flowed over the remains.

Peter spent the period between March 1697 and August 1698 on a visit to western Europe. By the standards of Muscovy this was a venture of startling originality – he was, in fact, the first Tsar ever to cross his western frontier except on a military campaign. Nor was such an escapade to be repeated by any other reigning sovereign before the nineteenth century. One of the Tsar's aims was to concert European action against Turkey, but he also planned to investigate European technical resources, to recruit foreign craftsmen and sailors – and in general to conduct an educational grand tour while continuing his apprenticeship in a dozen trades on the move.

With its dignitaries, interpreters, priests, dwarfs, bodyguards, pages, trumpeters, coachmen and footmen, his mission numbered some two hundred and fifty souls. The nominal head was Lefort, and the Tsar himself travelled as Peter Mikhaylov – an incognito which led to much confusion. There were times when he dressed as a Dutch sailor and objected to being treated as a monarch. At other times he resented being accepted as Peter Mikhaylov – at Riga, for example, where the Swedish governor-general was ill and failed to accord special honours to one who posed as a private individual. Further offence was caused in Riga when the Tsar took it upon himself to reconnoitre its defences, an intelligence operation especially outrageous coming from one whose father had besieged the city within living memory. Halted by a Swedish sentry with levelled flintlock, Peter took grave offence, and three years later made his reception in Riga an excuse for declaring war on Sweden.

The Tsar had a more cordial welcome in Courland, Prussia and Brandenburg, though his eccentricities soon became the talk of Europe. At Coppenbrügge two of the most cultivated ladies of the age – Sophie of Hanover and Sophie Charlotte of Brandenburg – gave a banquet for him. On meeting these princesses, Peter showed acute embarrassment; he covered his face with his hands and professed himself robbed of speech – only to keep the ladies at their dinner-table for hours, rising repeatedly to his feet to toast his own health, exhibiting hands calloused by hard work and explaining his plan to build a Black Sea fleet of seventy-five vessels. The sophisticated ladies found this intelligent, wild young man fascinating, and happily overlooked his uncouth table manners. Moving on to Holland, Peter worked for a week as ship's carpenter on the wharf at Zaandam, then proceeded to Amsterdam and obtained access to the East India Company's shipyards. His many Dutch visits included a saw-mill, a silk factory and an anatomical theatre at Leiden; when his followers showed distress at the sight of cadavers laid out for dissection, the Tsar forced them to bite into a corpse to teach them to be less squeamish – yet another demonstration of his appetite for western scientific method.

Peter left for England in January 1698 with a squadron of the Royal Navy. He climbed the mast of the flagship in mid-Channel, calling in vain on the portly English admiral to join him aloft. His stay in England lasted three and a half months. At Deptford he continued his nautical studies, and he visited Portsmouth; two mock sea-battles staged for him in the Solent reputedly caused him to say that he would rather be an English admiral than Tsar of Russia. He went to the Mint and the Royal Society, and to Woolwich, Greenwich and Oxford. In a long talk with the Bishop of Salisbury he showed that he could hold his own in theological discussion, while the wrecking of his lodgings – John Evelyn's house at Deptford – revealed him in his other familiar role of a royal hooligan who left behind bespewed walls, smashed floors, trampled lawns, ripped curtains and pictures riddled with pistol shots, besides furniture broken and burnt on a truly regal scale.

From England, Peter went to Vienna and met the Emperor Leopold I. But though the Tsar now felt sufficient self-confidence to conduct his own negotiations, he was unsuccessful in obtaining action against the Turks. Then, as he was planning to go on to Venice, news reached him from Moscow that the Streltsy were in revolt again. He decided to return at once, but delayed his journey through Poland long enough to plan with King Augustus II a joint Russo-Polish war against Sweden; hope of a united European effort against Turkey having failed, Peter was already turning his attention from the Black Sea to the Baltic. Augustus proved an agreeable drinking companion, and the two flamboyant monarchs took such a liking to each other that they exchanged clothes.

It was in this heretic western rig offensive to Orthodox eyes that Peter returned to terrorize Muscovy and cut its traditions to ribbons. Reaching his capital on 25 August 1698, he avoided the Kremlin and made straight for the German Quarter and his German mistress, Anna Mons. He spent the night at his barracks-village of Preobrazhenskoye. On the following day boyars and other fawning dignitaries flocked to pay homage in customary oriental style, but the hefty young Tsar hauled them to their feet even as they tried to execute the kowtow. Then he took scissors and cut off their beards. The boyar Alexis Shein (commander-in-chief) and Prince Theodore Romodanovsky (head of security police and responsible for order during Peter's absence) were the first to suffer this indignity. Peter later gave the office of barber to one of his court jesters. But the shearing of the boyars was no joke, and before long he had imposed a tax on the wearing of beards, though clergy and peasants were allowed to keep them. The Tsar also banned traditional long, flowing Russian dress in Moscow in favour of western European clothes, reaching for his scissors again to snip off some voluminous sleeves. Nor had the Tsar any further use for a traditional Russian Tsaritsa such as his wife Eudoxia. Although she had never interfered with his way of life and he was not thinking of marrying again, he removed their son (the Tsarevich Alexis) from her and effectively divorced her by sending her to a convent – in a particularly humiliating manner.

These scandals were nothing compared to the fate visited on the Streltsy. By the time of Peter's return his deputies had already crushed the rising, executed the ringleaders and banished the rest. The incident seemed closed – until the Tsar gave orders to bring the exiled Streltsy back for examination in the torture-chambers of the Preobrazhensky Chancery under Romodanovsky. Not punishment, but the extraction of information, was the chief purpose of this inquisition, which followed the custom of the country except that the number of those questioned was unusually large on the present occasion. The examiners first put the victim to the knout – slashing by a specially constructed flail of which the operative section was a rod of hardened leather; they then grilled the lacerated back over a slow fire. As long as life lasted they could continue to repeat this sequence, which rated as an infallible research technique for the investigation of ordinary crime as well as of treason and political offences. It was especially effective when the victims could guess what information their tormentor sought, as was the case in the present instance; even before leaving Vienna, Peter had concluded that his old enemies the Miloslavskys were behind the revolt,[1] and he meant to obtain evidence that the Streltsy were in league with his half-sister, the ex-regent Sophia.

The Tsar himself witnessed the agony of the tortured and probably put some of them to the question himself. His victims included women of Sophia's entourage in the Novodevichy Convent, and statements were extorted to confirm his instinctive conviction of her guilt. He confronted and interrogated her before compelling her to become a nun, confined in the convent under the permanent guard of a hundred soldiers. It remained to dispatch the surviving Streltsy, whose death was to be a spectacle which no Muscovite should ever forget. Two men to a cart and each carrying a burning candle, nearly two hundred victims came from Preobrazhenskoye to Moscow on 30 September 1698, while weeping wives and children followed the grim convoy. The Tsar proclaimed the sentence in person and had them publicly put to death; as he did some thousand of the Streltsy altogether – by beheading, hanging or the wheel – before the slaughter ended. His executioners left the corpses to dangle from the Kremlin walls, by the city gates and in front of the Novodevichy Convent – three directly opposite the window of Sophia's cell. Attacked by crows and filling Moscow with the stench of death, these grisly pendants festooned the cowed city for months before winter came to freeze them on their gallows.

It is probable that Peter personally cut off the heads of the first five victims at Preobrazhenskoye.[2] He also insisted that his associates do the same, and the favourite Menshikov reputedly boasted of beheading a score. Ever the eager student of anatomy, Peter also forced certain boyars to witness the dissection of one of the slain, accompanying these horrors with particularly brutal and violent carousals.

16 Master Autocrat: Peter I   1700-25

Peter's Northern War against Sweden occupied a large part of his reign (1700–21). His constant aim was to establish himself on the Gulf of Finland, thus regaining an area (and a potential outlet on western Europe) which Russia had already possessed at various periods in the past. However, first success in the conflict went to Charles XII of Sweden, who defeated Russia's allies Poland and Denmark and marched to the relief of Narva, which the Tsar had laid under siege. Menaced by a small Swedish army of a few thousand troops to his own thirty or forty thousand, the Tsar fled on the eve of battle after entrusting command to a foreign general whom the Swedes promptly routed. The Battle of Narva made Peter the laughing-stock of Europe. He seemed guilty of gross cowardice, absurd as it may appear to attribute such weakness to the great Tsar; but so many-sided was his nature that it need surprise no one if there were times when he excelled ordinary men in timidity as well as in courage.

Peter showed his customary resilience by mobilizing fresh troops and casting new cannon to replace those lost at Narva. Meanwhile Charles had turned his attention to Poland and Saxony, leaving the Tsar to capture an almost desolate area on the estuary of the River Neva – the site of St Petersburg. This offered Peter the outlet to the Gulf of Finland which he sought, but he could not regard his conquest as secure until he had defeated Sweden decisively in the field. He accomplished this far from the Neva estuary with the Battle of Poltava in the Ukraine on 27 June 1709. Here a Swedish bullet pierced the Tsar's hat – as if to emphasize his heroism and good fortune – while the wounded Charles, for once a less dashing figure, had to command his troops from the stretcher on which he lay in fever. Narrowly escaping capture, the king left the field to the Tsar and made his way to Turkey. Peter celebrated his triumph in Moscow in his usual florid style and Russia now took Sweden's place as a great power, though the war was to drag on for a dozen more years.

Until the eve of Poltava, Peter would have made peace on almost any terms which allowed him to keep his hold on the Gulf of Finland. He would have settled, in other words, for far less than he actually obtained; for in the end Russian victories made him master of Estland and Livonia as well as Ingermanland, giving

Arctic Ocean

0   400
Miles

SWEDEN

FINLAND

BALTIC SEA

Nystad

Kexholm
Cronstadt
St.Petersburg
Tartu(Dorpat)
Riga
Pskov
Novgorod

L.Ladoga
Önega

Soloyetsky Monastery
Archangel
Kholmogory

N.Dvina

Kama

Khlynov
(Vyatka)

Yekaterinburg

POLAND

W.Dvina
Smolensk

Monastery of the Trinity and St.Sergius

Kostroma
Tver
Yaroslavl

Moscow
Oka Tula

Nizhny
Novgorod

Kazan

Ufa

Tobol

Samara

Desna

Dniester

Prut

Voronezh

Kiev

Kharkov
Poltava

Dnieper

Bender

Ochakov

Danube

Taganrog

Azov
Sea

Bakhchisaray

Donets

Don

Saratov

Tsaritsyn

Volga

Yaik (Ural)

Azov

Kuban

Astrakhan

BLACK SEA

Terek

CASPIAN SEA

Constantinople

O
T
T
O
M
A
N

E
M
P
I
R
E

Derbent

Kura

Baku

ACQUISITIONS OF PETER THE GREAT (r.1682–1725)

PERSIA

European Russia 1689

Acquired under Peter the Great

~ARTHUR BANKS~

him the Baltic ports of Narva, Reval and Riga. Though Estonians and Latvians formed the majority of the population in these provinces, Germans were culturally and economically dominant, and Peter now passed from hiring Germans as technical experts to ruling them directly. His troops had begun the war by devastating Estland and Livonia, but on annexation by Russia these lands received the right of internal self-government and kept German as their official language. Peter thus provided Russia with a base for recruiting administrators. Over the next two centuries Baltic Germans were to serve the Tsars on such a scale that German names often figure more prominently than Russian among their high officials and generals.

The year 1711 saw a brief renewal of warfare against Turkey, embroiled with Russia by the routed Charles XII. Peter decided to strike a quick blow by invading Turkish territory, only to fall into a trap near the River Prut. Surrounded by a Turkish army outnumbering his own by about four to one, and thinking himself faced with capture and torture, he sent word to his Senate to ignore any instructions purporting to come from him in Turkish hands. In the event the Turkish grand vizier decided not to exploit his advantage, and for reasons which remain obscure. Peter thus received an unexpected reprieve – but had to return Azov, first conquest of his reign, to Turkey.

Ever eager for outlets to new seas, Peter led an expedition against Persia in 1722, which ended with the cession to Russia of Persian provinces on the western Caspian coast together with Baku and Derbent.

Peter was well over six and a half foot tall, being strong and well-built to match, and would have been radiantly good-looking but for certain physical defects – he was round-shouldered and swung his right arm in an unnatural manner as he walked, while his face and neck were prone to violent nervous twitchings. Horrifying grimaces often preceded the spasms of fury during which he would lash out with fists or stick. A tireless worker of phenomenal energy, and addicted to hard labour with hammer, axe or any other tool, he was also a great drafter of state papers, issuer of ukases and traveller over immense distances, often using a humble conveyance which would have been more suitable for an ordinary merchant. Even when walking he was always in a hurry, and forced lesser men to trot along by his side.

Disliking etiquette and uniform, Peter was untidy in appearance, often wore darned stockings or patched boots, and sometimes appeared in shirt sleeves on formal occasions. Though hating to be stared at by crowds, he was sociably inclined and democratic in the sense of dispensing ferocious joviality and crude bullying to one and all with no regard for social station. As many a prince and plebeian discovered, to be loved or hated by Peter was like being mauled by a

The Streltsy carry stones with which to build
a pillar in the Red Square commemorating their
services – a sequel to the successful mutiny
of 1682, which gave the regency to Sophia.
Miniature from Krekshin's *History of Peter the
Great* (eighteenth century).

The diamond crown (or 'hat') of Ivan v
(the feeble-minded younger brother of
Theodore iii), who was raised to the throne
by the revolt of the Streltsy in 1682.
He reigned as co-Tsar with his younger half-
brother Peter the Great until his death in 1696.

The Regent Sophia.
Daughter of Tsar Alexis
and half-sister to Peter
the Great, she was made
regent by the revolt of the
Streltsy in 1682, being
deposed by Peter and his
supporters in 1689.
By an anonymous artist,
early eighteenth century.

Prince Vasily Golitsyn.
Lover of the Regent Sophia,
he was also her chief
political support during her
regency; he led two
unsuccessful expeditions
against the Crimean Tatars.
By an anonymous artist,
late seventeenth century.

The boyar Leo Naryshkin (uncle of Peter the Great) who was put in charge of the office of foreign affairs after Peter and his supporters had seized power from the Regent Sophia in 1689. Seventeenth-century portrait.

(*overleaf*) The siege of Azov by Peter the Great in 1696 led to the capture of this Turkish stronghold after an abortive attack by the Russians in the previous year. Engraving, *c.* 1699.

Knouting, the traditional form of beating
which played a prominent part in the questioning
and punishment of suspects under the Tsars
until its abolition in 1845.

A cartoon from Peter the Great's reign showing
the compulsory clipping of beards instituted
by the Tsar after his return to Moscow from
his tour of western Europe in 1698.

(*opposite*) The execution of the Streltsy in
Moscow in September 1698 at the behest of Peter
the Great. Engraving of 1700.

The morning of the Streltsys' execution,
a nineteenth-century impression by V. Surikov.

Two etchings by Le Prince,
1765. (*left*) A soldier of
the Corps of Streltsy; they
mutinied against Peter
the Great and were savagely
punished by him.
(*right*) An officer
of the Streltsy.

The Battle of Poltava (1709) in the Ukraine,
Peter the Great's victory over Charles XII
of Sweden. This was Peter's most important
military victory and helped to establish Russia
on the Baltic coast.
Painting by Nattier (1685–1766).

bear. He freely lavished his blows, hugs and kisses without regard to age, sex, station or polite usage, and sometimes wept copiously in public.

The number of Peter's bastards was considerable, as also of his casual mistresses. One of these, the Lithuanian servant-girl Catherine, attained the status of acknow-ledged consort before becoming his wife, his Empress – and finally succeeding him to rule as Empress in her own right. Having entered the household of the favourite Menshikov as a trophy of war aged seventeen, she was said to have washed his shirts besides sharing his bed before she caught the Tsar's fancy in turn. Catherine was a strapping wench not conventionally beautiful, and accompanied Peter on all his later campaigns, being one of the few people who could calm his terrible rages. She bore him eleven children who all died in infancy except for Anne (mother of the future Peter III) and Elizabeth (herself a future Empress). Both these daughters were born out of wedlock before the year 1712, in which Peter married Catherine as his second wife.

Catherine's first protector, Alexander Menshikov, was another upstart, and became a prince after reputedly starting his career as a pieman. That there was an erotic element in the Tsar's relations with Menshikov – and possibly even with Lefort – is suggested by Wittram,[3] and is a reminder that rumour strongly attri-buted homosexual proclivities to the Tsar. There were occasions when he insisted on sleeping with his orderlies, but (according to another student of the subject) only in order to control the nervous twitching of his arms by gripping their shoulders.[4]

The Tsar's closest associates had a vast capacity for strong liquor, as had Peter himself. He could drink enough for ten, yet go on to do ten men's work. It was also his habit to make others drunk. A huge sconce in brandy was the penalty commonly paid by those found quarrelling at his table or preaching heresy in the boozy theological debates which he would provoke in his cups. It is still possible to inspect in the Kremlin armoury the Tsar's huge drinking-horn, a vessel so shaped that it was impossible to put it down unfinished without attracting atten-tion by spilling the contents. Foreign diplomats were not immune from these indignities. Nor were women, as might be observed in the Tsar's Summer Garden where St Petersburgers and their ladies sometimes took their ease informally . . . but at the risk of sudden eruptions of regal hospitality. After sentries had sealed all exits, guardsmen would close on the terrified burghers with tubs held at the ready, while officers of field rank ensured that no one flinched from drinking the royal health in bumpers of coarse spirit.[5]

Although Peter's closest associates needed no such encouragement to tipple, there was more to drinking with the Tsar than mere swilling. Peter himself planned the elaborate whimsical association of his boon companions called the 'most crazy, most droll, most drunken assembly', which his former tutor Nikita Zotov long presided over as 'patriarch' or 'prince-pope'. He promoted various cronies to 'cardinal' and 'archimandrite', not to mention other offices with grossly obscene titles. The paradox of indulging in detailed parodies of church ritual while remaining a firm believer and a considerable expert on ecclesiastical affairs was typical of Peter's character.

Of the care lavished by Peter on his drunken assembly, the marriage of 'Patriarch' Zotov at the age of eighty-four was typical. Dressed as King David, Prince Romodanovsky led the wedding procession in a sledge drawn over the frozen Neva by a team of bears, and the affair ended with the usual drunken orgy. Peter found it so enjoyable that he later staged the marriage of a succeeding 'patriarch' (another elderly toper) to Zotov's widow. The very consummation of this union of dotards took place in the presence of Peter and Catherine, and the fact that bride and groom enacted it only in mime owed less to considerations of good taste than to their advanced age, besides which they were too drunk to attempt anything more ambitious. Peter himself held the low rank of deacon in his mock hierarchy, and showed similar humility on the secular plane when he appointed Prince Romodanovsky 'king' or 'Caesar', and pretended to be one of his humbler subjects – submissively reporting such events as victory at Poltava and peace negotiations at Nystad to the mock monarch. Separating himself from his high rank in this way, the Tsar enjoyed relief from the cares of office.

All association with the rowdy monarch involved danger to life and limb – or so it seems from the endless anecdotes about his pranks. He fancied his skill as a dentist, with unfortunate results for any sufferer from toothache within reach, for the Tsar's great strength, speed off the mark and slapdash approach meant that he was liable to pull out a sound tooth before his patient could find voice to protest. To complain of any physical ailment in Peter's presence was to court disaster, for he dabbled in surgery too and was wont to call for his scalpel and operate on the spot. On other occasions flame and ice were his instruments. On the night of 1 April 1723 he caused the fire alarm to be sounded in St Petersburg; the people tumbled from their houses and rushed towards the blaze . . . to be greeted as April Fools on the Tsar's orders by soldiers stationed around a huge bonfire lit in the open. On an old gentleman of eighty, who imprudently refused an invitation to join a masquerade dressed as a devil, the Tsar played a rougher jape. If the story is to be believed, Peter had him placed on the ice of the Neva stark naked except for a cap with pasteboard horns.[6] The victim died, thus providing a typical punch line to a royal joke. It is unfortunately the case that very old men were among Peter's preferred butts.

Pushkin's poem *The Bronze Horseman* (written in 1833) brilliantly evokes St Petersburg and its founder, contrasting the Tsar with the wilderness of waters and the marshy river banks of the empty site where he stands obsessed by his grand design. From the town which he intends to found in this waste, he and his subjects shall threaten the Swedes; gain a firm footing on the sea; welcome the flags of all nations; and carouse without inhibition. All four aims were realized, as was a fifth also mentioned by Pushkin: 'Old Moscow was put in the shade by the younger capital like a purple-clad dowager by a new Tsaritsa.'

The Tsar founded St Petersburg in 1703 and transferred his capital there from Moscow in 1712. He made his greatest impact on his subjects and the world by the war which he fought for the site, by building his city there against all odds, and by the many consequences, direct and indirect, of the decision to move the seat of the government. It was an act of far-seeing statesmanship – or of grandiose folly. Russian historians have inclined to praise the statesmanlike vision, foreigners to stress the folly; but the far-reaching effects are not disputed by either.

Compared with Archangel, Russia's only sea port at the beginning of Peter's reign, the Neva estuary offered many advantages. It gave access to the Gulf of Finland and the Baltic, and thus a shorter sea haul to Russia's trading partners; was nearer to Moscow and the main Russian centres of production; and was ice-free for a longer period of the year. But it was first essential to drain the marshes and ballast them with wood and stone. Since these materials were scarce in the neighbourhood, it was necessary to bring them in by boat or peasant cart and even to import them from abroad. It was also necessary to haul food from far away – and all this with road communications so poor that there were times when no vehicle could approach by land. The many unbridged streams made movement impossible without constantly taking to the water – all very well for a Tsar who was so fond of boating, but others found it less to their taste. Worse still, the area was liable to flooding when westerly gales drove sea water up the Neva. Such a flood drowned hundreds, perhaps thousands, in the very year of the city's foundation, and Peter himself witnessed the next big flood three years later. He thought it amusing to see people stranded on trees and roofs.

Such considerations made the new port a doubtful prospect. But to conceive that same port, lodged in such an out-of-the-way corner, as the capital city of a huge empire seemed madness, especially in war-time. However, the Tsar had resolved to burst the bonds of Muscovy, and was never one to let mere impossibilities stand in his way. Condemned criminals and Swedish prisoners swelled the labour force of peasants rounded up to build their new capital and brought to the site from many parts of Russia under armed escort. Often lacking the most elementary tools, they dug at the soggy earth with their hands and carried it in the folds of their coats. Add to this the hazards of famine, fire, flood, scurvy, dysentery, lack of shelter and medical care, and it is easy to understand why the Neva swamps, a 'paradise' to the Tsar, were sheer hell to many others. Rising from the bogs, the new capital notoriously became the graveyard of its builders, though reliable mortality figures are not available.

Since it was the Tsar's way to dragoon the élite as well as the dregs of society, he also compelled princes and potentates to move to his new city and build stone houses there – the plan being to make the new capital entirely stone-built. But though the frontage of the Neva was indeed 'clothed in granite' (Pushkin), and many public buildings were magnificent stone edifices, the markets and suburbs were largely of wood and more resembled parts of old Moscow than a city of the future. Piety and defence were among Peter's first concerns in erecting public buildings. He made a beginning with the Peter and Paul Fortress – conceived as a bastion against the Swedes, but soon to become a prison for the Tsars' domestic enemies. Other early buildings were the admiralty with its well-known needle spire and the large naval dockyard which was employing up to ten thousand workers by 1715. Another early landmark was the Alexander Nevsky Monastery, where the remains of the saint were installed in 1724. It was then in a suburb of the city, and the long street which ran eastwards from it to the admiralty was to become the most famous in Russia – the Nevsky Prospekt, built and tended by Swedish prisoners. To embellish these efforts the Tsar recruited foreign architects, himself going into details of planning with his usual thoroughness.

Peter made St Petersburg the scene of many public spectacles with celebrations of victories, ship-launchings, dwarfs' weddings – any excuse for cannonades, firework displays, military parades and fancy dress, not to mention public knout-ings, breakings on the wheel and beheadings. Here too the darkest episode of his reign, the death of his son Alexis, took place in 1718.

Born in 1690, the Tsarevich Alexis grew into a clerkly, stooping, sickly person – everything most hateful to the great Tsar. It is true that the youth was also some-thing of a drunkard, but that virtue alone did not redeem his old-fashioned piety, aversion to war and general laziness. Peter could see all his work undone at the moment when such an heir should take the sceptre in his nerveless hands. Even to a living Peter the feeble Tsarevich posed a threat, for without even lifting an eye from his prayers the young man inevitably attracted the hopes of all who yearned for a quieter existence – certainly the majority of the population. The common people, clergy and boyars all tended to look at him as a deliverer from a hated tyrant; or from Antichrist, as Peter was widely regarded.

Until the age of twenty-five, Alexis proved an unsatisfactory son, but without being entirely hopeless. In his eighteenth year he began to perform duties involv-ing military supply, recruiting and the defence of Moscow. He did not disgrace himself; but his heart was not in the work, and it was typical that he should have been absent from the Battle of Poltava, perhaps because he was recovering from a chill. Peter sent him abroad in 1710 with two unwelcome assignments – to continue studying and to marry a foreign princess. Though many a later Tsarevich was to wed a German, the proposal offended Muscovite tradition dear to Alexis. However, he was willing, as usual, to do what was required, and fixed on Princess Charlotte of Brunswick-Wolfenbüttel as the least uncongenial among available brides. He took her to St Petersburg, where she did not enter into the spirit of the new Russia – or of the old either, retaining her Protestant faith and shunning contact with her adopted country.

Returning from abroad, the young bridegroom found the Tsar threatening to test by personal examination his progress in the studies which he had so sadly neglected. At the prospect of having to produce evidence of non-existent accomplishment in draughtsmanship while his terrible father stood over him, the young man panicked. As he later confessed under torture, he anticipated the ordeal by taking a pistol and firing at his right hand. But missed! And only gave himself a powder burn. To botch even a self-inflicted wound – it sounds more like an anticipation of Chekhov than the work of understudy to an autocrat. Of this misdemeanour Peter knew nothing until later, perhaps because it was at this time that he finally gave up all hope for his heir – relapsing into an ominous silence until, in October 1715, Charlotte bore Alexis a son (and herself died a few days later). In his new grandson and in a son born to Catherine and himself at about the same time, Peter obtained two reserve heirs. Both babies were named Peter, and Alexis had become expendable.

The tragedy could now proceed to its second act, which began with a letter from Peter to Alexis listing the young man's shortcomings and dwelling on his distaste for things military. 'It is by war [the Tsar pointed out in a rare lapse into historical generalization] that we have come out of darkness into light.'[7] Comparing Alexis with the bad servant in the Gospel who buries his talent, Peter told him that he must mend his ways or be cut off like a gangrenous limb. In reply the young man humbly expressed himself willing to face disinheritance. But Peter now presented stricter terms. It was no longer enough for the Tsarevich to retire from public life, the Tsar told him; he must do so irrevocably by becoming a monk. Alexis answered that he was willing to accept this condition too. There Peter let the matter rest for several months – a significant point; for although the Tsar later treated his son with great cruelty, he only did so after showing what was for him a considerable degree of forbearance. By August 1716, however, Peter's patience was exhausted. From Copenhagen, where he was engaged on military business, he sent the Tsarevich a curt ultimatum: Alexis had one week to decide whether to join his father or enter a monastery. He had no intention of doing either if he could avoid it. For form's sake he agreed to go to Copenhagen, but as soon as his carriage was safely across the Russian frontier, he headed for Vienna –

thus becoming the most important political defector in the history of the Tsars. At ten o'clock on a November evening he intruded, distraught and panting, on the Austrian vice-chancellor and blurted out his story. With some misgiving the Emperor Charles VI agreed to grant asylum.

Not until December did the Tsar have certain knowledge of his son's treachery and determine to lay his hands on the traitor at all costs. The young man's whereabouts were unknown, and it might have seemed a hopeless task to scour an entire continent for him, had not hopeless tasks been such a speciality of Peter's. It is still frightening to contemplate the single-mindedness with which the great Tsar harnessed guile, threats and will to his set purpose – the temper of his determination can be judged from detailed written instructions conveyed to his principal agent and covering every eventuality.[8]

The third act of the drama – the pursuit – had begun. Rightly suspecting that Alexis was somewhere in the Austrian Empire, Peter first decided to have him discreetly abducted and gave this task to a captain of his guards. But when reconnaissance showed that the Tsarevich had gone to earth in a fortress, the plot to kidnap him was abandoned in favour of diplomatic pressure. Peter Tolstoy now took over as chief huntsman. This unscrupulous negotiator mounted a programme of intimidation after obtaining permission from Charles VI to interview Alexis at his latest refuge, St Elmo near Naples. Tolstoy tempted the Tsarevich with the promise of forgiveness if he would only return to Russia. But should he refuse (Tolstoy told him) the Tsar was fully prepared to march against the Holy Roman Empire and capture him. Not that it would come to war. Rather than fight for the Tsarevich, the Emperor would certainly surrender him – an unfounded claim, but one which Austrian officials bribed by Tolstoy confirmed on the spot. Tolstoy also claimed that the Austrians were about to separate the Tsarevich from the Finnish serf-girl Euphrosyne who had accompanied him on his escape dressed in man's clothing – one touch of romance in an otherwise sordid tale. This threat was a shrewd blow at the young man's morale, for she seemed to be his only friend in the world, and was also bearing his child. The culminating stroke came with Tolstoy's assertion that Peter was on the point of leaving for St Elmo in person. His will now utterly paralysed, the spineless Tsarevich at last consented to return to Russia on condition that he might live privately and marry Euphrosyne. Tolstoy agreed. His orders were to bring Alexis back, and promises could always be reconsidered at leisure once Peter had his son in his clutches.

The last act – the kill – began with Alexis's arrival in Moscow in January 1718 and lasted six months. Peter formally arraigned his son as a prisoner before a gathering of notables in the Kremlin, and told him that he could only save himself by renouncing the succession, making full confession and naming all his sympathizers. Complying with his usual meekness, Alexis mentioned names which brought arrest and torture to many persons guilty less of plotting Peter's over-throw than of desiring it. The ensuing witch-hunt came to involve all the Tsare-vich's associates, including his personal manservant, friends among the clergy and other advisers. Taint by association reached Suzdal where Alexis's mother, the ex-Tsaritsa Eudoxia, had been cloistered for some twenty years – or so it had been thought until alarming intelligence emerged from that part of the world. The former Tsaritsa had not been comporting herself as a nun, it turned out, but had continued to wear secular dress and had become involved in a liaison with a Major Glebov. He now became a target for the Tsar's fury, suffering impalement wrapped in warm furs to prolong his agonies in a sub-zero temperature. Never, surely, has spite against the lover of a wife so long discarded been carried further. Eudoxia herself suffered banishment to a less permissive convent.

Meanwhile Peter kept Alexis under house arrest. The Tsarevich still hoped to escape with his life, but was finally caught up in the web of denunciation. Bribed, browbeaten or naturally co-operative, his mistress Euphrosyne bore witness against him, saying that he had proposed to dismantle the navy should he succeed to the throne, and to move his capital back to Moscow. This evidence helped to doom her lover. The Tsar had him imprisoned in the Peter and Paul Fortress in June, tried by a court of high officials and sentenced to death as a traitor. But traitors rarely died easily in Peter's Russia, and the Tsar did not spare his own son from torture, combining his usual vengefulness and determination to lay bare conspiracy with the purest scientific curiosity. Believing human nature to be infinitely ductile if subjected to reason and threats in sufficient quantity and force, Peter had harangued and threatened Alexis over a period of twenty years. Why, then, had the Tsarevich refused to change his character? It was almost an abstract problem to which the knout (believed to unlock all secrets) must surely provide an answer. Alexis received forty strokes in all, and since only a few blows were known to prove fatal it is not surprising that he died on 26 June from these beatings, and possibly from further ordeals too. His father's curiosity still re-mained unsatisfied, for the Tsarevich took with him to the grave his simple secret – that human nature is less flexible and more brittle than the great Tsar could conceive.

For that crowned impresario it was a convenient death, since even his hand might have trembled in staging the public execution of a son. The official explana-tion of the tragedy was death from natural causes, of an illness 'resembling apoplexy', and the sequel showed Peter at his most callous. He attended his son's funeral, but would neither declare court mourning nor abandon his usual carou-sals; nor did he cancel the annual celebration of the Battle of Poltava on 27 June. But perhaps the martyr was not worth many tears – his drunken asides, such as that expressing an intention to impale certain persons on assuming supreme power,[9] suggest that his own style of leadership might have resembled his father's in some of its less admirable aspects.

Peter's numerous reforms reflect many aspects of his restless nature, one striking feature being the intense degree of his personal involvement. Another is the lack of any unifying pattern, for many of the measures concerned were improvisations designed by the head of a nation at war to increase military efficiency. Peter cancelled some reforms before they had time to become effective, but others outlasted the Romanovs.

Among the more durable innovations was the new bureaucracy created by Peter's 'table of ranks' in 1722 – a hierarchy of fourteen grades for all servants of the state, military and civil, including court officials. Supplanting the old ranks of Muscovy (including the ancient title of boyar) the table remained in force until 1917. So did the senate, established by Peter in 1711 with nine members to represent him in his absence and designed to function as the highest legislative, administrative and judicial body in the state; it was still in being in 1917, though much restricted in its operations during most of its life. The division of the country into 'governments' (*gubernii*), of which there were eight when they were introduced in 1709, lived on at least in name until 1917 (and after), as did a particularly characteristic imperial Russian office introduced by Peter – that of provincial governor.

Another innovation to survive until 1917 was the holy synod, which perhaps marks Peter's biggest institutional break with the past. Inheriting the system whereby the Orthodox Church was governed by a patriarch, Peter allowed that supreme office to lapse with the death of the Patriarch Adrian in 1700. After a delay of twenty-one years during which he left the church without a fully established head, Peter replaced the patriarchate with the synod, which consisted of church dignitaries, on the principle that corporate bodies were less liable to be corrupt and unco-operative than were individuals; besides which the new organ was put under a lay administrator, the chief procurator. The principle of corporate authority was also embodied in a shorter-lived institution – that of the colleges substituted by Peter for the old *prikazy* (chanceries, or offices) with their partly regional spheres of activity. The colleges foreshadowed the ministries which took their place under Alexander I nearly a century later, but functioned on the principle of collective responsibility.

It was a basic feature of Peter's style to give his new institutions foreign names, and the Russian words for table of ranks, senate, provinces, synod and colleges do not have a Slavonic root among them. They were only a small part of a large glossary of imported foreign terms which swamped Russian vocabulary at the time. Such neologisms were by no means a mere flourish, for the Tsar always liked to base his work on a close study of foreign models – whether he was building a

Marble bust of Peter the Great by Carlo Rastrelli, and (*below*) a caricature by an anonymous artist.

Catherine, the former
Lithuanian servant-girl who
became Peter the Great's
mistress, wife, Tsaritsa
and Empress, and survived
him to reign briefly as
Catherine I.
Contemporary French print.

Another impression of
Peter the Great's mistress,
later wife and Empress,
Catherine. Engraving,
end of eighteenth century.

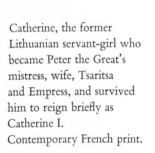

The wedding banquet
of Peter the Great
and Catherine, who were
married in 1712.
Early eighteenth-century
engraving.

Wedding of Volkov,
Peter the Great's dwarf,
in the palace of the
favourite Menshikov.
Engraving by A. Zubov
(b. 1682).

Peter the Great's fleet at Archangel.
The creation of a Russian navy was one
of Peter's many achievements, and he first
visited Archangel in 1693. Engraving of 1700.

Captured Swedish frigates entering
St Petersburg, an episode in the Northern
War of 1700–21 which ended in a Russian
victory. Engraving of 1720.

The Tsarevich Alexis
(son of Peter the Great),
who sought political asylum
in Vienna in 1716, but was
induced to return to Russia
where he perished in prison
– probably as the result of
knouting administered on
his father's orders.
Contemporary engraving.

Peter the Great, on his deathbed in 1725.
Late eighteenth-century engraving.

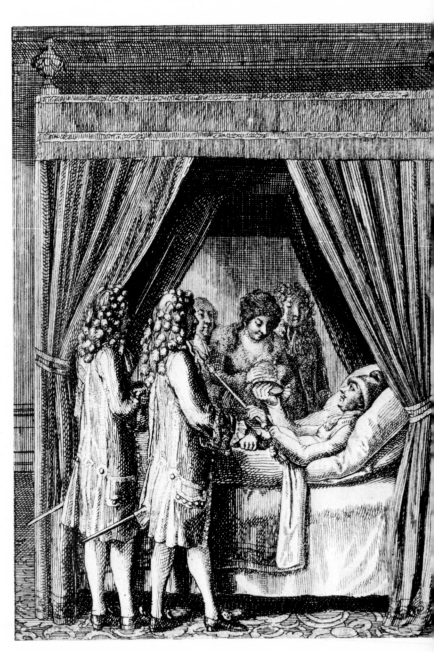

Catherine I, the first Empress of Russia,
succeeded her husband Peter the Great and
ruled from 1725 to 1727. Painting by Nattier.

Alexander Menshikov, the principal favourite
of Peter the Great and Catherine I. He was
dismissed from power by Peter II and died in
Siberian exile in 1729.
Marble bust by Rastrelli.

(*opposite*)
Peter the Great (r. 1682–1725),
detail from a mosaic
of the Battle of Poltava (1709)
after a contemporary engraving.

frigate, drafting an army manual or re-working the fabric of the state. During war with Sweden he secretly complimented his enemies by sending an agent to investigate their system of government. This was a promising target for administrative espionage, since Sweden too was an absolute monarchy – but one with a reputation for efficiency.

Though the Tsar did not found the Russian regular army, he extensively developed it. His Preobrazhensky and Semyonovsky Guards came to take a large part in non-military affairs, for he often used their officers to investigate abuses in high places. He also made his guards into cadres where future officers of all units must begin their service as privates. The Tsar greatly expanded the army as a whole, and himself played a prominent role in framing the new military regulations of 1716. As for the Russian navy, that more than anything else was his own personal creation; and he took extreme pains with the naval regulations of 1721, drafting and redrafting them in his own hand.

An effective war machine demanded a thriving economy, and Peter's efforts included the development of Russian industry – especially mining, metal-working and textile production. In the field of commerce he looked beyond immediate military motives and short-term aims in seeking new markets. Having established himself on the Baltic, he did not forget the Orient, but energetically pursued contact with China and India – even planning to send a naval squadron to Madagascar and set up a staging-post there for trade with the east. That his imagination was no more bounded by polar ice than by equatorial monsoons is shown by his order to Vitus Bering issued five weeks before his death and directing the explorer to undertake the expedition which eventually led to his discoveries in the far north-east.

Born into a country which reckoned time from the notional beginning of the world and started the year on 1 September, Peter brought Russia up-to-date by introducing the Julian Calendar in 1700. No longer 6,508 years ahead of the rest of the world, she now lagged eleven days behind countries using the Gregorian Calendar.

Peter's own erratic spelling did not deter him from reforming Russian orthography by shedding certain superfluous letters of the alphabet and helping to design a new type face to replace the ornate Church Slavonic print in which Russian books had hitherto been set. This streamlining of the alphabet was one among many tokens of the growing secularization of Russian culture. It was also on the Tsar's instructions that the first Russian newspapers began to appear in 1703, besides which he commissioned numerous translations, often vetting them himself; a modest linguist by the standards of some later Tsars (his only foreign languages being Dutch and German), he needed no special knowledge to ensure that a rendering was couched in plain man's Russian. His other cultural activities included the decree founding the Russian Academy of Sciences a year after his death, and the establishment of many humbler institutions of learning with a typical practical bias – schools of mathematics, artillery, navigation, medicine and engineering.

That Peter changed his subjects' appearance by banning beards and prescribing clothes of western European style has already been mentioned, but it must be stressed that he limited these innovations to officials and gentry – leaving to the peasants, priests and merchants the traditional beards and dress of Muscovy. For this reason Russians from Peter's time onwards tended to look as if they belonged to two different breeds. But the difference went beyond externals to embrace culture, education and general outlook on an increasing scale, and the growing rift between two Russian cultures was among the more unfortunate effects of Peter's reforms. No doubt it was inevitable if the country must be 'westernized' at such headlong speed. But was this after all so very desirable? Many of the Tsar's contemporaries regarded his policy of headlong westernization as a grave error – a point of view which some later historians and social thinkers came to share.

An egalitarian approach was an especially typical feature of the Tsar, for social, national and religious affiliations meant little to him, and Menshikov's rise from alleged pieman to prince had many parallels, as did Catherine's from Lithuanian servant-girl to Empress. Peter made a Portuguese Jew his chief of police in St Petersburg, and a former boot-black became procurator-general of his senate. Nor was the Tsar an inverted snob, for he was fully prepared to promote the less effete members of the old boyar families along with social upstarts.

The main levelling principle adopted by Peter was his imposition of lifelong service to the state on virtually all male citizens; besides which all officers, military and civil, must work their way up through the ranks, as had the Tsar himself by beginning as a drummer-boy. From time to time Peter required gentlemen from designated areas to present themselves in Moscow or St Petersburg for inspection and assignment to a branch of the service. He compelled their sons to attend special schools, and prohibited unsatisfactory pupils from marrying. Although the gentry was the most privileged class, it was not exclusive. Attainment of any of the eight highest grades in the table of ranks conferred the hereditary status of gentleman without regard to social origin; and this promotion was open even to such serfs as could take advantage of a provision granting freedom to those volunteering for the colours. However, it was more the shadow than the substance of equal opportunity and social mobility that Peter offered. He left the peasant masses in worse condition than he found them by impressing them comprehensively as soldiers, factory workers and builders – all callings in which mortality rates from overwork and ill usage ran high. Taxation fell especially hard on the peasantry with the establishment in 1718 of a heavy annual poll-tax from which gentry, clergy and merchants were exempt. But there were few members of the community who could feel safe from their Tsar. He regimented monks in their cells, and appropriated monastery funds to finance his wars, while taxing hats and baths along with beards and every other conceivable source of revenue.

Mass regimentation led to mass evasion, to counter which Peter encouraged denunciation by making half the property of a defaulter forfeit to any informer who reported him to the authorities; he thus created a network of spies, official and unofficial, whose reports often led to savage reprisals and punishments. But in this field too the Tsar revealed his broad egalitarian principles, sacrificing erring dignitaries as readily as common criminals. He had a vice-governor of St Petersburg knouted, and two senators had their tongues burnt out with red-hot iron. Condemned for extortion, a governor of Siberia was publicly hanged and his body left to dangle on the gallows for months. His downfall resulted from information laid by the chief fiscal – holder of a new office created in 1711 to keep financial and judicial matters under surveillance. That this arch-custodian himself later perished on the wheel (for committing some of the very offences which he had been appointed to detect) will surprise no one attuned to the intimations of totalitarian manners in Peter's Russia.

Not that Russia of his day was distinguished by the public decorum which is a marked feature of twentieth-century totalitarian behaviour. Peter's minions squabbled openly, and there were sessions of the senate during which they collapsed wrestling on the floor. One such feuder, Baron Peter Shafirov, held various high offices, but fell foul of other officials and was condemned to beheading on charges which included the misuse of public money. Led out to the scaffold, he laid his head on the block and the headsman swung his axe, which duly whistled through the air and came down – to strike the block, not the victim; thus the baron discovered that his sentence had been commuted. Such were Peter's methods of creating a tradition of public service. He might have been more successful if his choice of victims had been less erratic; for instance, that massive peculator Menshikov was not executed or exiled during the reign, as happened to so many lesser defaulters.

Happy to use any human material whatever, the Tsar was also prone to misuse it on a grand scale. It was in his reign, according to the author of a *History of Corporal Punishment in Russia*, that torture flourished more than at any other time in Russian history.[10] Peter's aim was not to make his punishments fit the crimes, but to intimidate the unco-operative; to which end brigands, thieves, embezzlers, political plotters, or those who merely expressed dissent from his policies, suffered barbarous punishments such as those mentioned above. Peter also introduced a new military penalty which was to play an infamous part in the history of later Tsars. This was the system whereby soldiers propelled offenders between the ranks, striking them with willow staves (*shpitsruteny*) as they stumbled past, and frequently awarding several thousand blows in this manner. Often fatal, this form of flogging could be imposed under military regulations for blasphemy and adultery, offences of which the royal commander-in-chief was surely as guilty as any man in his ranks. A yet more barbarous ordeal closely associated with the great Tsar was torture by the wheel, on which the executioner spreadeagled his victim after smashing each of his limbs in two places. Peter was the first Tsar to use this method on any considerable scale (against the Streltsy in 1698), and he later sanctioned it in his military regulations.

There is an extraordinary degree of coincidence in detail between the biographies of Peter the Great and Ivan the Terrible. Each sovereign began his reign as a child terrorized by violent and mutinous subjects. Each also began his military career with an unsuccessful campaign against a Turkic enemy in the east and turned failure into victory shortly afterwards. Both Tsars devoted their main military energies to fighting for an outlet on the Baltic, albeit with unequal effectiveness. Each led his armies in battle, and each also found occasion to follow a general tradition of Muscovite rulers by discreetly withdrawing his own person from danger when menaced by superior force. Other common features include an idiot brother or half-brother; great piety and religious erudition combined with systematic mockery of the outward forms of religion; and the appointment of mock heads of state. The two Tsars also shared a keen interest in printing, an addiction to drunken frolics with compulsory participation for victimized dotards, and a bizarre sense of humour dangerous to onlookers. Each killed his eldest son and heir.

Striking as these similarities are, the contrast between Peter the extrovert and Ivan the introvert is still more eloquent. Peter felt fully at ease in the seat of power, lacking Ivan's constant itch of insecurity; nor did he share the earlier Tsar's sense of brooding grievance or the passion for confessing his innermost thoughts in public. Both Tsars inflicted atrocities, but Ivan was the more creative terrorist, and also the more dedicated. His destruction of Novgorod and area far eclipsed in scope and variety the horrors of Peter's butchery of the Streltsy, premier domestic atrocity of the later reign. It is admittedly impossible to establish the exact scale of the earlier massacre, but it seems likely that the number of victims was fifty times that of the Streltsy slaughtered by Peter. More of a technician or practical man, Peter was comparatively pedestrian in approach, administering terror in doses less wildly disproportionate to the aim of maintaining the security of his realm and person – though it is also true that a keen interest in anatomical study and sheer high spirits came into play when he inflicted extreme pain. But Peter did not show the same personal concern as Ivan in dispatching his subjects with his own hand and choosing ingenious methods of death. The great Tsar was more content to execute and maim through the agency of others – and notably through the Preobrazhensky Chancery, which he gradually expanded from a mere regimental headquarters, giving it exclusive powers to arrest, investigate and judge political offences.[11] This was a far more rational and effective security organ than Ivan's Oprichnina.

If Peter was less cruel than Ivan, he was also more callous, as can be seen from the very different reactions of each Tsar to the death of his eldest son. It was in a moment of rage immediately regretted and long repented that Ivan struck down his heir, whereas Peter spent over a year having the Tsarevich Alexis hunted through Europe, took six months to kill him after luring him back to St Petersburg, and barely deigned to notice his passing after having him knouted to death. Thus Peter was less 'human' than Ivan, even if his general record was less inhumane; and it is perhaps for this reason that the earlier Tsar enjoyed more affection from his subjects than did his successor.

Coming to the throne a century and a half after Ivan, Peter was a far more modern ruler. He had many of the instincts of a twentieth-century totalitarian dictator – combining the repressive flair of a Hitler or Stalin with the clowning talents of a Mussolini or Khrushchev, and adding the drive of a Lenin. But fortunately for the world the giant Tsar lacked the elementary equipment available to these pygmies – such as the telephone and a comparatively high level of literacy among the ruled. Given these facilities, he would have shown humanity what a giant-size dictator was like. As it was, he made an impact on Russia greater than that of any other Tsar, or of any other Russian before Lenin. But it is also arguable that the great Tsar failed to achieve any fundamental change in Russian society, merely imparting a hysterical tempo and alien style to trends already well established at the time of his accession; for he did not invent the 'westernization' of Russia, only accelerated an existing process. Be that as it may, Peter easily qualifies for the title of great which mankind confers on so many of those who increase their country's international prestige at the expense of individual citizens' freedom and prosperity.

Peter received the formal title of 'Great' in the wake of celebrations following the Peace of Nystad, which ended the Northern War in 1721 and brought the climax of his glory. He himself bore the news of peace up the Neva, travelling on a brigantine which fired three cannon shots each minute. On his arrival in the capital, guns of the admiralty and of the Peter and Paul Fortress took up the salute. Twelve dragoons bore the news round the city to trumpet fanfares and drum rolls, and the ensuing carnival lasted a week. It was in October of the same year that the senate and synod met together in St Petersburg and resolved to press a trio of new titles on the monarch – Father of the Fatherland, Emperor of All Russia, Peter the Great. After due show of modesty, Peter accepted, thus in a sense putting an end to the history of the Tsars, for the Russian sovereign's formal title now began: 'Emperor and Autocrat of All Russia, Moscow, Kiev, Vladimir, Novgorod . . .' Henceforward he was, officially, Tsar only of Kazan, Astrakhan and Siberia. But the historic title of Tsar was too deep-rooted to wither away, and it continued to be used alongside Emperor until the dynasty ended.

Peter's was not the only promotion to follow the Treaty of Nystad. Russia herself, having started his reign as Muscovy in the minds of western Europeans, was now an empire. Though some of the powers took years to grant official recognition to the Tsar of Muscovy as Emperor of Russia, all were aware that Peter had made his country one of the most powerful on earth.

Peter died on 28 January 1725, his death, like that of most great men, giving rise to stories of varying authenticity. In the previous November he had leapt into the sea to save some soldiers endangered in a stranded boat, but it is not clear that this exploit hastened his end two months later. Less heroic was the persistent legend that he perished of syphilis; in fact it seems most likely that he died of a painful bladder complaint combined with cirrhosis of the liver.[12]

Part 4   Age of Empresses

17 Mixed Heritage

The period 1725–96 saw the Russian throne occupied by a sequence of seven sovereigns whose links are extremely complex.

They were all related in some way to Peter the Great – if only distantly and by marriage, as in the case of Catherine II. It may also be observed that female and male rulers chanced to follow each other in strict rotation. Succeeding in 1725, Catherine I became the first woman to rule Russia as titular sovereign, though there had been female regents in earlier periods. Once established, the principle of female rule became dominant for seven decades. During this time four Empresses held sway, male occupation of the throne being restricted to less than five years' reign in all – and that by a boy, a baby whose mother was regent during most of his brief reign, and an adult who seemed not quite a man. All the Empresses had their share of feminine characteristics, but none of the four is easily conceived as a member of the weaker sex. Each accomplished the feat – increasingly difficult for a Russian autocrat – of dying a natural death; whereas three out of four of their male heirs were murdered.

The seven rulers of the period all came to the throne during the operative period of the law of succession decreed by Peter the Great and dated 5 February 1722. This empowered the reigning sovereign to nominate as heir any individual of his choice – but with the clear implication that he would restrict himself to descendants or other relatives. The new principle replaced the previous established custom, not enshrined in law, whereby the throne had generally descended to an eldest son officially proclaimed heir and presented to the people by his reigning father at the age of fifteen. The new and more flexible system could only be expected to work well provided that each sovereign chose wisely, and provided of course that he did not omit to make his choice altogether, a prospect for which Peter failed to cater. Unfortunately all his eighteenth-century successors erred in

Genealogy of the Romanovs, with Dates of Rule

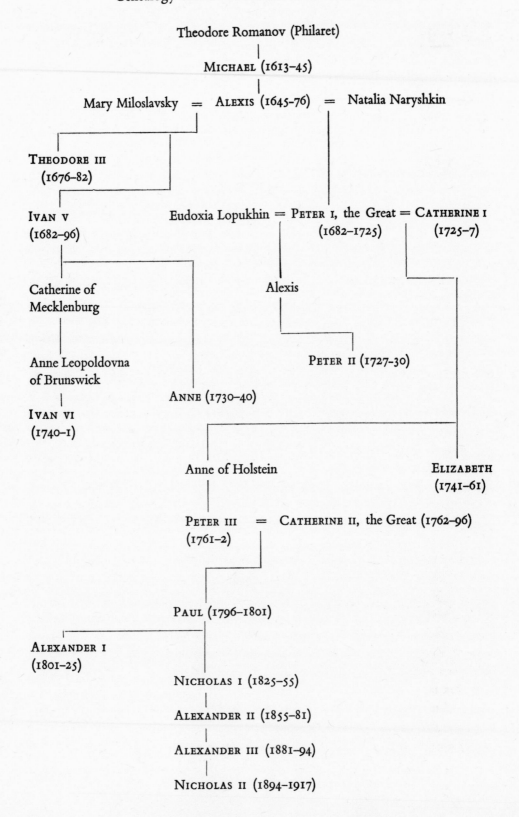

Theodore Romanov (Philaret)

|

MICHAEL (1613–45)

|

Mary Miloslavsky = ALEXIS (1645–76) = Natalia Naryshkin

THEODORE III
(1676–82)

IVAN V
(1682–96)

Eudoxia Lopukhin = PETER I, the Great = CATHERINE I
(1682–1725)   (1725–7)

Catherine of
Mecklenburg

Alexis

Anne Leopoldovna
of Brunswick

PETER II (1727–30)

IVAN VI
(1740–1)

ANNE (1730–40)

Anne of Holstein

ELIZABETH
(1741–61)

PETER III   =   CATHERINE II, the Great (1762–96)
(1761–2)

PAUL (1796–1801)

ALEXANDER I
(1801–25)

NICHOLAS I (1825–55)

ALEXANDER II (1855–81)

ALEXANDER III (1881–94)

NICHOLAS II (1894–1917)

one or other of these respects. Peter himself died without nominating any heir, and such choices as were made (the ladies being the more conscientious in discharging this duty) proved unsuccessful in the sense that usurpers or favourites exercised effective rule almost exclusively during the age of Empresses.

Peter the Great having died intestate, his widow Catherine succeeded him, elected by a gathering not legally empowered to appoint a new monarch (inevitably so since there was no constitutional provision for setting up such a body) and consisting of leading dignitaries who assembled in the imperial palace on the night of 27–8 January 1725. For the first but by no means the last time the two guards regiments stationed in the capital now played a role as arbiters of the succession. Of the two main candidates (Catherine herself and Peter's grandson Peter Alekseyevich), the guards supported the former – partly because her ally Menshikov had adroitly seized this moment to make good long-standing arrears in their pay, and partly because Catherine was popular with the army as something of an old soldier herself. Marshalled outside the palace by drum-roll, the troops of the Preobrazhensky and Semyonovsky Regiments were well equipped to win over any doubtful voters, especially when some of their officers filtered into a corner of the council chamber and began to influence the deliberations with threatening shouts.

Catherine was willing to reign, but lacked the ability or inclination to rule. Bawdy, kindly and a great brandy-drinker, she seemed more like the genial madame of a brothel than mistress of the largest empire in the world. She was also illiterate or barely literate – a handicap shared by her close ally Menshikov, who nevertheless became effective head of government. He was a shrewd manipulator whose horizons, bounded only by the limits of his own ego, were far-flung indeed. Thus a favourite became *de facto* ruler, by contrast with the reign of Peter the Great, who always overshadowed his favourites, however influential – Menshikov as much as any. By no means unknown in previous eras, favouritism now became – unofficially and with many fluctuations of fortune – more than ever a leading institution of the state, for Menshikov was only the first in a long sequence of such eighteenth-century potentates to wield great power.

19 Peter II 1727-30

Menshikov exercised much of his power through a body newly established in 1726 and consisting initially of six members – the supreme privy council. He also took precautions to safeguard his position after Catherine's death, which occurred in 1727. It transpired that she had willed her throne to the rival candidate of two years earlier (Peter the Great's grandson Peter Alekseyevich) in a testament approved as valid at the time, though later regarded as a forgery. Menshikov secured the betrothal of his daughter to the boy, who succeeded as Peter II at the age of eleven and took up residence in Menshikov's house. Thus the great favourite might have been destined for yet greater heights of glory, had he not contrived to annoy the capricious young Emperor by his overbearing manner. In 1727 Peter casually dismissed his prospective father-in-law. Menshikov now began a long journey into exile, accompanied by his daughter and a large retinue of servants and hangers-on, but pursued by relays of couriers who bore imperial orders gradually stripping him of his following and possessions. He died in Siberia in 1729, having borne these afflictions bravely, as fallen favourites often did. In success or failure – and their status was always precarious – they were a rugged breed.

With Menshikov's downfall the dominant influence passed to members of the Dolgoruky family, one of Russia's most illustrious princely houses. They now copied the fallen favourite's methods by betrothing a member of their own clan to the boy-Emperor. Meanwhile Peter had been spending much of his time on extended hunting expeditions and precocious flirtation – not least with his voluptuous aunt, the Tsarevna Elizabeth. While he thus neglected affairs of state, the Dolgorukys (who were opposed to Peter the Great's reforms) managed to assert their old-fashioned principles by removing the court and organs of government to Moscow. Their plans and the Emperor's projected marriage to a Dolgoruky received an abrupt check in January 1730, when Peter II contracted smallpox and died.

When Peter II died without naming an heir, the task of choosing his successor devolved to the supreme privy council which had ruled the country since Menshikov's fall and now consisted of eight members, being dominated by members of the Dolgoruky and Golitsyn families. At the suggestion of Prince Dmitry Golitsyn the council made its offer of the vacant throne to Anne, Duchess of Courland (daughter of Ivan V and niece of Peter the Great), conditional on her accepting less than autocratic power. This was the only serious attempt made in the eighteenth century to eliminate or restrict the Russian autocracy – by converting it into a kind of constitutional monarchy based on a bargain struck in advance with the sovereign elect. The council required Anne to give the following undertakings amongst others on pain of forfeiting her throne: not to remarry or nominate an heir; and not to make peace, declare war, appoint generals, grant estates or impose taxes without the council's consent.

Anne signed her name to these conditions in Mitau on 28 January 1730 and left for Moscow. But she quickly realized on arrival that the gentry as a whole was opposed to an arrangement which might suit the Dolgorukys and Golitsyns, but threatened to replace an absolute monarchy with an absolute oligarchy exercised by the council. By no means everyone felt that an octet of autocrats was preferable to a solo performer, and the rowdy support of guards and lesser gentry emboldened the new Empress to repudiate the conditions which she had accepted a month earlier. At a gathering of officers and dignitaries in her palace on 25 February 1730 she tore up the scrap of paper concerned. Becoming full autocratic Empress by this demonstration of imperial will, she dissolved the supreme privy council, and subjected the Dolgorukys and Golitsyns to persecution which ended for several of them on the executioner's block.

Anne succeeded to the Russian throne at the age of thirty-seven, having spent twenty years as the widow of Duke William of Courland. Marriage to a niece of Peter the Great had its occupational risks, and it had been the groom's misfortune to see his wedding staged by the bride's uncle in typically florid manner, a special feature being two colossal pies containing live dwarfs. They stepped out through the broached crust and danced a minuet on the table, incidentally setting the tone for Anne's personal style as ruler two decades later. The duke died soon after this nuptial orgy, not necessarily as the direct result of Russian hospitality. Since then the widowed Anne had largely resided in her duchy until her summons to the throne.

Stately and tall, Anne had the look of a true Empress, nor did she lack patience and common-sense on the rare occasions when she chose to deal with matters of state. But she preferred to sign official documents unread and govern through German proxies, two of whom had already risen to prominence under Peter the Great: Field-Marshal Münnich and Count Ostermann. However, both potentates suffered partial eclipse by a more recent arrival – the Empress's lover Ernst Bühren, or Biron, whom she brought to Russia from Courland, and who was favourite-in-chief throughout her reign. Openly despising Russians, he did not bother to learn their language and occupied no official position apart from that of court chamberlain. He became notorious for corruption and cruelty which attracted particular odium because he was an alien.

To protect her foreign-dominated government from a possible *coup d'état*, Anne created a third guards regiment, the Izmaylovsky – commanded by a Scot and partly officered by Baltic Germans. But odd whims indulged within her court and capital (transferred back to St Petersburg from Moscow soon after her accession) were her chief medium for exercising autocratic power. Sharing with her famous uncle a taste for firearms and displays of eccentricity, she kept loaded guns handy in her palace, and it was her unsporting habit to fire through the windows at birds in her garden – a pastime in which she required her ladies-in-waiting to take part. She was intellectually lazy but easily bored, and surrounded herself with gossiping women, dwarfs, hunchbacks, court jesters, cripples and other human curios.

Among Anne's favourite amusements was the ordering of whimsical marriages, and one of these contributed an especially gaudy splash of colour to her reign. Though the groom bore a proud name as one of the many Princes Golitsyn, he served the Empress as a buffoon, and she thought it amusing to marry him to another court butt – an outstandingly hideous Calmuck woman. For this purpose Anne ordered the construction of an ice palace on the frozen Neva. With its glacial columns, statues and balcony, it was over twenty feet high and nearly three hundred feet long. Ingenious *tableaux* wrought in coloured ice graced the scene and included a life-sized elephant mounted by an ice man in Persian dress, with a real man hidden inside to simulate the creature's trumpetings. Lit by countless candles, blocks of ice covered with blazing oil and ice dolphins spewing fire, the crystalline edifice offered a scintillating spectacle, but cold comfort to a bride and groom immured inside for the night after the ceremony with sentries posted to prevent escape. It says much for their ability to take a joke that both survived the rigours of the nuptial slab. A lavish carnival accompanied this grotesque pageant, vividly illustrating the lengths to which Anne could carry expensive buffoonery – and a reminder that her court was spending over half of the national income.[1] Perhaps it was fortunate that an Empress with such tastes left the ruling of Russia to others, however harsh and grasping.

21 Ivan VI   1740-1

After Anne's death on 17 October 1740, the eight-week-old baby Ivan VI – her great-nephew – succeeded as nominal Emperor, whereupon the government of Russia became a bone of contention between competing Germans who had managed to coexist with comparative decorum under the deceased Empress. These included Anne Leopoldovna (the Empress Anne's niece and the new Emperor's mother). Though a granddaughter of the Russian Tsar Ivan V, she was daughter of a Duke of Mecklenburg and thus half German, besides being married to a German who now also sought to influence Russian events – Duke Anton of Brunswick. The late Empress Anne had appointed yet another German, Biron, regent to the baby Tsar, but a classic *coup d'état* ended his regency after only three weeks. On the evening of 8 November 1740, he gave dinner to Field-Marhsal Münnich without realizing that anything untoward was afoot – only to suffer arrest later that night on the field-marshal's orders. Münnich's adjutant burst into the regent's bedroom at the head of a detachment of Preobrazhensky guardsmen who carried him kicking and punching out of the palace wrapped in a blanket. He was taken to Schlüsselburg Fortress as a prelude to trial and Siberian exile.

During the rest of Ivan VI's thirteen-month reign, his mother Anne Leopoldovna was regent. She disliked appearing in public and left little trace on Russian policy or imagination. Nor did Münnich, the strong man of the hour, long survive as power behind the throne after toppling Biron. He fell through the efforts of a rival German already mentioned – the resourceful Ostermann, effective ruler of Russia during most of 1741. To his sway, as to that of all other German potentates and favourites – including all members of the house of Brunswick – the Tsarevna Elizabeth's *coup d'état* of 26 November 1741 put an end for the next twenty years.

Daughter of Peter the Great and Catherine I, the Tsarevna Elizabeth had remained single despite her father's campaign to marry all his younger female relatives into the princely houses of Europe. He had wished to see her as queen to Louis XV of France, and it was with such an exalted union in mind that she learnt to speak French and dance the minuet – but very little else. Neither accomplishment seemed especially apt when – in default of any suitor more august – arrangements were made for her to wed the Bishop of Lübeck. But he unfortunately died before the wedding could take place, leaving Elizabeth to enjoy the life of an unattached Emperor's daughter in St Petersburg – a function for which nature had equipped her generously. A big, bouncing young woman with large, lustrous, blue eyes, rich auburn hair, a voluptuous figure and superb complexion, she was sometimes called the loveliest girl in Europe. Though her charms may have seemed a little obvious and she had a tendency to put on weight, she was irresistible to men and surely the most sexually attractive Russian Empress. Her love life maintained the strenuous standards set by both her parents, and has evoked some censorious paragraphs from her Victorian English biographer Nisbet Bain, as well as the worldly innuendoes of her more revealing Polish chronicler Waliszewski. But love affairs were only part of the full physical life led by the athletic Tsarevna, who also enjoyed hunting, riding, dancing, sledging and skating. Her manner was easy and spontaneous, and she was widely popular – not only with the muscular young guardees who competed for her favours. She rarely read a book and found politics boring; but to lack intellectual interests is not necessarily to be stupid, as she showed when she occasionally chose to use her brain.

Her claims to succeed Peter II in 1730 had arguably been greater than those of her cousin Anne of Courland and as the most serious rival for the throne during Anne's reign, Elizabeth had wisely chosen to behave with great caution. The Empress's agents watched her closely, but she managed to avoid trouble, showing respect to her crowned cousin and to Biron. Kept short of money, the Tsarevna was unable to indulge her more extravagant tastes; but she contrived to escape the convent, destiny of so many ladies who became inconvenient to a reigning sovereign. The thought of Elizabeth as a bride of Christ is indeed daunting. She

Coronation procession of the Empress Anne
in Moscow, 28 April 1730.

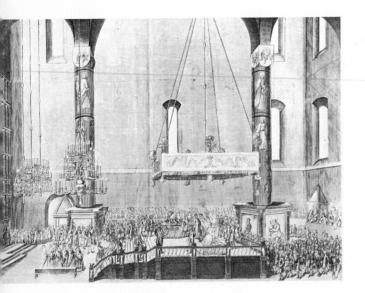

A niece of Peter the Great, the Empress Anne ruled from 1730 to 1740, largely through the agency of German favourites.
On becoming Empress she denounced the conditions limiting autocratic power on which she had accepted the throne.
Bronze statue by Rastrelli.

The coronation of the Empress Anne: a scene inside the Uspensky Cathedral, where all the Tsars, Tsar-Emperors and Empresses of Russia were crowned. A contemporary engraving.

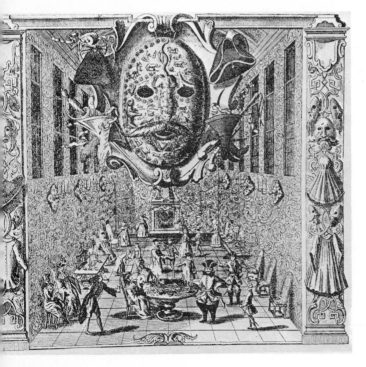

Scene from a masquerade at the court of the Empress Anne, who was well known for the staging of lavish and extravagant spectacles. A contemporary engraving.

A contemporary engraving celebrating the birth
of Ivan VI on 23 August 1740. After a reign
of thirteen months which ended on
26 November 1741, he was deposed in the *coup*
which brought the Empress Elizabeth to power.

№ 30. Видъ въ проспектие Успенской соборной церькви и перед оной площади и прочему спро

The coronation of the Empress Elizabeth
with the Uspensky Cathedral in the centre.
A contemporary engraving.

(*opposite top*) Daughter of Peter the Great, the
Empress Elizabeth (ruled 1741–61) came to
power by a *coup d'état*. She was celebrated for
her patriotism and piety as well as for the size
of her wardrobe and her pursuit of the gay life.
Painting by L. Tocque.

(*opposite bottom*) The *coup* of 26 November 1741,
which brought the Empress Elizabeth to power.
Contemporary print.

Stanislaus Augustus, King of Poland
(r. 1764–95), was one of Catherine II's
lovers as Count Poniatowski before
succeeding to the Polish throne.
Painting by Bacciarelli.

Platon Zubov (1767–1822) was the last
of Catherine the Great's favourites and took
part in the assassination of the Emperor Paul.
A portrait by Lampi.

(*opposite*) Three future sovereigns of
Russia. Peter III (ruled 1761–2);
Catherine II, the Great (ruled 1761–
96); Paul (ruled 1796–1801). Painting
of 1756 by R. M. Lisiewska.

(*top*) Gregory Potemkin, Prince of Tauris,
most influential of Catherine the Great's many
favourites and possibly the most flamboyant
Russian in history. By H. Löschenkohl.

Peter III, who ruled for six months in 1761–2
before being deposed in the *coup* which brought
his wife Catherine to the throne.
A mosaic portrait of him as Grand Duke after
an original of 1758.

Countess Elizabeth Vorontsov (1739–92),
mistress of Peter III, in whose favour
he threatened to depose his wife Catherine,
sending her to a convent.

had 'not one bit of nun's flesh about her',[2] as the English minister to St Petersburg reported; while the Spanish ambassador put the same thing in a different way when he remarked that Elizabeth showed 'no shame in doing such things as bring a blush to the least modest cheek'.[3]

Between the reigns of the two strong rulers Peter I and Catherine II, foreign diplomats in St Petersburg were able to intervene in Russian affairs with extra-ordinary freedom, and the *coup d'état* which overthrew Ivan VI and his regent Anne Leopoldovna owed part of its inspiration to the French ambassador, the Marquis de la Chétardie, who wished to end the foreign policy pursued by Ostermann. Secret negotiations took place between Tsarevna and marquis – largely through the French adventurer Lestocq, Elizabeth's personal physician and politically the most important of her early favourites. These dealings might have come to nothing had they remained secret. But they attracted the attention of the regent, who summoned Elizabeth to an interview on 23 November 1741 at which she confined herself to warnings – and foolishly so, for she alarmed the Tsarevna without rendering her harmless. The next day brought Elizabeth further cause for concern when she learnt that the guards regiments were ready to march against Sweden, which had declared war on Russia in the previous July. Since the guards were Elizabeth's main supporters, the proposal to remove them from the capital looked like a prelude to her arrest. She therefore faced the choice between seizing power at once and spending the rest of her life in the nunnery for which she was so ill suited.

Elizabeth proved equal to the crisis – a hazardous adventure, even if the spirit of light opera seems to have presided over this, as over so many other eighteenth-century Russian palace revolutions. Her tactics were to strike boldly and silently at night with a unit of the Preobrazhensky Guards, the Grenadier Company. She first sounded certain members of this unit in secret, and when they readily swore to support her she felt encouraged to appeal to the company as a whole. Leaving her palace with a few close advisers between 1 and 2 a.m. on the morning of 26 November, she wore a cuirass and carried a silver cross as her sledge sped through the snows of St Petersburg on its way to the Preobrazhensky barracks. Here she picked up a short pike and had the drums slit lest anyone should beat the alarm; but the guards were hers – from a combination of personal loyalty, hope of reward, patriotic dislike of foreign domination and unwillingness to face a winter campaign against Sweden. Parties were detached to seize Ostermann and Münnich – the two German potentates most to be feared – while Elizabeth herself made for the Winter Palace, where (according to some accounts) she personally roused the regent from sleep and arrested her. Among others seized and taken to Elizabeth's palace were the baby Tsar and the regent's husband, Duke Anton of Brunswick. Meanwhile soldiers and dignitaries were hurriedly swearing loyalty to the new Empress on all sides and she hastened to proclaim herself colonel of the guards.

Appearing on a balcony of the Winter Palace, the seductive usurper evoked loud cheers from the crowd despite bitterly cold weather.

Elizabeth was a warm-hearted person by the standards of her age and circle. But her kind impulses were apt to remain mere impulses, as the deposed regent, the infant ex-Tsar and their family learnt to their cost. The usurping Empress first took the humane decision that these members of the house of Brunswick were to proceed to German territory – where, after all, they really belonged. They accordingly set out for the western frontier. But Elizabeth changed her mind and sent couriers with orders to arrest them. Detained at Riga, the Brunswickers languished in a near-by fortress for about a year, and were then brought to central Russia; a further change of plan saw them removed to imprisonment at Kholmogory in the bleak north. It was here that the ex-regent died after bearing more children destined for the prison cell, while the deposed boy-Emperor remained under especially close guard – isolated from his family – to be transferred in 1756 to Schlüsselburg Fortress. Monarch for thirteen months before his second birthday, this most luckless of Tsars spent all his remaining life as a captive kept in official ignorance of his whereabouts and even of his own identity; he was also, according to one authority, the first person in Russian history to suffer solitary confinement.[4] Forced to hide behind a screen whenever anyone came into his cell, he hardly ever saw a human being except for the specially appointed gaolers who ill-used him. His eventual fate under the Empress Catherine II must be described later.

While the Preobrazhensky grenadiers and others received promotion and rich rewards for their part in bringing Elizabeth to power, leading figures of the previous reign stood trial. Münnich and Ostermann were among those sentenced to a cruel death – the former to quartering, the latter to breaking on the wheel. Proclaimed by drum roll in the streets of St Petersburg, the execution was staged on the morning of 18 January 1742 – staged, but dramatically countermanded at the last moment by the sudden announcement of an act of imperial clemency typical of the Tsars. The gouty elder statesman Ostermann suffered an assault on his nerves which he withstood with dignity. First informed that he was merely to be beheaded – not subjected to the agony of the wheel – he obediently placed his neck on the block. One executioner held him by the hair, while another took the axe from a piece of sacking . . . when the presiding secretary flourished a piece of paper and announced: 'God and the Empress have spared thy life.'[5] He suffered exile to Siberia instead of execution, as also did Münnich, who treated the grim pantomime of his trial, condemnation and last-minute reprieve with sublime contempt. As for the rabble of St Petersburgers who had flocked to see German heads roll, they were furious to miss so exciting a spectacle, and troops had to quell their protests.

Münnich suffered banishment to Siberia, now vacated by the Empress Anne's fallen favourite Biron, who received permission to live in exile in European Russia. At a posting-station near Kazan the paths of the rival potentates happened to cross and they exchanged bows without speaking[6] – though certainly neither had forgotten that Münnich had so recently overthrown Biron as regent. Ostermann died in exile. But Münnich – most robust, perhaps, of all Russian eighteenth-century favourites – lived on to obtain pardon from Peter III and return to European Russia at the age of nearly eighty in time for Catherine II's seizure of power. The fate of Ostermann and Münnich is a reminder that Elizabeth reputedly took a vow on the night of her bid for power never to sign a death sentence if she should succeed in becoming Empress.[7] The alternatives which she permitted are hardly evidence of humanitarianism, the ordeal of Ostermann being by no means the most savage; but her practices at least contrast favourably with the bloody executions of the Dolgorukys and others carried out under the Empress Anne.

Though her accession ended an era of foreign domination, Elizabeth was no xenophobe – as witness the cosmopolitan entourage of minor figures who escorted her on her ride to power on the night of 25–6 November 1741. These ousters of German influence in Russia included the aspiring Empress's German music teacher Schwartz; a Sergeant Grünstein of the Preobrazhensky Guards, who was of German Jewish origin; and the French émigré Lestocq. It must be added that the influence of French fashions and manners on the Russian court was considerable during Elizabeth's reign, while a growing interest among the Russian élite in French culture and the French language was also a feature of the period.

Elizabeth by no means dispensed with favouritism, but her two main favourites – a Ukrainian Cossack and a Russian – were far from pretending to supreme power. The former, Alexis Razumovsky, attracted attention in the Ukraine as a good-looking chorister and went to sing in the choir of the imperial chapel in St Petersburg, where he became the Tsarevna Elizabeth's lover. There is also evidence that they may have married in secret shortly after her accession and that they had a daughter. In any case the handsome Alexis openly appeared with his imperial mistress as if he had the official status of consort, while remaining charmingly untouched by delusions of grandeur. Granted high military rank as a perquisite of his position, he was modest enough to remark that no one could possibly take him seriously even as a lieutenant – let alone as the field-marshal which he had just become.[8] He was admittedly something of a drunkard and liable to lay about elder statesmen with his whip when hunting; but by the standards of eighteenth-century favourites these were mild peccadilloes.

Ivan Shuvalov, who succeeded as reigning favourite in 1749 but without entirely replacing Razumovsky, was of similarly angelic disposition. He too left grand policy to others, preferring the role of patron to artists and scholars, and helping to found Moscow University in 1755. But his term as Elizabeth's reigning lover did affect politics to the extent of helping his two politically minded cousins, Alexander and Peter Shuvalov. The former was in effect Elizabeth's chief of political police in his capacity as head of the secret chancery. This had replaced Peter the Great's Preobrazhensky chancery (abolished under Peter II) – an example of the way in which the main Russian political security organ has continually changed its name over the centuries without necessarily changing its methods. Alexander Shuvalov's brother Peter was still more influential, administering internal affairs and inventing a howitzer of disputed efficiency, while amassing a large personal fortune and even larger debts by corrupt practices typical of an eighteenth-century Russian statesman. To such practices Elizabeth's chancellor, Alexis Bestuzhev-Ryumin (responsible for foreign affairs until his downfall in 1758) was no stranger either.

The beautiful Empress was always eager to improve on nature and would spend several hours a day at her toilette. She was a keen student of French fashion, and the figure most commonly quoted for her reign is that of the fifteen thousand dresses found in the imperial wardrobes after her death. She would not wear the same dress twice, and had the habit of changing her clothes several times a night during the many sumptuous balls which she continued to grace, still dancing vigorously even when she had begun to look more like an imposing matron than the most beautiful girl in Europe.

One special feature of the Empress's entertainments was the staging of masquerades at which all the women appeared as men and all the men as women. Arrayed as a Cossack hetman, a French musketeer or – out of compliment to her father – a Dutch sailor, the gorgeous sovereign outshone all beauties of both sexes at these transvestist junketings. Though her voluptuous charms had many admirers (not least the grand duchess and future usurper of the throne, Catherine), she was intolerant of rivals. When a certain Natalia Lopukhin appeared at a court ball wearing a pink dress and with pink roses in her hair, Elizabeth took this as a deliberate challenge, since pink was her own preferred colour. Reaching for her father's weapon, a pair of scissors, she snipped off the roses and boxed the culprit's ears. But the Empress had by no means finished with this particular victim, later convicted of conspiring with the Austrian ambassador. Elizabeth caused her to be knouted and lose her tongue, though this was technically an act of clemency, for it involved commuting a death sentence passed by the senate. It is perhaps as typical an example of Elizabeth's double-edged kindness as can be quoted.

In contrast with her successor Catherine II, Elizabeth led a disorderly life, following an erratic daily timetable in keeping with the generally slipshod atmosphere of her court. She rarely slept before dawn – conceivably as a precaution, since she of all people was least likely to forget that the hours of darkness were sacred to the *coup d'état*. When not dancing or otherwise celebrating at night, she would surround herself, like the Empress Anne, with elderly female companions who were engaged to gossip and tickle the soles of her feet – a process which afforded her nervous relief. The supposed influence of these *gratteuses* on high policy gave rise to reports that they could be bribed to put in a word with the Empress during the watches of the night.

Elizabeth liked to travel in state, and her imperial progresses often involved many thousands of people and horses, as when she periodically transferred her court and seat of government to Moscow for a matter of months. This confused peregrination involved hosts of flunkeys and the mass removal of furniture, which travellers of the period commonly carried with them wherever they went. Damp, draughty, ill-built palaces which were liable to burn down and the many other inconveniences of the Empress's surroundings combined curiously with the ostentation which gave her court the name of the most luxurious and licentious in Europe. To these elements she added extreme piety as a devout member of her church, assiduous in her attendance at divine service and making pilgrimages on foot to various shrines.

What with dancing, love affairs, devotions, dressing up and the care of her fading health and waning beauty, the Empress led a full and energetic life; but one which left her little time for concerns of state. It was a constant complaint of her high officials that they could not obtain her signature to important documents, not so much because she was careless – for she by no means took such matters lightly – as because she could rarely find a spare moment. According to report, the Empress once failed to sign a treaty with Austria because a wasp happened to settle on her pen at the critical moment and distract her attention, after which six weeks passed before she again found time to write her name.[9] But though such stories were common, Elizabeth was not entirely frivolous. Deeply-felt patriotism and considerable force of will lay behind her policies in at least two directions – her efforts to regulate the succession to the throne in a manner to be described below; and her personal insistence that Russian military activities against Prussia should maintain their momentum during the Seven Years' War. In most other spheres she was a creature of temporary impulse – easily swayed by appeals for mercy, but also by insinuations against third parties leading to their disgrace and exile.

Highly conscious of being Peter the Great's daughter, the Empress often alluded to her illustrious parentage, but did little either to develop or to dismantle her father's policies. Yet Russia advanced in strength and international influence during her reign. Perhaps the main advantage of this and of the immediately preceding four reigns, despite their many frivolous elements, was to leave the country relatively free from interference such as had been continually supplied by her greatest Emperor. Under Peter's heirs, Russia was thus able to recover to some extent from excess of firm government.

23 The Grand Duchess Catherine 1744-61

The titles grand duke and grand duchess, once borne by the Muscovite sovereign and his wife, devolved to junior members of the reigning family in Russian imperial times – that is, mainly to the sovereign's children and their consorts. It was, accordingly, as the Grand Duchess Catherine that the future Empress Catherine II, or Catherine the Great, held the position of second lady in Russia during the last seventeen years of Elizabeth's reign. By no stretch of the imagination could Catherine be called a Russian, having been born as Princess of Anhalt-Zerbst on 21 April 1729 and christened Sophia-Augusta-Frederika. Nor was Anhalt-Zerbst a likely nursery of Russian empresses, being only a petty German princedom. However, that only helped to recommend Sophia to the Empress Elizabeth when she decided to find a bride for her nephew Peter, heir to the Russian throne. A princess as lowly as Sophia (it was argued) would not venture to intrigue, but would submit entirely to her husband's will – for which misconceptions the Grand Duke Peter was later to pay with his life. Though his wife was a charming, affectionate young woman, it was unwise to come between her and the powerful ambition which she secretly cultivated for many years.

Her marriage to the grand duke came about as follows. In January 1744, Princess Sophia's mother received a letter inviting her to present her daughter with all possible haste to the Empress Elizabeth in Russia. Leaving Zerbst in great excitement and secrecy, the ladies travelled in modest incognito by way of Berlin. They entered the Russian Empire, and at Riga received an elaborate welcome which included cannon fire and a military escort. The vastly swollen cortège rolled on in great state to St Petersburg – and thence to Moscow, where Elizabeth had established her court for the time being.

The Empress was delighted with the fourteen-year-old Sophia, who seemed to take to her future husband at first and with Teutonic thoroughness set herself to study for the role of wife to a Russian heir. She acquired instructors in the Russian language, but fell seriously ill a few days after her arrival – the effect, as she carefully allowed it to be known, of studying Russian in a freezing room in the middle of the night. Her life seemed in danger for a time, and there was talk of summoning a Protestant pastor; but Sophia said that she would rather see an Orthodox priest

Even *in extremis*, it appeared, she did not forget what role she had set herself to play. This devotion to Russia endeared her to the Empress, who showed her great kindness during her illness. Humbler Russians were also impressed.

On 28 and 29 June 1744, Sophia duly embraced the Orthodox faith; was affianced to the grand duke; became a grand duchess; and changed her name to Catherine Alekseyevna. Though a grandson of Peter the Great, her fiancé considered himself a German, and had come to Russia in 1742 on much the same terms as his bride – he had arrived as the Protestant Karl-Peter-Ulrich, Duke of Holstein, and had embraced Orthodoxy to become the Grand Duke Peter Feodorovich. But the change meant little to him. He always felt like a foreigner in Russia, sneering at his adopted country as a godforsaken, uncivilized place. Catherine once said that he was as discreet as a cannon shot; and she had good reason to know since the couple had barely met before Peter was naïvely confiding that he was really in love with one of his aunt's ladies-in-waiting and would rather have married her. Catherine had to remind herself that she was really betrothed to the throne of Russia rather than to this mentally retarded, sickly, lanky, ugly, stupid, boastful, sadistic youth – though it must be added that much of the evidence about Peter comes from sources violently hostile to him, his wife not least among them.

Elizabeth staged a prodigious marriage celebration in St Petersburg on 21 August 1745, but was so eager to see the union blessed with offspring that she hustled Catherine off to the nuptial couch when the wedding ball was barely under way. The groom, less ardent, arrived two hours later – remarking fatuously that the servant would indeed be astonished to see the two of them in bed together.[10] Still an ignorant and innocent young girl, Catherine vainly awaited enlightenment on her wedding night, for the most eligible bachelor in Europe proved a dismal failure as husband, as at everything else. He even achieved the seemingly impossible feat of being unfaithful and impotent at the same time. Impotent or not – the point has never been established beyond doubt – he had several purported love affairs, but has not been proved to have fathered a child in or out of wedlock. According to Catherine's own account, her marriage still remained unconsummated in 1752.[11] Meanwhile the Empress Elizabeth could see the years roll by with no sign of Catherine becoming pregnant; and for this failure to produce an heir she tended to blame the duchess rather than the duke. If the girl could not rouse her husband, it must be her own fault – Elizabeth could not remember having such difficulties with her own men. Catherine thus spent much of her time on bad terms with the Empress who controlled her fate.

Closer acquaintance revealed no compensating qualities at all in the spineless grand duke. He refused to grow up. That he should continue to play with toy soldiers in his late twenties was bad enough; but for Catherine to enter his room and find, as she once did, that he had solemnly court-martialled and hanged a rat for eating some of these playthings, was downright unnerving. What with Peter's incessant violin-playing (discordant to Catherine, who had no ear for music) and the pack of hounds which he installed next to her room in the Winter Palace, he kept the place in constant uproar. To the stink, the yelping and the crack of his whip as he trained or viciously punished these brutes, many other nuisances were added. When drunk, which he frequently was, he was liable to beat his favourites as well as his dogs. He would flirt with ladies-in-waiting, loll around gossiping with servants and play all manner of tiresome japes; he once drilled holes in the door of the Empress's dining-room so that he and his sniggering cronies could spy on her as she supped with her intimates.

The grand duchess felt lonely and abandoned, but did not surrender to despair. She was fond of dancing, and took part in the many magnificent receptions, masquerades and balls held at Elizabeth's court. There were also outdoor sports. When residing at the palace of Oranienbaum on the Gulf of Finland, she would rise at three o'clock in the morning to go duck-shooting in the reeds by the canal; and return to find her husband snoring off his previous night's drinking bout. A better horsewoman than many suspected, she would set off demurely riding side-saddle, as the Empress ordered – not so much because she thought it ladylike as because she believed it less likely to cause a miscarriage. But once out of sight of the palace windows, the dashing grand duchess would throw a leg over, having devised a special convertible saddle, and canter off astride like a man.

Catherine was a healthy young girl who thrived on affection, love and physical passion – commodities which her wretched spouse (whether impotent, sterile or neither) could not supply. The time came when she needed something more resembling a man. Nor was there any lack of candidates. Though not beautiful, she was lively and attractive, with a slim build and dark hair. In 1752 she became the mistress of Sergey Saltykov, an otherwise insignificant young courtier; and after two miscarriages she eventually gave birth on 20 December 1754 to the heir so impatiently awaited for nine years by the Empress Elizabeth. Whether the baby Paul was Saltykov's child or the Grand Duke Peter's no one was inclined to ask aloud. So far as Russia was concerned, Paul was a Romanov. But to the young mother the birth was no happy event. Now that she had at last performed her function, she was expendable and no one bothered to pretend otherwise. Barely had the child been safely delivered before the midwife bore him triumphantly away on the Empress's orders. Catherine remained weeping and abandoned for hours, exhausted after a difficult labour, lying in a draught from two badly fitting windows, and with no one to bring her even a glass of water. Forty days passed before she received permission to see the infant, and then only briefly. Further contact was restricted to occasional supervised visits, and she had no say in his upbringing.

A new lover, Count Poniatowski, helped Catherine to ignore such ill usage, as did the development of strong intellectual and political interests. She became a compulsive reader – graduating from novels to historical, political and philosophical works, and paying special attention to two French contemporaries, Montesquieu and Voltaire. Such matters meant nothing to most of Elizabeth's courtiers, but Catherine did come to share the concern of that circle for political intrigue. At first persecuted as an enemy by the powerful chancellor Bestuzhev-Ryumin, she allied herself with him when he realized that she was not an ally of Prussia. She was in fact more the instrument of England, obtaining loans or bribes from one British ambassador in respect of services to be rendered later. It was the Grand Duke Peter who acted as the agent of Prussia, Russia's opponent in the Seven Years' War, which broke out in 1756. Regarding Frederick the Great as his master, he had once kissed a bust of the Prussian king in public to demonstrate this; and he was soon compounding bad taste with high treason by sending Frederick copies of the orders despatched to Russian commanders in the field.

24 Peter III 1761-2

With Elizabeth's death on Christmas Day 1761, Peter III succeeded as Tsar-Emperor. Thirty-three years of age, he became the first male Romanov to mount the throne as an adult during the first century and a half of the dynasty. Not that there was anything notably mature about his attitude, but his very childishness made him, in a sense, the purest possible breed of autocrat. Whereas his successors (not least Catherine herself) constantly took their subjects' reactions into account – if only in order to keep them under more effective control – Peter would indulge his lightest whim without caring what anyone might think. During the very weeks when the deceased Empress was lying in state, her newly elevated nephew's carousals continued unabated. Meanwhile Catherine, a sober figure in black, was spending several hours a day on her knees by the coffin, well knowing that the contrast between roistering Tsar and mourning Tsaritsa would not pass unnoticed. Peter further antagonized the church by his habit of misbehaving during divine service – shouting, walking about, even poking out his tongue at officiating priests. As monarch he promoted drastic changes in church organization which did not have time to take full effect – prohibiting certain icons, insisting that priests shave off their beards, favouring Protestant and other outlandish practices, and decreeing the confiscation of church property.

All this was nothing to his folly in provoking the guards. At a time when any prudent ruler would have made it his first task to conciliate these powerful garrison units of the capital with their tradition of making and breaking Emperors, Peter went out of his way to antagonize them. He took them out of the uniforms given to them by Peter the Great and dressed them in hated Prussian rig, while continuing to show preference for the Germans and other aliens of his household troops. Celebrating his accession by hurriedly making peace with Frederick the Great, newly defeated by Russia, Peter invited the Prussian king to name his own terms as if he were the victor, not the vanquished, and thus idly threw away the achievements of his own armies at Zorndorf and Kunersdorf. No less misguidedly, Peter decided to attack Denmark – intending to conquer Schleswig and join it to his Duchy of Holstein. But what Russian soldier would willingly risk his life for such a cause as that? Against such tactless plans must be set one measure which,

189

however unjust or misguided, earned Peter great popularity with the most influential section of the community – that exempting the gentry from all obligation
to serve the state in peace-time. Thus Peter III reversed one of the most fundamental principles of Peter I: that of compulsory service for all. The event was a
landmark in the developing ascendancy of the gentry which continued throughout
the age of Empresses.

To Catherine the six months of Peter's reign were a nightmare. He repeatedly
threatened to put her in a convent, while continuing to flaunt his liaison with
Elizabeth Vorontsov – a squat, sallow, squinting, pockmarked, rowdy girl, and
Catherine's very opposite. For years he had been threatening to marry this soul-
mate once his wife was out of the way, and as reigning monarch he could now
easily dispose of her. Nor could Catherine easily protect herself, being in an
advanced state of pregnancy by her latest lover, Gregory Orlov. Though the
flowing fashions of the day might help to conceal her condition in early 1762, she
hardly felt poised to overturn an empire. But in the event her latest liaison was
to bring Peter's downfall. Gregory Orlov was a fiery lieutenant, the hero of the
guards and renowned for his bravery in battle; he was also celebrated for having
seduced the mistress of his general, who conveniently died before he could punish
this breach of good order. The young officer was apt to be lucky in this sort of
affair, and he also had four brothers. All guards officers, all formed in the same
heroic mould, they secretly set themselves to win their comrades-in-arms for
Catherine's cause.

Could Catherine bear her child without the Tsar's knowledge? To this end she
employed a stratagem based on Peter's love of watching the fires which so often
broke out in his capital. A servant of Catherine's agreed to set light to his own
conveniently sited wooden house on receiving a signal from the palace. Labour
began, the signal was given, the diversion duly created and the baby safely
smuggled away.[12] This took place on 11 April. A month later the drunken
Emperor publicly humiliated Catherine at an official banquet, calling her a fool in
front of four hundred distinguished guests who included foreign ambassadors. She
shed some tears and tried to pass the episode off, but now privately resolved to
dispose of Peter, or rather to lend her discreet support to the various conspiracies
which his folly had provoked and which had come into being independently of
her. It was the idea of deposing Peter III rather than of raising Catherine II to the
throne which inspired many of the plotters.

While preparations for a *coup d'état* secretly continued in St Petersburg, the Tsar
and Tsaritsa left the capital separately. Peter installed himself with his mistress and
suite some twenty miles to the west in the palace of Oranienbaum, and Catherine
stayed in the mansion of Monplaisir at Peterhof about five miles nearer in. Her

supporters were still not completely ready to strike, but learning that one of their number had been arrested on 27 June they decided to act at once, fearing that he might betray details of their plot under torture. In the small hours of 28 June, Alexis – most resourceful of the brothers Orlov – quietly left St Petersburg by carriage with one companion. He reached Monplaisir at six o'clock in the morning, woke Catherine and told her that she must leave straight away for St Petersburg to be proclaimed Empress. She put on a black dress and jumped into the carriage. A few miles from St Petersburg, Gregory Orlov met them with another carriage and fresh horses, adding a gallant lover's protection as the little party sped further towards the capital on its dangerous mission.

It was as they entered the village of Kalinkina, headquarters of the Izmaylovsky Guards, that they reached the point of no return. Would the soldiers welcome Catherine as Empress? Or arrest her as traitor to the Tsar whom they had all sworn to obey six months earlier? Summoned by drum roll, the men at once made their sympathies clear by shouting and cheering. They pressed round Catherine, kissing her hand, calling her little mother. The commanding officer came out and knelt before her in homage, and the regimental chaplain also appeared to add the blessing of the church as all quickly swore loyalty to a new autocrat. From Kalinkina, Catherine pressed on to the capital, flanked by the triumphant Izmaylovs. Soon the other two guards regiments, the Semyonovsky and the Preobrazhensky, also joined her – and with that the issue was decided so far as the capital was concerned.

At about nine o'clock, barely three hours after beginning her dash from Peterhof, Catherine heard herself acclaimed Empress in a short church service at the Kazan Cathedral. Then she went to the Winter Palace in an open carriage. She appeared on a balcony, cheered by an excited mob, and showed the people her seven-year-old son Paul. The infant grand duke's presence lent a veneer of dynastic respectability to the affair, though his own claims to be autocrat were far better than his mother's. But the atmosphere was not conducive to such pedantic reflections. The shouts and laughter of the delighted crowds, the drum rolls and blaring trumpets of the military, and the church bells ringing out their peals of triumph – all helped to make it more like a public holiday than a revolution.

Unaware of these events, the Emperor Peter had gone to keep a rendezvous with his wife at Peterhof. He arrived in the early afternoon complete with his usual hangover and an imposing suite which included his mistress, two field-marshals and the Prussian ambassador. But where was Catherine? Her absence seemed to have the most sinister implications, as was fully confirmed when news of the successful *coup d'état* filtered through from St Petersburg, leaving the Emperor completely at a loss. After some deliberation he decided to sail about four miles across the Gulf of Finland to the island base of Cronstadt, headquarters of the

Russian navy. It also had an army garrison, and if Peter could rally these forces to his side he might win back his throne. He therefore set off late at night with his dwindling suite of followers. But Cronstadt harbour turned out to be blocked by a boom. Approaching by dinghy, Peter ordered the duty midshipman to remove the obstacle in the name of the Emperor, but was told that Russia now had no Emperor, only the Empress Catherine. The beaten monarch hastily returned to his galley, skulking down with his women as his pathetic expedition made an undignified retreat.

Not knowing how Peter was occupied, but intending to crush him without delay, Catherine set out for Peterhof at ten o'clock on the night of 28 June at the head of her guards. It was a picturesque scene and much enlivened one of St Petersburg's 'white nights'. Catherine wore the borrowed jacket of a Semyonovsky officer; she carried a sabre and rode astride a white horse, while her eighteen-year-old friend Princess Catherine Dashkov cavorted by her side in similar array. Though a sister of Peter's mistress Elizabeth Vorontsov, the Princess had all along been an enthusiastic supporter of Catherine; she played a considerable part in the *coup*, but perhaps more as a mascot than as a principal. In any case the expedition did not last long. Two letters reached Catherine in quick succession from Peter. In the first he offered to share the throne with her as equal partner; in the second he merely requested permission to leave for Holstein with his mistress. Ignoring both, Catherine had a formula of unconditional abdication conveyed to him; he was to copy it and sign. When he had done so, she had him taken under arrest to his near-by estate at Ropsha with Alexis Orlov as his gaoler, there to await transfer to Schlüsselburg Fortress.

Catherine returned to St Petersburg in triumph, to be greeted once again by excited crowds, military bands and the pealing of church bells. Now undisputed autocrat, she had carried out a 'ladies' revolution' in which no one had been killed. Vodka, not blood, flowed freely in these joyful days, and the exultant mob raided the liquor stores to such effect that the Empress later agreed to compensate retailers to the tune of over twenty thousand roubles.

The ladies' revolution did not remain untainted by violence. On 6 July the new Empress suddenly received an incoherent note from Alexis Orlov, Peter's custodian at Ropsha. The only clear fact to emerge from this drunken scrawl was that the deposed Tsar 'was no more'; Orlov or his minions had presumably murdered him, and in any case he was dead. Convenient as Catherine found the deed, there is no evidence that she ordered it.

The struggle between two Germans for the throne of Russia was over.

25 Catherine II, 'the Great' 1762–96

For seizing power from her husband Peter III, Catherine had the overwhelming motive of self-preservation, but she could have offered no such justification for thrusting her infant son Paul to one side instead of having him proclaimed Emperor with herself as regent during his minority. However, the fact is that this double usurper was a woman of towering ambition in her intelligent and highly controlled fashion. She wanted all power for herself. Her ambition coincided to some extent with Russia's advantage, at least where international standing and territorial expansion were concerned. But where no such identity of interests existed, stagnation or worse often resulted – especially in the position of the peasants who were the submerged majority of her subjects. They also presented Russia's most formidable social problem, and one which her policies only aggravated. The thirty-four years of her rule thus left the empire more of a slave state than it had been when she took command. So had the rule of Peter the Great. But while Catherine only paid lip service to her subjects' welfare, Peter seems to have felt a more genuine concern than she for the interests of the community as he understood them – even if his sympathy often expressed itself in cruelty foreign to Catherine's nature. Peter's active concern for Russia had helped to earn him the title of Great, which was in any case formally conferred upon him, while Catherine's claim to the same honour is less securely based. Though her foreign contemporaries exercised their Gallic wit by calling her 'Catherine le [sic] Grand', the use of the title Catherine the Great has now declined, at least among professional historians.[13]

By temperament Catherine was well adapted to the role of Empress and could take rapid decisions when necessary, but was also able to bide her time and compromise. As a civilized woman she did not like torture and executions, but did not shrink from sanctioning such measures when she thought her throne in danger. And though she always preferred to use as little violence as she considered necessary, it was often a considerable amount. She was suitably majestic on ceremonial occasions, but relaxed and gay in private. Rising and retiring early, she followed a methodical daily routine, and showed much stamina whether prosecuting affairs of state, drafting proclamations and decrees or gracing public occasions, writing plays and letters, planning wars or diplomatic *coups*, patronizing the arts or pursuing an active love life. Although much of her background recalls *The Prisoner of Zenda*, she did not much resemble a character from historical romance, being more urbane and level-headed than her entourage. And though she often gave way to tears – like Peter the Great – she was a resilient and adult person. Thus the throne of the Romanovs, a great provoker of childish caprice and megalo-maniac excesses, came to be filled for a third of a century with style and zest by a strong-minded and high-spirited Empress, but one who was also extremely self-centred.

One of Catherine's first concerns on the throne was to avoid falling victim to a *coup d'état* such as she herself had so recently staged. Lest conspiracy become a habit, she hastened to reward those who had swept her to power, loading them with promotions, decorations, roubles, estates and serfs on a tariff related to the impor-tance of each individual. The total largess dispensed in this way to forty individual 'elect of the people', as she termed them, came to over five hundred thousand roubles and eighteen thousand souls. As Bilbasov remarks with understandable sarcasm, the people's elect were rewarded for their services by receiving large numbers of slaves from among the very people which had supposedly elected them in the first place.[14]

As part of this distribution of favours, all five Orlov brothers were created counts at the time of Catherine's coronation in Moscow. The magnificent cere-mony was celebrated on 22 September 1762 before a score of bishops and twice as many archimandrites to the delight of Muscovites flattered and dazzled by sumptuous decorations, fireworks, carnival atmosphere and open-handed bounty in the form of six hundred thousand silver coins, conveyed to the old capital in oak barrels, to be tossed to the crowds. Catherine devoted great care to stage-managing the occasion, remembering that Peter III had made the mistake of not having himself crowned at all. She conciliated the clergy by her bearing at her coronation and by the respect which she showed to the church on pilgrimages undertaken soon afterwards to the Monastery of the Trinity and to Rostov. She also cancelled Peter III's decree confiscating church property. But within a few years her attitude towards the church hardened. She had the Metropolitan of Rostov, a turbulent champion of ecclesiastical rights, arrested and sent to a remote monastery; and she soon felt strong enough to reintroduce the secularization of church property. The clergy had first been encouraged, then put firmly in its place.

Among the various social classes it was the gentry whose support Catherine consistently sought as a matter of policy throughout her reign. Not only did gentlemen provide the medium in which palace revolutions fermented; they also owned, officered and policed a high proportion of the millions of peasants who

194

Catherine II, the Great. A German princess, she usurped the Russian throne from her husband, Peter III, in 1762 and ruled until her death in 1796.

supplied the country's wealth by their exploited labour, and provided the recruits for the lower ranks of Catherine's armies. Her decision to support the gentry was thus well calculated to tighten her control over Russia, but at the expense of a peasantry further degraded, humiliated and enslaved.

Soon after usurping the throne the Empress had thus begun to ensure that neither common people nor clergy nor her fellow-conspirators of 1762 were likely to endanger her position. She was also lucky enough to be disembarrassed of the single individual who most menaced her throne after the death of Peter III – the former Emperor Ivan VI who had reigned as an infant in 1740–1 before being dethroned and imprisoned. At the time of Catherine's accession he was still suffering solitary confinement in Schlüsselburg Fortress. But he was still alive in folk memory as 'Ivanushka', and there was every reason for successive monarchs to concern themselves with him, for he might be made the means of deposing them if he should ever escape from Schlüsselburg. Officially termed the 'nameless prisoner', he was officially ignorant of his place of confinement and identity – but was known to speak of himself as a prince. Catherine found an opportunity to interview him in the first year of her reign, though what passed between the two remains largely a mystery. Did the young man guess that his well-dressed visitor with her strong German accent was responsible for his plight? It is possible, for there is evidence that he was not just the stuttering idiot which successive rulers liked to think him.

The nameless prisoner was in the personal custody of two officers. Hating their assignment and often drunk, they had standing orders to kill him at once if any attempt should be made to free him. Catherine herself confirmed this instruction, originated by Peter III, adding another of her own – that no doctor was to treat the captive if he should fall ill. In 1764 the standing orders proved their worth when a Lieutenant Mirovich (a member of the Schlüsselburg garrison who nursed a strong personal grievance) chanced to learn who the nameless prisoner was and plotted to free him, take him down the River Neva to the artillery head-quarters in St Petersburg and there proclaim him Emperor. This was never more than a lost cause, but Mirovich turned out the Schlüsselburg guard and called on the bewildered soldiers to free their imprisoned sovereign. He also gained control of a cannon. But in the meantime Ivan's two gaolers had done their duty by stabbing him in his cell. With his sovereign dead, Mirovich allowed himself to be arrested and suffered public beheading after trial. It was the first execution in St Petersburg for twenty-two years,[15] a salutary reminder to any who might scheme to serve Catherine II as she had served Peter III. Moreover, a second rival sovereign had now been despatched, and again without the Empress having to play Lady Macbeth.

It remained to suppress sundry pretenders. Among these Yemelyan Pugachov had more success than some half dozen others who tried to pass themselves off as Peter III during the reign. It was in 1773 and among the Cossacks of the River Yaik (since renamed Ural) that he first raised the standard of a rebellion which swiftly spread to take in peasants, factory serfs and non-Russian peoples east of the Volga, including Tatars, Bashkirs, Calmucks and Kirghizes. Pugachov referred to Catherine as his wife and set up a mock court among minions to whom he gave the names of her leading statesmen; but this did not conceal the fact that his was a murderous class struggle of the submerged masses against the gentry. The revolt flared by fits and starts, and there were times when Pugachov had a force of twenty to thirty thousand irregulars under his command. His feats included the capture of Kazan, and the winter of 1773–4 saw Moscow itself in panic; with most of the regular army away fighting the Turks, nothing seemed to prevent Pugachov from bursting into the old capital itself.

Catherine's first reaction to the outbreak was characteristic – what would Europe think? Having displayed Russia to her foreign admirers as a benevolent despotism where happy rustics basked in idyllic pastoral conditions, she found it embarrassing to contemplate these same peasants hanging, burning and torturing their benefactors. But it would have required more than an ignorant Cossack to ruffle the Empress. At the height of the rebellion she continued a series of philosophical discussions with Diderot (now her guest in St Petersburg), showing a *sang-froid* justified when regular troops crushed Pugachov's rising in late 1774. Betrayed by his henchmen and brought to Moscow in an iron cage, the partisan chief suffered public quartering and decapitation. Catherine lightened the sentence in one particular, secretly ordering that the severing of the head should precede the quartering – not follow it, as was the proper sequence. She had the great guerrillero's limbs exhibited on wheels in four suburbs of the city, and his chief associates beheaded, hanged or knouted.

Pugachov represented a real threat to Catherine, but the same could not be said of another pretender of the period – the self-styled Princess Tarakanov. This beautiful but mentally unstable girl of unknown origin may not have been Russian at all, and had wandered Europe under other titled aliases before going to Italy and claiming herself a daughter of the Empress Elizabeth and the rightful occupant of Catherine's throne. It chanced that Alexis Orlov was in the Mediterranean at the time as admiral commanding the Russian fleet against the Turks. On Catherine's explicit instructions to kidnap the 'princess' by force or guile, he pretended to support her cause and to be in love with her, thus luring her on to a Russian vessel at Leghorn. Gunfire and shouts of 'Long live the Empress' greeted her as she came aboard . . . to be seized, locked in a cabin and delivered to the Peter and Paul Fortress in St Petersburg. Catherine had her searchingly interrogated, and she died shortly afterwards – reputedly of tuberculosis. The episode shows how sensitive the Empress remained to the most insubstantial dangers even after a decade of consolidating her power.

Catherine combined the brutal use of power in defence of her throne with great skill in passing as an enlightened ruler imbued with lofty ideals. As one authority puts it, she erected self-advertisement 'into a system of government',[16] a striking example being the *Instruction* which she drafted in 1765–7 as a directive to a legislative commission charged with framing a new code of laws. The *Instruction* did not purport to be an original contribution, based as it largely was on Montesquieu's *L'Esprit des lois* and other foreign sources, including the writings of the progressive penologist Beccaria. Nor was Catherine foreshadowing drastic changes, since she proclaimed autocracy as the principle of Russian government and did not propose to emancipate the serfs – though her proposal to put their relations with their owners on a firm legal basis was far-reaching in a country where the masters' whim was paramount. Overloaded with rhetoric on such topics as justice and equality, besides being based too exclusively on western European experience, the *Instruction* was far from being a practical guide to reform. Nor was the motley legislative commission competent to frame laws on the basis of this or any other document. Consisting of over five hundred delegates of different classes (excluding serfs, but including many non-Russian subjects of the empire), it did not succeed in drafting any of the proposed code before being, in effect, dissolved in 1768. As this episode shows, Catherine was an eager initiator of bold designs, but her interest easily evaporated.

While committing her concern for serfs to paper, the authoress of the *Instruction* was engaged in making conditions harsher for the living serfs of her empire. 1765, the very year in which she started work on the *Instruction*, saw her empowering masters to send their slaves to permanent hard labour in Siberia. Two years later she ordained knouting and hard labour for serfs who should present complaints against their masters. She continued to give away relatively free state peasants as serfs, and by the end of her reign the number of citizens thus enslaved by the authoress of the *Instruction* came to about a million souls.[17] Peter III's manifesto freeing the gentry from service obligations had already removed any moral justification which serfdom might have had under Peter the Great, who at least made both gentry and peasants serve the state. Catherine not only maintained the privileges granted by Peter III, but further reinforced the gentry's rights in a charter of 1785, so that her reign became famous as the golden age of the Russian gentleman.

Catherine's *Instruction* came more into its own outside Russia than on native soil, being published in over a score of editions and in the main European languages. The French government declared it a prohibited import – a propaganda triumph for Catherine, since it clinched her reputation as an enlightened autocrat with the outside world, which did not know that the document had all along been virtually banned in Russia itself. Voltaire called it the 'most beautiful monument of the century',[18] though he might more accurately have called it the century's most successful confidence trick. As the episode shows, an autocrat or dictator can often count on the enthusiastic support of foreign savants – provided that he exercises power with sufficient brutality, at a safe distance, and with vociferous claims to be inspired by noble motives. Not that Catherine was a hypocrite in the sense of deliberately seeking to mislead, for she clearly felt herself engaged on a serious project of great importance during the many laborious hours devoted to copying out her *Instruction*.

As Empress, Catherine remained remarkable for the continued variety and vigour of her love life. Her most important paramours were Gregory Orlov, Gregory Potemkin and Platon Zubov, whose sway coincided with the spring, summer and autumn of their imperial mistress's reign respectively.

The liaison with Orlov proved most durable, beginning some years before the *coup d'état* which he helped to mount and lasting until 1772. He wished to marry the Empress, but she had no intention of sharing her throne, and the course of this association began to run untrue. Accustomed to dominating women, the virile young officer found his iron will confronted by another – more flexible but of tempered steel. Catherine's energies contrasted with the handsome Gregory's sloth, but she could spare him little time from affairs of state and he took to having other mistresses on the side. Tiring of him in the end, she sent him on a mission to the Turks and took a certain Alexander Vasilchikov as substitute. She also had new locks put on her doors and posted extra sentries – for an Orlov was capable of anything, as she had good reason to know.

The new lover was the first in a series of nonentities who came to enjoy the Empress's favours. But barely had this sequence of faceless men begun before it was disrupted by one who was far more than a male concubine: the prodigious Potemkin. As the only lover endowed with greater energy than the Empress herself, he also became unique because of the special relationship which he maintained after his position as reigning paramour lapsed in 1776. He personally selected many of the young men who successively occupied his vacated position for a year or two at a time until Platon Zubov – a recruit not of his choosing – took over as final favourite of the reign. While Catherine grew older, her lovers remained perennially young, most of them being in their early twenties. Even as a girl she had always had lovers younger than herself, but the gap naturally grew ever wider as her life proceeded; Zubov was nearly forty years her junior.

A patriotic Russian by adoption, Catherine chose Russian lovers except for the Pole Poniatowski (before her accession) and the Croat, or Serb, Zorich. But as a good German by origin she imposed a marked degree of order on her love life, and the appointment of a new favourite came to follow a precise drill. The Empress's personal doctor would first inspect a potential recruit, since she feared venereal disease. Then a special officer, Countess Bruce – who came to be known as l'éprouveuse – personally tested the young man's prowess as a lover. She seems to have had a vocation for the task, but did not fully grasp the nature of her brief, since it was only before a candidate's appointment that she was expected to evaluate his virility – not afterwards, as she discovered to her cost when surprised by the Empress with a reigning favourite, Ivan Rimsky-Korsakov. This led to the commissioning of a new éprouveuse who (it was hoped) might show a more decent respect for the conventions. The Empress would appoint a new favourite personal adjutant-general and install him in chambers with a special staircase communicating with her own quarters. She would also bestow a large dowry in money, land and serfs. Her constant escort, he might not leave the palace without permission; nor might he associate with other women – a clause which one of the young men, Alexander Mamonov, infringed when he fell in love with a girl of his own age and begged Catherine to release him from his duties so that he could marry. She behaved graciously, if in questionable taste, insisting on giving the bride away herself and no doubt reflecting that the empire still had an adequate stock of handsome young guardsmen.

Potemkin was in a class of his own among Catherine's lovers – huge of stature, ill-proportioned and ugly, but with great vitality. Called Cyclops, because he was blind in one eye (from assault by Alexis Orlov, according to rumour), he consumed estates, serfs, jewels, honours, titles, roubles and women on a grandiose scale. This great magnifico often sported robes encrusted with precious stones, but might also be seen in an old dressing-gown – a man of extremes whose broad Russian nature contrasted with the disciplined style of his crowned German mistress. In another century Potemkin might have found his true level directing a film 'epic'. At Bender in 1791 when commander-in-chief against the Turks he imported orchestras, girls and jewellers in quantity, besides an entire *corps de ballet* and over five hundred personal servants. The grand tycoon set up court beneath the battlefield, roistering and wenching in underground halls specially excavated by his soldiers. From these orgies he would periodically emerge to defy Turkish bullets, a style of trench warfare all his own. His bullying manner as commander in – or rather under – the field found full play in his treatment of a subordinate general, a Prince Dolgoruky whose wife he had seduced. Daring to protest, the high-born cuckold found himself gripped by the sashes of his decorations and hoisted in the air in front of his brother officers by the giant fornicator. 'Wretch!

[Potemkin shouted] I gave you and the others these decorations! You don't deserve them either! You're all a load of muck, and I have every right to do what I like with you and yours!'[19] Were these the words of a madman or of a genius? Was Potemkin a coward? Or immensely brave? No one could be sure, but at all events he retained a freedom of manœuvre and moral ascendancy over Catherine such as no other favourite enjoyed.

In 1787 Catherine made a six-month journey to New Russia, including the Crimea – vast, recently annexed territories ruled by Potemkin as newly created Prince of Tauris. In the dark of January with the temperature well below zero the Empress set out from her palace at Tsarskoye Selo for the south and the spring. She shared with her current lover a huge sledge containing several compartments, drawn by thirty horses and escorted by nearly two hundred other sledges and vehicles. They consumed peaches and champagne in the snows, and at night great bonfires lighted their way. Within a few weeks the party was sailing down the Dnieper in a fleet of some four score vessels, Catherine travelling Cleopatra-like in one of three huge barques gorgeous in red and gold. Now the renowned Potemkin villages swam into her ken. The great showman had forcibly uprooted the population of near-by areas to serve as a living backcloth and make it seem that his Empress was gliding through a prosperous, newly-colonized paradise – in fact a wilderness of empty steppe. Buildings had sprung up on the river banks, while other picturesque habitations further off were mere two-dimensional stage scenery. Once the Empress had passed by, the props were packed up and the dazed villagers sent home. This violent transplanting desolated entire provinces, taking a heavy toll in human life.[20]

Unconcerned with the seamy side of the operation, invited notables from western Europe joined the imperial progress – to be suitably regaled on a grand tour which brought together the Emperor Joseph II of Austria and Catherine's former lover Stanislas Poniatowski (now King of Poland) as well as ambassadors, generals and smaller fry. They visited the site of Yekaterinoslav, future capital of the area, the old Tatar city of Bakhchisaray and the new harbour of Sevastopol – not to mention attendance at banquets, firework displays and numerous other celebrations. On the return journey the party witnessed a re-enactment of the Battle of Poltava staged by fifty thousand soldiers on the original site.

Ostentation on this scale was beyond the scope of lesser beings such as Catherine's last lover, Platon Zubov – the conceited, ambitious young fop whose ascendancy belongs to the decadent period of the reign. Such was his sway over the ageing Empress that the highest in the land would wait for hours in his ante-chamber. He received suppliants *en masse* – often standing with his back to the petrified audience while flunkeys groomed his *coiffure* before a large mirror. His pet monkey, a nimble creature about the size of a cat, liked the taste of powder and wigs; it would leap from head to head of the assembled notables, busily nibbling while the recipient of such signal honour scarce dared to breathe. On a wider stage, Zubov's interest in foreign affairs created no less alarm, saddling Russia with an ill-judged military adventure against Persia; but by now Catherine had lost the knack of calling her favourites to heel.

Although Potemkin may have been the only lover whom Catherine fully respected (and there is evidence suggesting that they were secretly married), she was fond of all her young men. She was affectionate as well as sensual by nature, and would speak of them effusively as her children or pupils. There was something of the indulgent headmistress about her, and the gossips of Europe went too far when they called her the Messalina of the North.

As a typical sovereign of her period, Catherine pursued territorial expansion by conquest and diplomatic trickery without considering the wishes of the peoples concerned. It was in the south that Russia gained most benefit when victories over the Turks carried her frontier to the Black Sea, bringing in the areas which included the Crimea and received the name of New Russia. Catherine thus added a new coast-line to the outlet on the Baltic conquered by Peter the Great. She also had further designs on Turkey in the south-west, including the seizure of Constantinople where she intended her second grandson to rule, having earmarked him for the role and named him Constantine in anticipation. But this ambition remained a mere dream. Larger but less beneficial increases in the empire's territory came at the expense of Poland. Having helped to place her ex-lover Stanislas Poniatowski on the Polish throne in 1764, and thus already made the country something of a Russian puppet, Catherine went on to seize large tracts of Polish land by the partitions of 1772, 1793 and 1795. In so far as the areas concerned were peopled predominantly by Orthodox believers, they could arguably be ruled better from St Petersburg than from Warsaw. But by also taking more specifically Polish lands, Catherine stored up difficulties for Russia – including Kościuszko's rebellion during her own reign, and the recurrent Polish troubles which plagued her successors.

To love of power and men, Catherine added a third passion – for the arts. As patroness on a grand scale, she imported noted architects to Russia, among whom were the Italian Giacomo Quarenghi and the Scot Charles Cameron. She created the most important museum of her day when she founded the Hermitage in St Petersburg, for which her agents in many parts of Europe bought canvasses by Van Dyck, Rembrandt, Raphael, Titian and other masters. The Empress also commissioned works of art, of which Falconet's equestrian statue of Peter the Great is most celebrated; she chose the plinth herself – a colossal natural rock

ACQUISITIONS OF CATHERINE II (r. 1762-1796) AND ALEXANDER I (r. 1801-1825)

(*left*) Catherine II, the Great, leaves for Peterhof on 28 June 1762 at the head of her guards to arrest her husband, Peter III. (*centre*) Catherine on her way to Kherson during her six-month tour of the Crimea and southern Russia in 1787; (*right*) a scene from one of the lavish entertainments staged by Catherine's lover and most important favourite, Gregory Potemkin, whom she made Prince of Tauris.

Peterhof, the Tsars' residence on the Gulf of Finland about 20 miles west of St Petersburg, figured in the *coup* which brought Catherine II to the throne in 1762. A contemporary engraving.

(*opposite top*) The coronation of Catherine II, which was celebrated with great pomp in Moscow and took place on 22 September 1762. Painting by S. Torelli.

A mosaic portrait of Catherine II, dating from 1763 – the year after her usurpation of the throne.

The meeting between Catherine the Great and the Emperor Joseph II of Austria, which took place on 18 May 1787 when Joseph was Catherine's guest during her tour of southern Russia. Water-colour by Löschenkohl.

(*opposite*) Catherine II takes communion: part of the ceremonial of her coronation.

(*opposite*) An allegorical portrayal of Catherine the Great travelling through her Empire.

Russian victory over the Turks in 1770.
Catherine II's wars with Turkey resulted in
the acquisition by Russia of large territories on
the Black Sea Coast, including the Crimea.
A contemporary engraving.

Workmen moving the granite block, weighing
1600 tons, which was selected by Catherine II
at Lahta on the Gulf of Finland to become the
base of Falconet's equestrian statue
of Peter the Great in St Petersburg.
From a Russian engraving of 1770.

(*opposite*) The Bronze Horseman, a monument
to Peter I, the Great, was set up in St Petersburg
in 1782 by Catherine II. The equestrian statue
by Falconet took twelve years to complete.

Scene from the play *Oleg* by Catherine the
Great. The Empress wrote over a dozen plays.

Catherine the Great playing with her grandsons,
Alexander (the future Alexander I)
and Constantine.

(*opposite*) A portrait by Lampi of Catherine the Great by her throne.

Russian life at the end of the eighteenth century:
(*top*) Moscow Fair; (*bottom*) ice hills (toboggan
runs).

weighing sixteen hundred tons which she noticed at Lahta on the Gulf of Finland and had transported with great difficulty to St Petersburg.

Catherine promoted linguistic study and learning generally, by encouraging the foundation of the Russian Academy and fostering the existing Academy of Sciences, while she herself energetically practised the art of writing. Her literary output is more impressive for bulk than originality, and includes the *Instruction* mentioned above, over a dozen plays in Russian and French, many articles and essays, fairy tales for children, memoirs and correspondence, besides which she edited a satirical journal. Such were the products of a restlessness which, she said, overcame her whenever she set eyes on a freshly-cut quill pen.[21] Towards the end of her reign she also turned her energies to the hounding of rival scribes. It was one thing for the sovereign herself to satirize the customs of her country; but for a subject, Nicholas Novikov, to do the same was a different matter, and she imprisoned him without trial in Schlüsselburg Fortress, from which he obtained release only after her death. A yet severer fate threatened Alexander Radischchev, who assaulted the institutions of autocracy and serfdom in his account of *A Journey from St Petersburg to Moscow*. Sentenced to death but reprieved, he suffered transportation to Siberia on the orders of Voltaire's illustrious pen-friend, who seems to have believed that liberal views were like crowns – an adornment for the monarch's own head not to be flaunted by mere commoners. A revulsion (shared by several successors on the Russian throne) against the French Revolution stiffened such reactionary postures of the Empress in the degenerate last years of a reign glorious in its outward manifestations, but far less so in other ways.

The Age of Empresses came to a sadly humdrum end when, on 6 November 1796, the Semiramis of the North suffered a fatal stroke while seated on her commode.

26 Paul 1796–1801

Inheriting the throne at the age of forty-two from his mother Catherine II, the Emperor Paul made an outstanding contribution to the history of the Tsars by enacting a new law of succession. He promulgated it on the day of his coronation, 5 April 1797, and it superseded Peter the Great's discredited enactment of 1722, that empowering each sovereign to nominate his own heir. The new measure grounded the succession on the principle of male primogeniture – assigning the crown to a deceased monarch's sons in the first instance, and thereafter to his brothers, the eldest taking precedence. Remaining in force until the end of the dynasty, this law gave Russia a sequence of five more Tsar-Emperors; and with the notable exception of the crisis of December 1825 (to be described below) dynastic upheavals hinging on the succession issue now passed from the Russian scene. But although the exclusion of female rulers helped to discourage scandals such as had attended the accession of so many eighteenth-century monarchs, it by no means rendered nineteenth-century Russia safe for autocracy, for three of the last six Tsars were to meet a violent death.

The new law owed much to Tsar Paul's resentment of his deceased mother, last of Russia's sovereign Empresses. Since the boy's very birth on 20 September 1754 amid inauspicious auguries already chronicled, mother and son had never been on good terms, for little affection could develop between Catherine (then grand duchess) and a child whom the Empress Elizabeth immediately removed from her. The seven-year-old Tsarevich was almost a stranger to his mother when she usurped the throne, besides posing a serious threat to her position since his title to rule was better than her own. It was therefore natural that Paul should grow up to fear and mistrust Catherine. Believing that she had cheated him of his birth-right, he honoured the memory of the martyred Peter III, who was possibly his father only in name. This was a situation ripe with improprieties, which

Catherine herself did little to remove – returning the Tsarevich's fear and suspicions with contempt, isolating him from affairs of state and allowing her
favourites to sneer at him openly.

As Tsarevich, Paul resided chiefly on his estate at Gatchina some thirty miles
south of St Petersburg. He was contentedly married to a former German princess,
and became absorbed in the task of establishing a small militarized state within his
domain. Admiring the Prussian military style (as had Peter III before him), he
formed an army of several thousand soldiers whom he dressed in Prussian uniforms
and personally drilled. Eventually all his four sons (the two future Tsars Alexander
I and Nicholas I, and the Grand Dukes Constantine and Michael) came to share
Paul's obsession with uniforms, parades, badges of rank, gaiter buttons and kindred
trivialities. Passing into Alexander I and through Nicholas I, this militarist streak
distinguished later Romanovs too.

While Paul occupied himself with the affairs of his private army, the Empress
Catherine secretly decided to bar him from the succession in favour of his eldest
son Alexander, whom she informed of this intention, receiving his guarded consent; but before she had taken any definite steps in the matter her sudden death
intervened. Not pausing to grieve over his mother, Paul immediately collected
her papers, and probably burnt any documents willing the succession to Alexander.[1]

With the ferocity born of three decades' frustration, Paul now grasped supreme
power. He emerged as impulsive, erratic and irritable, and became increasingly so
throughout his reign, until many of his subjects were whispering that he was mad.
Whether or not he was indeed so, as certain foreign diplomats reported,[2] he
accomplished the feat of becoming a laughing-stock and bogyman at the same
time – a source in both capacities of countless anecdotes.

The practice of awarding savage punishments on the spot lent terror to the
Tsar's many military inspections. His short figure, turned up nose and harsh
falsetto voice might have seemed comic on the stage, but were far from entertaining on the drill-ground – his favourite arena for displays of caprice. An officer
would come on parade knowing that the Emperor might make some trivial or
fancied misdemeanour the pretext for sending him straight to Siberia in one of the
sealed carriages kept in readiness expressly for this purpose. Though it is unlikely
that Paul, when inspecting his troops, ever gave one famous order attributed to
him ('Files, by the right, to Siberia . . . quick march'),[3] he did compel distinguished
generals to attend lectures on elementary tactics given by juvenile upstarts. Meanwhile senior officers who had marched with Catherine's field-marshals saw themselves ousted by mediocrities who had won their spurs with the preposterous toy
army of Gatchina. As for members of the military rank and file, they received
poor food, frequent beatings and outlandish uniforms so tight that the wearers

could not rise to their feet unaided if they fell over – not to mention ordeal by regimental barbers who curled and plaited their hair, saturating it with a paste of lard, flour, brick-dust and kvass, and leaving it to congeal in an evil-smelling crust.

Nor were civilians immune from the Tsar's vicious caprice, as the ill luck of Pastor Seider showed. Having a small lending library near Riga, he chanced to place an advertisement in a local paper asking for the return of a book which he had issued on loan, an inoffensive work with the misleadingly suggestive title *Power of Love*. Apprised of this, Paul conceived the whim of having the pastor arrested, and though the man of God did evade the appalling ordeal of the knout – by presenting his watch to the official flogger, according to one version of the story – he was conveyed in chains to the mines at Nerchinsk in Siberia.[4]

The Tsar directed his main animus against the gentry, the very class which seven successive sovereigns had so greatly favoured since the death of Peter the Great. Exempt from corporal punishment at the time of Paul's accession, Russian gentlemen now found themselves rendered liable to flogging, nostril-slitting and the cutting out of tongues as if they were mere peasants. Paul also plagued the gentry with his fads about dress, banning tail-coats, waistcoats and round hats as indications of sympathy with the French Revolution. When he drove out, the occupants of other carriages or sledges were required to halt and descend to make the prescribed obeisances in an alert and soldierly fashion. Since the Tsar had a regular hour for driving about St Petersburg between noon and one o'clock, prudent citizens avoided the streets altogether at that time.

The Emperor enjoyed greater popularity outside his capital. Fancying himself as a protector of the common man, he tried to help serfs by regulating the amount of compulsory labour due to their owners. But while such measures remained largely a dead letter, he was consigning relatively free state peasants to slavery – giving them away to his favourites by the hundred thousand on a scale unknown even under his mother's jurisdiction. As for foreign affairs, Paul showed a frivolity undisciplined by much sense of geographical, military or religious reality when he sent a Cossack army to conquer India and began dabbling in the concerns of the Maltese Order of the Knights of St John – freakish policies such as antagonized almost every nation in Europe and harmed Russian trade. Meanwhile foreigners might not enter Russia, Russians could not travel abroad, the borrowing and import of foreign books came under a ban, and native book production dwindled almost to nothing.

Paul was feared, but not universally hated, being affectionate, lively and fond of children. Ladies appreciated his delightful manners when he was graciously inclined, though he was small and ugly, in marked contrast to his nine children. These were all (excepting only his second son Constantine) handsome, tall and robust; and with such impressive progeny – four sons and potential heirs among them – a less neurotic ruler might have faced the future serenely. But it is typical of a Tsar whose nature fed on suspicion that he plotted against his closest relatives, conceiving the plan of immuring them in fortresses or convents except for his favourite daughter Catherine. She was to marry Prince Eugene of Württemberg, a thirteen-year-old visitor who had caught the Tsar's fancy, after which Eugene would become heir to the throne – doubtless to be imprisoned himself in the course of Paul's next attack of paranoia. Such were the designs of one who had begun his reign by promulgating a clear law of succession specifically intended to make manœuvrings of this kind impossible.

It is arguable that Paul was a statesman in potential despite his many aberrations. Schiemann says that the Tsar's decisions were determined by principles, not by personal interests: 'This is the crucial difference between his conduct and that of his mother, whom principles could certainly serve as the means to an end . . . but who never let herself be blinded or inhibited by them.'[5] An ideal sovereign might have combined the eccentric son's conscientious promptings with his self-centred mother's keener sense of political reality.

Since none could conceive what savage blow the autocrat might strike next, it can easily be understood, if not excused, that Paul's eldest son Alexander lent some support to the conspiracy which led to his father's murder on the night of 11–12 March 1801. Alexander's attitude was largely passive, the two main plotters being the disgraced statesman Nikita Panin and the military governor of St Petersburg, Count Peter Pahlen. But, as it happens, none of these three ringleaders took part in the actual murder, though Pahlen sent the assassins into action. Panin was absent in exile from the capital, while Alexander himself remained inactive not far from the scene of the crime.

Several dozen conspirators took part, among whom was Platon Zubov, the last of Catherine's favourites. They met for a late supper party on the fateful night, and some were drunk as they toasted their venture in champagne and set off for the Emperor's residence – the grim, fortress-like Michael Palace recently constructed on his orders. Gaining access to this building without hitch, they made straight for the Tsar's bedroom. A scuffle at the door awoke him and, according to one of many conflicting versions of the incident,[6] he had time to hide himself in the fireplace behind a screen before the officers broke in. The room seemed empty until someone pulled the screen away, and the Tsar's bare feet appeared at the bottom of the chimney in which he was standing. Then the assassins hauled him out petrified with fear and begging for mercy in his nightgown and cotton nightcap, and a confused altercation followed during which one conspirator struck the Emperor on the temple with a heavy golden snuff-box. Paul fell struggling to the ground. Trampled, beaten and finally strangled with a scarf, he was a great while giving up the ghost, and many of those engaged in the fracas could not clearly make out what was happening. Finally General Bennigsen, seemingly the only assassin to have kept his head, assured himself that the Tsar was indeed dead, and had him dressed in uniform and tidied up in so far as that was still possible. The official version was that Paul had suffered an apoplectic fit, but this enjoyed little credit at the time, for the conspirators went round openly boasting of their bloody deed.

St Petersburgers were beside themselves with joy, and strangers kissed each other on the streets as if it were Easter Day. The offending round hats and other articles of dress banned by the murdered Emperor reappeared, worn in public to the cheers of onlookers; and by nightfall festive citizens had drained every available bottle of champagne in the capital.

27 Alexander I

Alexander I came to the throne burdened with feelings of guilt, such as were to haunt him all his days, for the murder of his father. Though involved in the *coup d'état*, he had co-operated cautiously, seeking assurances that the Emperor's life would be spared. Yet what could such guarantees conceivably have been worth? Rulers of Paul's character are not simply deposed, but must be physically exterminated, as Alexander surely realized. Had he, however, denounced the conspirators to his capricious father, his only reward might have been to spend the rest of his days as Paul's prisoner in the Fortress of Schlüsselburg.

At the time of Paul's assassination his heir was sleeping or feigning sleep in his quarters in the same palace. Roused by one of the plotters, the first person to call him 'your Majesty', Alexander showed horror at the announcement of his father's death and seemed to lose all self-control. But once he and his advisers had rallied their forces they lost little time in undoing the mischief of the previous reign. On the same night a courier left to recall the Cossack army sent by Paul to conquer India. Alexander quickly sanctioned steps to conciliate the English and persuade them not to proceed with a naval bombardment of Cronstadt and St Petersburg apparently threatened by Nelson's fleet. Of no less urgent interest to St Petersburgers was the proclamation whereby Alexander undertook to govern in the tradition of the grandmother who had wished to designate him as her heir. He honoured this implied promise to abandon Paul's methods by rehabilitating over twelve thousand people banished or dismissed from their posts in the previous reign. Alexander also abolished Paul's secret police and censorship, lifted the ban on foreign books and travel, and most of the Pauline ordinances about dress and deportment. The young Tsar also intended to free the serfs and relax the principle of autocratic rule, or so for a time it seemed. But with Alexander things rarely were what they seemed, for behind the smile of this charming young man a most devious intelligence lurked.

He had begun to show his talent for duplicity in early youth, when the Empress Catherine planned his upbringing in detail. Her son Paul having been smothered with care by old women in stuffy apartments, she exposed her eldest grandson Alexander (born on 12 December 1777) and his younger brother Constantine to the rigours of fresh air, cold baths and an English nanny. Doting on the boys, especially Alexander, she personally taught them to read and write. In her eyes Alexander was always good-tempered and obedient, with a quick intelligence – the ideal child, she thought. Not all his tutors shared that view, however. The boy's chief skill was one which his adoring grandmother did not quite divine, though sharing it herself: a knack of pleasing exceedingly when he chose – but while keeping his own counsel. Alexander's naturally oblique approach gained further encouragement from the rift between his reigning grandmother and his parents. Catherine's headquarters at the Hermitage in St Petersburg was a centre of wit and dissolute morals high-mindedly condemned from Paul's virtuous, barrack-like establishment at Gatchina. But the significant point is that Alexander could feel at home in both camps, for the boy already had the art of being all things to all men.

As one of Alexander's tutors, Catherine appointed the Swiss Frederick LaHarpe, whose republican views made him a strange choice as mentor to a future autocrat. It was his habit to talk by the hour of human rights and dignity, freedom, enlightenment and the common weal, while Alexander listened entranced to this impressive virtuoso performance. But LaHarpe did not make him work; he did not set the boy practical problems or even supply him with information about the vast country which he was one day to rule.

When Alexander was not yet sixteen, Catherine arranged for him to marry Princess Louise of Baden, who took the name Elizabeth. Though admired for her beauty and charm, she did not long succeed in keeping Alexander faithful to his marriage vows – or much longer (according to rumour) in respecting her own. The young Tsar was renowned as an irresistible ladies' man, and it would be a difficult task indeed to document all his love affairs. It is therefore understandable that one biographer, Maurice Paléologue, should have adopted the convention of implying or stating in his *Enigmatic Czar* that Alexander made love to almost every attractive or otherwise celebrated woman who crossed his path, including the ex-Empress Joséphine of France, her daughter Queen Hortense and his religious consultant the Baroness Krüdener. Alexander has also been credited with homosexual and incestuous leanings – besides the charge of encouraging his wife to become the mistress of one of his close friends and even to embark on lesbian relationships. The young Emperor thus acquired some reputation as the first lecher of his realm, and even as its most august pimp. A less fanciful item in the catalogue of Alexander's supposed love affairs was his liaison with Mary Naryshkin – a Polish beauty and wife of a complaisant Russian court official – his openly acknowledged mistress for some fifteen years.

Alexander was destined to scale greater heights of international prestige than any

The Emperor Alexander I (r. 1801–25). Portrait by Jacques Louis David.

other Tsar, reaching the summit of his career on 19 March 1814, when he rode into Paris acclaimed by many peoples for his martial prowess and magnanimity in victory. Hailed as an Agamemnon among kings and as the saviour of Europe, the Russian Emperor was above all the conqueror of Napoleon, to whose defeat he had perhaps made a larger contribution than any other individual. The Tsar entered Paris with princes, generals and statesmen from many parts of Europe, all of whom he far outshone in the splendour of his achievement and imperial presence. Tall, fair, blue-eyed, imposing and celebrated for his good looks, he rode the light grey mare Eclipse – Napoleon's present from the days of their alliance – and was flanked by the glittering Cossacks of his escort. The event was all the more spectacular in marking so dramatic a reversal of fate, taking place as it did less than eighteen months after Napoleon's own victorious ride into Moscow of September 1812. But the Russian's was the more brilliant triumph. In Paris, Alexander was surrounded by international pageantry at its most splendid, not by empty streets, burning buildings and the smell of future defeat. The girls of Moscow had never mobbed Napoleon, but excited Parisiennes pressed through Alexander's escort and persuaded his officers to hoist them on the cruppers of their horses so that they could see the Russian Emperor.

As victor over the world's greatest military genius, Alexander had obtained a military diploma without parallel, and the question arises as to how far he owed this distinction to accidental circumstances and how far to his own proficiency in war. On the lowest level of the military art, that of the parade-ground, his enthusiasm and competence left little to be desired. Like later Romanov Tsars, he never seemed tired of inspecting his troops while on his travels; and he rarely missed the changing of his guard at the Winter Palace when resident in St Petersburg.[7] But active service was less his element. The Battle of Austerlitz in 1805 gave him a discouraging baptism of fire when he overrode the counsels of his cautious commander-in-chief and engaged Napoleon prematurely. A resounding Russian and Austrian defeat followed, in the course of which Alexander fled from the field with a small escort. No great horseman, he jibbed at jumping a small ditch, dismounted, sat down at the foot of a tree and gave way to tears, covering his face with a handkerchief.[8] But this moment of weakness was untypical of a Tsar who was not, as the incident might suggest, a physical coward.

No doubt his unhappy experience at Austerlitz was in Alexander's mind when, at Russian army headquarters in 1812, he accepted a formal recommendation presented by three senior advisers to leave the scene since his presence threatened to hamper his commanders in their efforts to resist Napoleon's invasion. Thereafter Alexander delegated the handling of his armies to others, and though he accompanied the Russian forces on the Napoleonic campaigns of 1813-14, he did not seek the laurels of a fighting general. However, so far as higher military and

L

diplomatic strategy is concerned, he kept the reins firmly in his own hands. It was his contribution on this high level which became a decisive factor in saving Russia and other countries from domination by Napoleon.

In the diplomatic field, Alexander had the presence and adroitness to treat as superior or equal with any statesman in Europe from the Emperor of France downwards. Other hereditary crowned heads found themselves eclipsed – as at Tilsit in 1807, when the King of Prussia waded his horse into the River Niemen and gazed mournfully through the rain at the lavishly appointed raft in the middle of the stream where the Emperors Alexander and Napoleon were parcelling up his realm.[9] Seven years later it was Napoleon's turn to have his territories divided at the Congress of Vienna, where Alexander played the role of victor-in-chief in a dazzling pageant of negotiations, receptions, banquets and intrigues both diplomatic and amorous. On the European stage he had graduated from inexperienced *jeune premier* to seasoned matinée idol, well equipped to put such veteran performers as Metternich, Talleyrand and Wellington in the shade. Napoleon himself paid tribute to the Tsar's histrionic talents by calling him the Talma of the North, thus comparing him with a celebrated French actor of the day. Napoleon further stressed Alexander's subtle deviousness in negotiation by calling him a Byzantine Greek; and also paid the more dubious compliment of saying that if Alexander had been a woman, then he, Napoleon, would have fallen in love with him.

Besides charm and histrionic skill, Alexander's ten-year duel with Napoleon also reveals a less immediately obvious characteristic of the Tsar – his extreme stubbornness in clinging to certain basic principles of policy while appearing to pursue different aims. Defeated at Austerlitz and elsewhere, and compelled to treat with the Emperor of France at Tilsit and Erfurt, Alexander had entered into alliance with the French and joined the continental system directed against England. This policy of friendship for Napoleon was unpopular with the Russian court, the gentry and the people in general. An anti-French party arose in St Petersburg, and the Tsar's prestige slumped to the point where there was talk of serving him in the same way as his father Paul. But he still kept his own counsel. Privately agreeing that Napoleon was not to be trusted, he considered it politic to feign the naïve enthusiasm of an eager young man for the French Emperor, whose downfall he was contemplating at the very time when the two rulers were exchanging their most fulsome compliments. In Alexander's struggle with Napoleon, the Russian Tsar's ability to wear a charming mask and play a waiting game eventually vindicated his comment made in a letter of 1808: 'Bonaparte maintains that I'm no better than an idiot, but he who laughs last laughs best.'[10]

During the French invasion of Russia in 1812, Alexander showed great obstinacy in waiting for initial defeat to turn into victory. As Napoleon thrust farther and farther towards Moscow, the Tsar clung to the view that time, terrain and climate were on Russia's side, and he had sufficient force of character to keep his head when many of his relatives and advisers were apparently losing theirs. His most obvious contribution to the Russian cause at the beginning of the campaign lay in the stimulus given to national morale by his visit of July 1812 to Moscow, where he rallied patriotic forces and received an enthusiastic reception. He then returned to St Petersburg to spend a frustrated period, absent at the end of August from the bloody battle of Borodino which opened the road to Moscow to the French, and bitterly criticized when Napoleon entered the former Russian capital on 2 September. Then Alexander again incurred strong censure for ignoring no less than three peace overtures sent to him by Napoleon from Moscow. But the rout of the French grand army during its winter retreat, begun on 7 October, justified his policy in full.

Alexander's fortitude is further illustrated by his personal decision, taken against the advice of many members of his entourage, to pursue Napoleon after the beaten remnants of the grand army had extricated themselves from Russian territory in December 1812, and to carry the war to a victorious conclusion in the heart of France. This decision has incurred the criticism of Russian historians, including the Tsar's own distant relative, the Grand Duke Nicholas Mikhaylovich.[11] Alexander's justification is the likelihood that any truce with the French would only have been temporary, and that Napoleon would have been certain to lead his armies back over the Niemen sooner or later to avenge 1812. The campaigns of 1813–14 made this impossible, after which diplomacy supervened, with the Tsar continuing to play a brilliant role.

The Congress of Vienna came between Alexander's two prolonged visits to Paris – as the victor of 1814 and again (after Napoleon's final defeat) in 1815. Russian armies were too far east to fight in the Battle of Waterloo. But not wishing the British and Prussians to push him into the background, the Tsar made a dash through enemy-held territory with a small detachment of Cossacks to Paris in order to assert his presence there as soon as possible. On 29 August, after his army had caught up, he staged a massive parade of 150,000 men and 500 cannon on the Plain of Vertus. Eight altars stood there, and an elaborate religious ceremony accompanied the parade, supervised by Alexander's spiritual adviser of the moment – the Baroness Krüdener, whose sober blue serge dress and straw hat contrasted with her extreme mystical exaltation. Alexander described this as the most beautiful day of his life, and he said that his heart was full of love for his enemies.[12] The Tsar's forces no doubt did impress these enemies, but they did not frighten the Duke of Wellington, who said that his small army would be capable of pointing the Russians in any desired direction before they could make a move.[13]

Curiously enough, Russia's crowned leader during the war against Napoleon was among the least patriotic of Tsars, at least in the narrow sense. He would never, it seemed, appoint a Russian to command an army if he could find a German general to fill the post. At the Congress of Vienna there was only one Russian among his close advisers, who consisted of a Pole, a Greek, a Corsican and several Germans. Alexander did not even learn to express himself clearly in Russian, preferring to speak French. He also offended national sentiment by failing to visit the field of Borodino on home territory, whereas he did not omit to inspect the foreign sites of Wagram and Waterloo.

Alexander's charm and obstinacy were suitable weapons for the confounding of Russia's enemies on the field of battle and in the conference chamber. But it is unfortunate that he also used them against his own subjects, and in a manner so oblique and elusive that he remains a notoriously enigmatic figure among the Tsars. Was the 'blessed one' (as he was called) a hypocrite in the sense of deliberately cloaking sinister designs in an aura of sweetness and light? Or is it more instructive to regard him as two different people – the one a sincere advocate of humanitarian principles, the other a remorseless oppressor?

Typical of this ambivalence was the Tsar's obsession with the mirage of a Russian constitution – that is, with the idea of abolishing the autocracy and replacing it with a monarchy limited by legally established guarantees. He developed this theme before his accession, saying that he meant to grant Russia a constitution on becoming Tsar, after which he would retire to live as a private citizen on the banks of the Rhine. In the last year of his reign he was still harping on his continuing intention to grant Russia fundamental laws,[14] having made little tangible contribution towards such aims beyond entrusting various individuals with the task of drawing up draft legislation which was not enacted. Though he did admittedly permit certain constitutions to function within his empire, it was typical that the beneficiaries of this concession to the democratic principle were not Russians, but Finns and Poles incorporated within the realm. Alexander became Grand Duke of Finland in 1809, after annexing the country from Sweden; and in 1815 he acquired the greater part of the former Grand Duchy of Warsaw, which became known as the Kingdom of Poland. The Russian sovereign now styled himself King of Poland, which did not prevent him from infringing the constitution granted to the Poles in 1815. Whatever he understood by a constitution, limitation of his own power does not seem to have been part of it.

With regard to the peasants, Russia's most grievous social problem, Alexander failed to take any effective preliminary steps in the direction of their emancipation from serfdom. Though it is true that he liberated the serfs of his Baltic provinces, this took place in a fashion sadly characteristic of his methods. The peasants in question received their 'freedom' on terms which left them worse situated, and more dependent on the local landowners, than before. Meanwhile the Tsar was

congratulating the gentry of Estland on understanding that 'only liberal principles can serve as a basis for the happiness of the peoples'.[15] As this episode illus-
trates, whenever Alexander aired his liberal principles someone was always liable
to suffer.

Though the reign often appears as a gradual decline from liberalism to oppression, the former phase was the more tentative and brief, and was virtually confined
to the first few years of the new administration. These saw the initiation of important reforms in the sphere of education and also witnessed the sway of the so-
called unofficial committee of 1801-03. Consisting of the Tsar himself and four
young friends, this informal body was whimsically nicknamed a caucus of
Jacobins – a compliment to its supposed inflammatory temper. Its only important
achievement, however, was to establish ministries in place of the earlier colleges
as a basis for the administration. This was a useful measure, but hardly a revolutionary one, especially as the appointment and dismissal of ministers was in the
hands of the autocrat himself, who thus came to function as his own prime
minister. In any case, the unofficial committee's main stumbling-block, as noted
by one of its members, was that Alexander became very stubborn as soon as
anyone disagreed with his preferences.[16] It was also typical that the new Tsar encouraged his senate to adopt a more independent attitude in discussing legislation – only to react angrily when that advisory body took him at his word by
criticizing a minor enactment. In keeping with this trend, Alexander was also
quick to re-establish under different auspices a security police authority such as he
had abolished on his accession.

The contrast between liberal word and reactionary deed recalls Catherine II,
who was similarly devious. But Alexander suffers by comparison with his grandmother, if only because he was better placed to institute far-reaching reform –
being the acknowledged sovereign, not a foreign usurper. In fairness to the blessed
Tsar it must be added that the Russian situation presented particular difficulties
to a potential reformer. Reforms could arguably come only from above in Russian
conditions – that is, from the autocrat himself. Unfortunately, it was the very
institution of autocracy which (together with serfdom) stood most in need of
reform, and for Alexander to have renounced his autocratic power would presumably have meant leaving the country at the mercy of a gentry more reactionary
than any Tsar. Such a reform might therefore have ended the chances of further
reform.

As things were, such concepts as freedom and equality remained in the realm
of soothing sounds presided over by Alexander the liberal. With the world of
harsh reality, the autocrat's sphere, they must never connect. Any attempt to join
these opposing poles was potentially dangerous, as was illustrated by the downfall
of Michael Speransky, most important associate of the Tsar in the years 1809-12.

Entrusted by Alexander with translating his exalted ideas into concrete realities, including the framing of a constitution, Speransky drafted detailed proposals, among them the project of a council of state such as was set up in 1810 to advise on legislation. But Speransky's talent for bringing word and deed into contact proved damaging to his career, though it is also true that the intrigues of powerful enemies contributed to his downfall. In March 1812, when he was at the height of his power, he was suddenly summoned for a two-hour private audience with the Tsar of which neither party has left an account. As Speransky was leaving, Alexander ran after him to say good-bye, his face stained with tears. Despite this display of emotion, Speransky arrived home after the interview to find two high police officials waiting with a carriage ready to take him into exile there and then on the Emperor's instructions.[17]

The last decade of Alexander's reign provides an anti-climax to its earlier glories. These years witnessed the disintegration of the Tsar's personality, one symptom of this being the development of pious obsessions bordering on religious mania. Once relatively ungodly, the Tsar first conceived this new interest in about 1812 and became a dabbler in mysticism, an obsessive quoter of biblical texts, a font of sanctimonious abstractions and a devotee of prayer whose calloused knees witnessed the rigours of his devotions. He sought consolation from a succession of prophets, including his childhood friend Prince Alexander Golitsyn (a converted rake like himself), renegade Catholic priests, English and French Quakers and members of the Russian sect of the self-castrating *Skoptsy*. The Baroness Krüdener, already mentioned, was prominent among these religious consultants. She dramatically obtained audience with Alexander in the middle of the night at Heilbronn in 1815, was constantly closeted with him in Paris later in the year, and harangued him on matters religious to the point where she afterwards received credit for founding the Holy Alliance; but wrongly so, for that institution – so liberal in theory, so reactionary in practice – bears the authentic stamp of the blessed Tsar himself. Her exclusive influence on the Emperor lasted only a year, for it was a feature of Alexander's obsession that the sway of one saintly adviser was always liable to yield to that of some new and more exotic successor. Perhaps the most grotesque in the sequence of these visionaries was Archimandrite Photius, a fanatic of Russian Orthodoxy somewhat resembling the comic Father Ferapont in Dostoyevsky's *Brothers Karamazov*, though a comparatively young man. Alexander at once fell under the spell of this zealot, to such effect that the archimandrite was able to blast Prince Golitsyn, that rival seer of long standing, out of his position as combined minister of education and religious affairs by pronouncing on him a curse so potent that it effected his transfer to the relatively humble office of postmaster-general. But though it is easy to condemn the blessed Tsar's religious aberrations, it must also be remembered that the Russian monarch's office was one of the most difficult, dangerous and lonely in the world, and it is understandable that he should have sought spiritual support – if also regrettable that the search led him into such strange byways.

An outstanding feature of Alexander's later years was the ascendancy of General Count Arakcheyev, who came to wield vast powers based on his personal standing with the Emperor. Their association dates back to the last years of Catherine's rule, when Arakcheyev was an artillery officer at Gatchina. He treated his subordinates with appalling brutality, and reputedly bit off a man's ear on parade[18] – an act outrageous even by the bluff soldierly standards of the Tsarevich Paul's private army. But with all his defects, Arakcheyev was also a man of great moral strength, able and willing to act as a bulwark between the youthful Alexander and his eccentric father's rages. During Alexander's reign, Arakcheyev's influence increased after temporary eclipse until in the early 1820s he became virtual dictator over the country. Hated and fawned upon by one and all, he dismissed ministers and generals, issued laws, promoted mediocrities and dispensed rebukes – a drab, minatory presence whose bristling hair *en brosse*, staring eyes and gaunt, hunched figure in threadbare cloak could demoralize the most glittering assemblage. He was also a scourge of the common people, notorious as a monster of cruelty and lechery – especially on his private estate at Gruzino, a community of some three thousand souls which he made into a hell on earth. His courtyard housed a vat of brine in which sticks and rods stood ready for use in the frequent beatings of serfs in his stables, more serious offenders being taken to near-by army headquarters to be dealt with by military floggers. Only Alexander's death, it seemed, prevented Arakcheyev from turning the whole of Russia into a large-scale Gruzino, though it is also true that he was a capable administrator and passed as honest by the standards of the day.

Had the Tsar absent-mindedly surrendered control of Russia to a man whom he was too unworldly to recognize as a ruthless oppressor or sadistic monster? Such is the impression which the angelic Emperor himself probably sought to convey – for though the relationship between Tsar and general was complex and elusive, it seems clear that Alexander always held the whip hand. To a great extent the blessed one knowingly assumed the ugly role of tyrant by proxy, and without modifying the smiling posture of a gentle sovereign whose mind was fixed on higher things than the knoutings and regimental floggings ordained by his chief henchman.

The imposition of an unpopular new system – that of military settlements or colonies – against the opposition of many advisers including Arakcheyev himself, showed the autocrat at his most stubborn. Like so many of Alexander's oppressive measures, the plan derived from motives of benevolent liberalism. He intended to reduce expenditure on the army, while also enabling his soldiers to exchange the rigours of the barrack-room for the amenities of family life. Arakcheyev commanded the project, and since his own estate was near Novgorod, it was found convenient to set up some of the first military settlements in that district. Male peasants of military age in the designated areas found themselves put in uniform. Their beards shaved and their hair cropped, they became military conscripts, but without ceasing to be serfs – a form of dual bondage, since they were required to combine normal farming activities with arduous military training. On these unhappy serf-soldiers of the locality unmarried soldiers from outside were billeted, becoming soldier-serfs. Women and children also came under military discipline, which reached such lengths that each homestead was liable to a daily kit inspection of household and farming utensils. Defaulters of either sex were subject to military floggings such as so often proved fatal. When the military settlers mutinied at Chuguyev in southern Russia in 1819, Arakcheyev suppressed the rising with extreme brutality for which he and the Tsar exchanged pious regrets by correspondence. But such setbacks did not deter Alexander, who planned to extend the system of colonies until it embraced his entire military establishment. He had resolved – or so he reputedly stated – to set up his colonies even if he must first pave the road from St Petersburg to Chudovo (on the way to Moscow) with corpses. By the end of his reign the system embraced over three hundred thousand colonist-soldiers, and it remained in force for some years after his death.

Alexander rarely showed himself more enigmatic than in his handling of the political secret societies which arose in Russia after the Napoleonic campaigns. By the early 1820s such conspiratorial groups (forerunners of the Decembrists) existed throughout large parts of the country. They were loosely organized but by determined men, largely army officers dedicated to overthrowing the autocracy. Though the Tsar held many of the threads of these conspiracies in his hands, he would not take effective action against them – remarking with some justice that the conspirators were merely expressing the kind of sentiment which he himself had held in youth; and that it was therefore not for him to punish them.[19] This easy-going attitude contrasts with his ferocity in crushing a trivial but very different disturbance of the same period – the mutiny in October 1820 of common soldiers of the Semyonovsky Guards in St Petersburg. They were guilty only of minor insubordination provoked by an unpopular colonel, and there was no political aspect to the affair. Yet when Alexander received news of the Semyonovsky mutiny during the international conference at Troppau, he persuaded himself with Metternich's approval that it was part of a general conspiracy involving the Carbonari and an empire of evil controlled by a satanic genius.[20] Arranging to have the Semyonovsky mutineers punished with the monstrous severity of Russian military law, he personally decreed that certain of the accused

The Emperor Paul, son of Catherine the Great,
came to the throne in 1796
and was murdered on the night of 11–12 March
1801 in the *coup* which led to the succession of
his son Alexander I. Portrait by Lampi.

A caricature of the Emperor
Paul after the work of
a Russian artist who
is said to have been punished
with Siberian exile for this
portrait. Engraving of 1804.

The Emperor Paul as Grand
Duke with his wife,
the Grand Duchess and
future Empress Mary.
Alexander I was their first
and Nicholas I
their third son. Watercolour
by H. Löschenkohl.

The Emperor Alexander I. After succeeding his
murdered father, Paul, Alexander I became
chiefly famous as the liberator of Europe from
Napoleon after the French had occupied Moscow
for a time during the 1812 campaign.
Contemporary French print.

The Empress Elizabeth, wife of Alexander I,
from whom he was partially estranged during
most of his reign.
Painting by Monier.

'Precipitate march of the flying Russian army to help the Prussians', a contemporary French cartoon of the Napoleonic wars.

(top) An English cartoon showing Alexander I and Napoleon at Tilsit in 1807, embracing on the raft where their negotiations took place, while the King of Prussia tries to rescue his crown.

A Russian soldier disposes of a French invader,
an episode from the 1812 campaign.
From a Russian folk-print.

The meeting of three monarchs in Prague in
1813. Alexander I (on the right) joins hands
with the Emperor Francis II of Austria and
King Frederick William III of Prussia.
A contemporary print.

Alexander rides in triumph into Paris
on 19 March 1814, the moment of greatest
international renown attained by any
of the Tsars.
A contemporary engraving.

The Russians in Paris, a contemporary French caricature commemorating the presence of Alexander I's troops in the French capital in 1814 and 1815.

The Moscow Kremlin in 1815.

General Count Alexis Arakcheyev (1769–1834),
the chief favourite of Alexander I's reign,
was generally regarded as a cruel monster.
Etching from a portrait of 1818.

should receive six thousand strokes and be sent to the mines.[21]. He thus showed himself as heartless in stamping out phantom phobias as he was lax in countering real danger.

Another puzzling feature of Alexander's last years is his handling of the succession problem. He himself had no legitimate male issue, and the eldest of his three younger brothers, the Grand Duke Constantine, was therefore heir presumptive. However, Constantine was unwilling to succeed, and sent Alexander a formal letter to this effect in 1822. In the following year Alexander signed a manifesto giving official expression to Constantine's renunciation and declaring the Grand Duke Nicholas (next brother in line) successor to the throne. But the Emperor unfortunately insisted on keeping this arrangement secret, with the result that Constantine continued to bear the official title of Tsesarevich, while no one outside a very narrow circle suspected that he had ceased to be heir. Whatever the reason for Alexander's insistence on secrecy – perhaps a wish to reserve the right to change his mind – this uncertainty, combined with his failure to crush the widespread political conspiracies of the 1820s, helped to involve his successor in a dangerous crisis.

The Tsar's death in 1825 at the age of forty-seven came as a shock, for it was the Empress Elizabeth whose health had given more cause for alarm at the time. Her doctors required her to spend the winter in the south, and for some reason the choice fell on Taganrog. This small port on the Sea of Azov had few claims to be regarded as a health resort, but the imperial couple took up residence there in September, newly reconciled after a long period of estrangement. There was a suggestion of a second honeymoon about the expedition, except that the restless Alexander soon set off to tour the neighbourhood on his own. It was while inspecting the Crimea that he contracted typhoid. He returned to Taganrog, where he died on 19 November 1825.

Did Alexander in fact die as reported – or did he contrive to disappear and survive to an advanced age in Siberia as the holy man Fyodor Kuzmich, or as an anonymous hermit in Palestine? These and other rumours gained wide currency, and the inscrutable Tsar thus continued to justify his reputation by taking his secrets with him to the grave.

News of the Emperor Alexander's death in Taganrog reached St Petersburg on 27 November 1825 and led to a dynastic crisis such as the Emperor Paul had attempted to avert by his law of the succession. For several years the formal renunciation by the Tsesarevich Constantine of his right to the throne had remained secret, as mentioned above. The general assumption therefore was that Constantine would inherit, especially as the Grand Duke Nicholas, next heir in line, immediately took the oath of allegiance to the Emperor Constantine and sponsored its administration in the capital and elsewhere. Despite this, Constantine not only remained firm in refusing the succession, but also – most unhelpfully – refused to leave Warsaw, where he was resident as Russian commander-in-chief of the Polish army . . . and had himself already sworn allegiance to Nicholas. Only after the exchange of several lengthy messages by courier between Warsaw and St Petersburg did Nicholas decide to claim the crown for himself, by which time a dangerous situation had developed.

Nicholas had apparently done more than was reasonable to secure the throne for Constantine. It is not clear, however, whether his own reluctance to reign was chiefly due to distaste for high office, concern for constitutional probity or fear of the guards stationed in the capital, with whom he had made himself unpopular by excessive severity in command. Be this as it may, he eventually attempted to end over two weeks of interregnum by invoking the hitherto secret document in which Alexander I had designated him heir, and by requiring the loyalty oath to be sworn anew to himself – not a moment too soon. The senate and synod complied, just as they had sworn to obey Constantine nearly three weeks earlier. But would the St Petersburg garrison do likewise? First signs seemed favourable as reports of the swearing-in of the guards began to reach the Winter Palace one after the other in the early morning of 14 December. But then a harassed general burst in to report that the First Battalion of the Moscow Regiment had mutinied, wounding certain senior officers. Many of the men, with some subalterns, marched to the Senate Square about half a mile to the west of the palace, where they formed up several hundred strong. The Decembrist revolt, sometimes termed the first Russian revolution, had begun.

This event differed from the numerous eighteenth-century palace upheavals aimed simply at replacing one personality on the throne with another, for the Decembrists were chiefly concerned to enforce institutional changes. Not that they had a common political platform. Some merely wished to establish a constitutional monarchy in place of the autocracy, while others planned to set up a republic, and certain extremists meant to begin by murdering the imperial family. In accordance with eighteenth-century tradition, aristocrats or gentlemen – mainly officers, serving or retired – were the prime movers. Such were the Decembrists proper. As for the rank and file which followed them, Russian private soldiers understood little about civil rights and constitutional government, their dissatisfaction bearing more on the harsh conditions of the service. The Decembrists played on such grievances, pretending that Constantine had intended to improve army conditions, but had been thrown in chains by the usurper Nicholas. Tempted by a bait which combined appeals to their self-interest, altruism and sense of drama, the troops came out into the Senate Square to cheer for Constantine – and also for 'Constitution' (a feminine noun in Russian), some of them apparently convinced that this was the name of Constantine's wife.[22]

By occupying the square, the Decembrists aimed to cut off the senate building from the Winter Palace; they might then hope to induce the senate to proclaim a provisional government consisting of leaders of the revolt. However, by the time when they occupied the square these tactics offered little prospect of success, since the senate had already sworn allegiance to Nicholas earlier on the same morning – a setback which did not deter certain other units from filtering through to join the men of the Moscow Regiment. By noon the number of mutineers in the square was over two thousand, with some civilian sympathizers. Not all the Decembrist leaders were present, however, and none of them seemed to know what to do.

An ornamental soldier celebrated only for his exploits on the parade-ground, Nicholas was resplendent in the uniform of his Izmaylovsky Guards as he now led men into action for the first time – and against his own subjects. But it was several hours before he joined combat. With bullets whistling about him, the new Tsar underwent his baptism of fire – reconnoitring the area of the Palace Square on horseback and exposing himself to danger of assassination by accosting rebel soldiers in the streets. He personally directed some, who told him that they were 'for Constantine', to the Senate Square[23] – almost as if he were rehearsing a military tattoo. But the Senate Square did not prove an inspiring rallying point, since this was no weather for a revolution – a gloomy winter's day with the temperature well below zero and a cruel north wind sweeping across the frozen River Neva. Standing there hour after hour, the men were cold, hungry and bewildered. It was less like storming the citadels of power than taking part in another interminable parade – if a somewhat disorderly one, for some of the mutineers were drunk.

Meanwhile Nicholas was making strenuous efforts to end the crisis without further bloodshed. He ordered loyal units to block approaches to the Senate Square, while his emissaries made prolonged attempts to persuade the rebels to surrender. The new Emperor's tactics probably erred on the side of forbearance and indecision rather than of undue haste. In the end, however, he decided to strike, and commanded his cavalry to charge – an attempt which ended in fiasco, for the horses were not properly shod and slipped on the frozen surface, while the riders had paraded without their swords. Then the Tsar ordered up artillery, and shouted the order to fire after giving the mutineers one last chance to surrender. Cannon opened up with canister shot. The rebels broke and fled, leaving at least fifty dead on the bloody square. The rest, crowd and soldiers mingled, pelted away in panic-stricken flight. Some tried to cross the Neva, only to come under fire as cannon balls smashed the ice and plunged them to drown in the freezing waters. That night loyal troops bivouacked in the square by camp fires. Falconet's huge equestrian monument to Peter the Great, erected by Catherine the Great, loomed through the flames; rearing horse and grim rider stood firm on their granite base – a reminder that the Russian autocracy was still in the saddle. The scene was hurriedly cleaned up during the night, blood being swabbed off the square or smothered in clean snow, while through holes specially hacked in the ice of the Neva the police thrust bodies – including, it was believed, those of the wounded.

The new Tsar spent the night following the rebellion interrogating the conspirators in the Winter Palace, having them marched in to face him with their hands tied behind their backs. This investigation continued over several months, more than a hundred and fifty suspects being questioned during the first week alone. Nicholas meant to unravel all the threads of the plot, varying his approach to suit each individual. But whether he chose to bully or charm, it soon appeared that he sought revenge rather than justice. He sent detailed orders about the prisoners' treatment – which dungeon should hold each individual; what sort of food he should receive; whether he should wear shackles or not, and if so whether they should be hand-fetters or foot-irons or both.

The trial of the Decembrists took place in their absence and without their knowledge, on the basis of elaborate court proceedings largely prearranged by the Tsar. It was he who decided, in effect, to hang the five ring-leaders – an execution which took place on a bastion of the Peter and Paul Fortress in the early morning of 13 July 1826, being carried out with scandalous incompetence. 'My God, they can't even hang a man decently in Russia,'[24] was the comment of one of the temporarily reprieved victims, whose legs had been broken in the bungled preliminaries. Meanwhile the Emperor had withdrawn to his residence at Tsarskoye

Selo as if to wash his hands of the affair, but received news of events in the fortress by courier at half-hourly intervals. On the next day he had the Senate Square purified from the pollutions of 14 December by a special religious service.

Nicholas was not a merciful man, and he did little during the three decades of his reign to relieve the lot of *mes amis du quatorze*, his typically sardonic phrase for the many exiled plotters of 14 December. But there has been a tendency to exaggerate his severity towards them. Though many of the condemned suffered acute hardship in Siberia and gave way to very natural despair, others were able to import such items as libraries and grand pianos from European Russia, enjoying a measure of freedom in exile and active in such fields as education, medicine, ethnography and local administration. Harshly as they were treated, it is misleading to refer to them as if they were victims of a twentieth-century concentration camp.

Born on 25 June 1796, Nicholas was the third son of the Emperor Paul, but hardly knew a father who was assassinated when the boy was only four years old. After a few years under the care of women (he contracted his lifelong dislike of Poles from a Scottish nanny), he was taught by men, though his mother still attempted to supervise his education. Her main aim was to wean the grand duke from the passion for military trivia which he shared with his younger brother Michael. However, it proved impossible to demilitarize the two imperial brothers. Even as adults they continued to show less interest in the art of warfare than in such matters as the positioning of buttons and the technicalities of arms drill.

Nicholas always remained an army officer at heart. Impeccable in uniform, he could not easily be imagined in a dressing-gown and preferred to sleep on a camp bed, using a thin palliasse stuffed with hay. He early received high military office, becoming inspector-general of army engineering and commander of the Second Guards Division while still a grand duke. But his heart remained on the parade-ground where every soldier knew that his Emperor could pick up a musket and slam it through all forty-eight motions of the regulation arms drill as deftly as the smartest corporal of the guards.

Erect, well-groomed and six feet three inches tall, Nicholas was by any standards a superb specimen of an Emperor, and rated as the most handsome man in Europe even when he had reached middle age and taken to wearing a toupée. He was nearly fifty years old when Queen Victoria received him during his visit to England in 1844. She noted his magnificent appearance and manners, but added that she found the expression of his eyes terrifying, and had never seen anything like them before.[25] A similar if somewhat more prejudiced impression was recorded by the Tsar's leading Russian political opponent, Alexander Herzen, who first saw Nicholas in 1826 when he rode into the city of Moscow to be crowned:

'He was handsome [Herzen wrote], but his good looks made you want to shiver
.... The swiftly receding forehead, together with a lower jaw overdeveloped at
the expense of the cranium, expressed inflexible will-power and feebleness of
thought, and more cruelty than sensitivity. But the eyes were the main thing.
They were wintry eyes without warmth or pity.'[26]

Wintry or not, the Tsar was happily married (as witnessed by some tender
passages in his correspondence) to the Empress Alexandra, formerly Princess
Charlotte of Prussia. There were, however, times when he showed impatience with
her physical frailty. Moreover, he was the first male in his Empire as well as the
most handsome man in Europe. Flirtatiously inclined and charming when he chose,
he had too strong a sense of duty to enjoy love affairs on the scale of his grandmother, the Empress Catherine. But the names of two mistresses are known, both
ladies-in-waiting. The more important was Barbara Nelidov, who bore him several
children. Long before he eventually overcame his scruples, his interest in her had become so obvious that members of his entourage were asking each other why the Tsar
could not simply take the young woman as his mistress and have done with it.[27]

Though Nicholas professed to regard Peter I as his model, keeping a bust of the
great Tsar on his desk, the underlying aim of his policy was to preserve the
status quo – a programme shortsighted, cynical and unduly harsh, besides proving
unworkable after his death. It was not unintelligently conceived, however, since
the continuing low general level of education in the population and the long-
standing tradition of corruption among officials were only two among many
factors which made fundamental reform seem a lost cause at this time.

Reactionary though he assuredly was, Nicholas was no reincarnation of a
seventeenth-century Tsar, for his conservatism was highly militant and he was
above all a working monarch. In the darkness before a winter dawn, he might
sometimes be glimpsed through a ground-floor window of the Winter Palace
poring over state documents by the light of four candles.[28] He was assiduous in
diplomatic negotiation, attendance at social functions and support of Orthodoxy,
being always careful to visit local churches and cathedrals on his travels in the
provinces and punctilious everywhere in discharging his ritual duties. His letters
and memoirs abound in references to God indicating that he looked to the deity
as his immediate superior in the chain of command – a divine generalissimo always
prepared to back up His more soldierly junior commanders. A restless traveller on
official business, Nicholas covered some ninety thousand miles during the first
twenty-five years of his reign.[29] About a sixth of this total was accounted for by
visits to foreign countries, including Prussia, Austria, England and Italy. But most
of his journeys were part of a recurrent tour of inspection of his empire, which he
treated as a vast military command. Driven by his restless energy, he would often

set out at midnight, and he followed the common Russian custom of travelling round the clock. He beat the unofficial sovereign's record for the four hundred and eighty-six miles between Moscow and St Petersburg with a time of thirty-eight hours – compared with Peter the Great's forty-eight hours, and Alexander I's forty-two.[30]

During these tours of inspection, the Tsar would descend on some unsuspecting office or institution to denounce breaches of order and good discipline; he would exile one official, dismiss another or rebuke a third before moving on elsewhere. Such raids menaced high and low without respect to age and nationality. He once pounced on a boys' school and dismissed a master because a pupil was leaning on an elbow during a history lesson, though listening attentively.[31] Another school in St Petersburg installed alarm bells for sounding whenever the imperial carriage appeared in the street outside. One one occasion an unfortunate foreign tutor, reported for the misdemeanour of sitting down during an Orthodox church service, was put in a strait-jacket on the Emperor's personal order and confined to a lunatic asylum in St Petersburg before being expelled from the empire.[32] It is, therefore, not surprising that another visitor to Russia, the Marquis de Custine, went about in fear of Siberian exile despite his French nationality and noble rank, and though the Emperor treated him graciously whenever they met.[33]

Always the junior commander at heart, Nicholas flourished in an atmosphere of action and orders. When his Winter Palace caught fire in December 1837, he left a ballet performance to direct the fire-fighting, abandoning it only when some thirty or forty men had been killed, and ordering the exact restoration of the gutted building in its original magnificence within a year. This was asking the impossible, for it had originally taken eight times as long to build the palace under the Empress Elizabeth. Such, however, was the force of autocratic will that the builders missed their target by only a narrow margin.

The severe cholera epidemic of 1830-1 led to riots which provoked the Tsar's personal intervention in Moscow and St Petersburg. He went to Moscow to tighten the quarantine regulations, and dismissed one doctor because his hospital happened to report more fatalities than any other; after which no Moscow hospital reported any deaths whatever for some while. By the time when he left the area, the Tsar and his anti-cholera precautions had begun to seem more deadly than the disease itself. When the epidemic later reached St Petersburg, serious disturbances broke out, whereupon the Tsar drove to the main trouble spot. Undaunted either by rioters or fear of infection, he harangued a crowd of five thousand as though they were delinquent recruits: 'Down on your knees! Kneel down and cross yourselves! Who do you think you are? A lot of Frenchmen or Poles? Call yourselves Russians?'[34] The Emperor then explained that his own brother Constantine had recently died from cholera – and burst into tears; for though he was so icy and unemotional on the surface, he often wept in public. Rarely, however, was his commanding officer's eye so blinded by sentiment that he missed an act of insubordination. On the present occasion one man had failed to doff his hat, and the Tsar had him arrested.

Most celebrated, perhaps, of all Nicholas's acts of personal intervention was his reported decision to settle arguments about the route of the projected railway from St Petersburg to Moscow by taking a map and drawing a straight line with ruler and pen between the two cities, even incorporating three kinks at points where the tips of his fingers happened to jut out.[35]

Since Nicholas could not be everywhere at once, he tried to terrorize his subjects into unthinking obedience, and made this attitude plain in a military order of the day issued nearly eight years before he became Tsar: 'The slightest dereliction [he warned his command] will be punished with the full severity of the law, and will never under any circumstances be excused.'[36] He followed this maxim throughout his reign, and supported it with execution, imprisonment, exile and flogging. Imprisonment varied from incarceration for life in a fortress of European Russia or Siberian gaol, to temporary detention in the guardroom of some local garrison unit. There were also various grades of exile – more tolerable on a family estate for a Turgenev or a Pushkin; less so for Decembrists, Poles and others sent to bleak outposts in eastern Siberia. The ugliest feature of the penal system was corporal punishment – deceptively mild name for the savage floggings from which the gentry (for example, the Decembrist leaders) were immune, but which many members of the 'unprivileged classes' suffered, including some of the unfortunate troops whom the Decembrists persuaded to mutiny. The court balls of the period, with their bejewelled ladies and glittering guards officers, must be seen against a drab background where sweating peasant soldiers beat other peasants to death.

A particularly severe orgy of beatings followed the suppression of the mutiny by military colonists in the Novgorod area in 1831. After troops had quelled the rising, the Tsar gave instructions to court-martial the offenders. So many floggings through the ranks did the courts order – of 1599 persons, to be precise – that it became necessary to cut willow-staves by the cartload, and the total of officially recorded fatalities from various forms of beating was one hundred and twenty-nine.[37] In many instances the families of the victims had to witness their agony. Having visited the area of the mutiny and ordained these atrocities, the Emperor coolly noted in a letter that God had rewarded him for his journey to Novgorod 'by granting my wife to be delivered successfully of a son several hours after my return'.[38]

Nicholas was directly responsible for these horrors because he repeatedly ordered

The Grand Duke Constantine (second son
of the Emperor Paul), who renounced the
throne in favour of his younger brother
Nicholas. English caricature, 1826.

(*opposite*) The Emperor Nicholas I as Grand
Duke with the Grand Duchess Alexandra and
their eldest son, the future Emperor Alexander
II. Contemporary print.

Nicholas I drives along the embankment of the
River Neva.
After a painting by Sverchkov.

Scenes from the coronation of Nicholas I
in Moscow in 1826. (*top*) The public announcement of the coronation; (*bottom*) the feast given
to the people by Nicholas I.

(*top*) The return of their Majesties to the
Granovity Chamber after the coronation
ceremony;
(*bottom*) The departure of their Majesties from
Moscow.

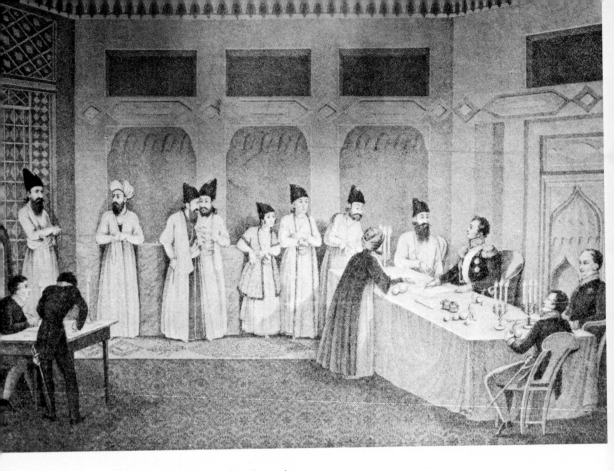

The signing of the Peace of Turkmanchay on
10 February 1828 after the defeat of Persia by
the Russians. After a painting by Mashkov.

Russian officers of the
reign of Nicholas I, most
military-minded of all
the Tsars.
From M. A. Demidoff's
Voyage, 1840.

(*opposite centre*) Nicholas I
and his staff attend the
Grand Review in Windsor
Great Park during his visit
to England in 1844.

(*opposite bottom*) Russian
landowners and their serfs.
French caricatures show
a contrast with the
idyllic picture of rural
life generally portrayed
in Russian sources.
From G. Doré, *Histoire de
la sainte Russie*, 1854.

The five Decembrists hanged on a bastion of the Peter and Paul Fortress in St Petersburg on 13 July 1826: Pestel, Ryleyev, Muravyov, Kakhovsky and Bestuzhev-Ryumin.

Nicholas I, from a contemporary print.

the application of the law in its full rigour, personally ratifying or changing many of the sentences – and thus deciding exactly how many blows the victims should receive.[39] Although nothing can be said in defence of such cruelty, history has dealt unjustly with Nicholas's reputation by comparison with that of Alexander I, whose personal responsibility for sanctioning widespread floggings with their attendant fatalities was possibly no less. Yet Alexander has gone down to posterity as the blessed Tsar, whereas his successor became known as *Nikolay Palkin* ('Nicholas the Stick'). Harsh as the system was, both Tsars did at least inherit it – they did not devise it. And both did at least render it slightly less inhumane. Alexander abolished the slitting of nostrils, and Nicholas banned the knout in 1845 – after Alexander had condemned knouting as 'inhuman cruelty' and set up a committee to consider its abolition – but kept it on the statute book all the same. Alexander and Nicholas also inherited the system under which the majority of their subjects were in effect slaves as serfs or state peasants. Each Tsar recognized the condition of the peasantry as needing reform, and Nicholas once described serfdom as a 'palpable and obvious evil'.[40] However, neither was willing or able to dismantle the system, though both contemplated change and introduced minor innovations. Meagre as their achievements in improving peasant status were, Nicholas was at least a less ineffectual protector of the peasantry than was his predecessor.

If history has dealt less kindly with the later Emperor's reputation, this is perhaps due to his failure to combine severity with noble phrases on the scale of an Alexander I. Nor was Nicholas's reputation enhanced by occasional flashes of a gallows humour all his own. His personal touch is well illustrated by the affair of two Jews caught illegally crossing a river on the south-western marches of the empire in 1827. Reporting to the Tsar, the local acting governor-general recommended the imposition of the death penalty. But Nicholas rejected this advice, writing that the culprits were each to be driven twelve times through the ranks one thousand strong. 'Thank God [the Tsar went on, not entirely accurately] we have never had capital punishment and I shall not be found introducing it.'[41] Recounting this episode, Schiemann correctly points out that twelve thousand blows were in effect equivalent to the death penalty, and in its most hideous form – but adds that this 'obviously did not occur to the Tsar'.[42] Yet Nicholas had commanded a guards division, and well knew what twelve thousand blows signified. He surely did not make the remark innocently – it was in fact one of the occasions when the grim monarch came near to cracking a joke.

The mock execution of Dostoyevsky and twenty others in St Petersburg in 1849 furnishes a better known example of such gruesome humour. After the accused had received sentence of death for offences which included participation in a political discussion circle, the Emperor commuted their fate to imprisonment

– but secretly, thinking it educative or amusing for them to go out believing that their last hour had come. In the Semyonovsky Square in St Petersburg on 22 December the Tsar's officials and troops enacted every detail of a real execution – down to the customary drum rolls, the funereal chasuble worn by the attendant priest, and the robing of the condemned in the special white shrouds in which, for convenience of disposal, they were to meet their doom. This sadistic farce continued even after the soldiers of the firing squad had received the order to take aim at the three prisoners first scheduled for dispatch. Only when they faced the levelled muskets did another drum roll herald the announcement of the commuted sentences.[43]

As this episode reminds one, the Tsar was a great hounder of writers. He began his reign by hanging a minor poet, the Decembrist Ryleyev, and by starting a campaign of petty harassment against a major one, Pushkin. At the time of the Decembrist revolt, Pushkin had been living in exile, but his name began to figure more and more during the investigation of the conspiracy as that of its poetical inspiration. Noting this, the Tsar suddenly summoned Pushkin to his presence. Small of stature, with dark, curly hair and sidewhiskers, exhausted from four days and nights of travel, cold and no doubt frightened, the greatest Russian of the age faced his tall and immaculate master. The Tsar asked him about his relations with the Decembrists, and Pushkin frankly admitted that he would have joined them if he had been in St Petersburg at the time – a dangerous confession had not the Emperor realized that a tame poet might become an asset to him. Though of unsoldierly appearance – his turnout particularly sloppy on this occasion – Pushkin made a good impression on Nicholas, who remarked at a ball later in the evening that he had just been talking to the cleverest man in Russia.[44] The poet for his part was charmed by the Emperor, especially when Nicholas proposed to act as Pushkin's personal censor – thus freeing him (or so it seemed) from the irksome interference of the ordinary censorship. However, the Emperor's patronage came to involve constant persecution through his police chief; and without freeing Pushkin from the regular censorship either.

The thirty years of Nicholas's reign were a period of severe repression, whether or not one accepts the division of his rule into three phases of increasing rigour – those provoked by the Decembrist revolt of 1825; by the Polish and other European revolutions of 1830–1; and by the European revolutions of 1848–9. These dates were only three high points in a series of provocations great and small which the Tsar stood ever poised to punish, whether he faced an entire revolutionary people in arms or a single ill-disciplined Russian schoolboy.

Three agencies of control in particular bear the stamp of the Tsar's personality: the censorship, a specially created police organization and the army.

A variety of bodies exercised censorship. They included an ecclesiastical censorship and that conducted by the security police, as well as a committee charged with the censorship of censors – apart from which almost any department of state could interfere with the printed word if it judged its own interests to be affected. But the chief censor was the Emperor himself. That there should be a strict ban on all adverse criticism of his person and government was only natural. But this was not enough for a Tsar who found even his subjects' approval an impertinence. 'Neither blame nor praise [he ordained in characteristic style] is compatible with the dignity of the government . . . One must obey and keep one's thoughts to oneself.'[45] Whether his subjects' opinions were loyal or disloyal mattered little to the Tsar in comparison with the enormity of them holding any opinions at all.

It was to discourage such tendencies that Nicholas founded his 'higher police', a political security force consisting of two branches – the corps of uniformed gendarmes and the Third Section, which came directly under the Tsar as a branch of His Majesty's imperial chancery. The head of the Third Section controlled the gendarmes and also a network of spies and *agents provocateurs*. General Benckendorff planned this apparatus, and became its first chief. It is not easy to think of him as a scourge of freedom, since he was somewhat incompetent and more of a ladies' man than the Himmler or Beria of his age; but his loyalty and obedience were not in doubt, which is what chiefly recommended him to Nicholas. In theory the political police was to help the population rather than to control it. When Benckendorff asked for general policy instructions, the Tsar is said to have held out a handkerchief and replied: 'Here is your directive. The more tears you wipe away with this handkerchief, the more faithfully you will serve my ends.'[46] Hence the gendarmes' style of operating more in sorrow than in anger. Polite young men of good family staffed the corps, with the result that a defaulting gentleman at least had a chance of being taken into custody by someone capable of addressing him in decent French.

Despite the importance of his censorship and political police, it was above all on the Russian army that Nicholas relied, and it was the army which became the most characteristic institution of his régime. A drill-sergeant at heart, perhaps, the Emperor could yet bend generals to his will and made great use of them to manage civilian affairs. That his reign has been called a quasi-military dictatorship by the Tsar is not surprising when one remembers that there was a period in the 1840s when no less than ten out of thirteen ministers of the crown were generals. Nicholas's army could present a military pageant as spectacular, probably, as any other army of his time could stage. Its mere size was awesome by the standards of the day, besides which the Russian soldier could deliver as smart a goose-step as any other soldier in the world – marching along with a full glass of water on his shako and not spilling a single drop. But such circus tricks could not compensate for inferior weapons, shortage of ammunition and over-emphasis on parade-ground evolutions. Military morale was low, the troops being peasants pressed into service for twenty-five years' harsh usage, feared in the Russian villages as a fate worse than death.

Besides suppressing mutinous Russians, the imperial army also served to crush peoples who formed an unwilling part of the Empire. It put down the great Polish revolt of 1830–1 after the Poles had gained some successes. The victorious Tsar set up a citadel with guns which could reduce Warsaw to ruins at any sign of further trouble – and that he would do so without flinching no Pole could doubt. He also presided over victorious wars against Persia and Turkey in the late 1820s; and in 1849 he lived up to his growing reputation as gendarme of Europe – sending Russian troops to support the Habsburg Monarchy by putting down the Hungarian revolution. But though Hungarians, Turks, Persians and Poles all suffered defeat, Nicholas's armies were less effective against the independent Caucasian mountaineers, who defied him throughout his reign. Above all it was the Crimean War of 1853–6 which revealed the inefficiency of the imperial drill-sergeant's military and administrative machine. When Nicholas died of an affliction of the lungs on 18 February 1855, his system had clearly failed to justify itself – as had the official ideology of his reign: autocracy, Orthodoxy and Russian nationalism.

In many ways the Emperor's policies had produced an effect opposite to that intended, for methods so despotic and often ludicrous in their details antagonized even the most moderately inclined of Russians. The result was that revolution became and remained a more attractive cause in Russia than it might ever have been if the supreme gendarme had not stamped out the faintest sparks of fancied insubordination so ferociously over nearly a third of a century. The Emperor's very zeal in defending the house of Romanov thus contributed to the eventual doom of the dynasty. Eager to destroy revolution, he helped to make it respectable.

Part 6   Decline and Fall

29 Alexander II   1855-81

Eldest son of Nicholas I, the Emperor Alexander II (born 17 April 1818) was to go down to history as the liberator of his serfs and as a reforming Tsar, though his career as heir to the throne had given little promise of such developments. When the dying father – true, almost with his expiring breath, to the military style of the dynasty – told his son 'I hand over to you my command'[1] he chose words well designed to evoke an echo in the Tsarevich, for Alexander shared the fixation on military trivialities which had now distinguished five Emperors in succession. Like so many predecessors on the throne, he was fascinated less by the art of war in general than by the evolutions of the drill ground as enshrined in Prussian military doctrine. He visited Berlin and Potsdam at the age of eleven, and cavorted on parade in Cossack garb before receiving from King William III the appointment of Colonel to the Third Prussian Uhlan Regiment – after which the boy insisted on wearing his new Prussian uniform for the rest of his stay. As Alexander grew older, his military studies impressed the Emperor Nicholas as too superficial, and instructions were given to make the Tsarevich 'a soldier in his soul, otherwise he'll be lost in our age'.[2]

Alexander was not to develop into a tough, straightforward army officer like Nicholas I. More complex and malleable, he seemed in some ways to resemble his uncle, the Emperor Alexander I, rather than his father. But the younger Alexander had a kinder heart than either of these predecessors on the throne, and the tears which sprang so easily to his eyes derived from warmer sympathies. He would try to help the unfortunate and oppressed, as on the occasion when he was walking by a canal with his tutor at the age of thirteen, and chanced to catch sight of an ailing (or drunken?) elderly workman who lay there groaning under a dirty mat; he rushed to comfort the old man, wiped away his tears and left him a gold coin.[3]

Alexander's kindness as Tsarevich impressed Herzen when the two happened to meet in Vyatka, Herzen's place of exile.

The heir's appearance [Herzen wrote] did not express the narrow severity or cold and merciless cruelty of his father. His features were more indicative of benevolence and apathy. He was about twenty years of age, but was already beginning to put on weight.[4]

That the bulky Tsarevich's sympathies went beyond mere facial expression was proved when he later interceded on Herzen's behalf with the Emperor. The encounter with Herzen took place during the journey through the Russian Empire undertaken by Alexander as grand duke in 1837, when he spent seven months visiting thirty provinces and penetrated as far east as Tobolsk – the first Romanov heir or Tsar ever to set foot on Siberian soil. True to his kindly nature, Alexander took this opportunity to confer graciously with surviving Decembrist exiles now beginning their third decade of banishment. Once again the Tsarevich appealed to the Tsar on behalf of his persecuted subjects, with the result that Decembrists found their lot lightened in certain ways. But for a general amnesty they had to await Alexander's coronation, when the survivors at last returned from exile – as did Dostoyevsky together with others banished in 1849.

Alexander's inspection of the Russian Empire in 1837 was a rapid tour largely devoted to official engagements, and these naturally continued to loom large in the extensive foreign travels which he made in 1838–9. The expedition lasted some sixteen months, and the young grand duke's programme embraced almost every country in western Europe excluding France and the Iberian peninsula. He took dinner with Queen Victoria in Buckingham Palace, but his visits to Germany proved the most productive, leading to his betrothal to Princess Mary of Hessen-Darmstadt. Although the Russian Emperor and Empress opposed the match at first, preferring a union with the house of Karlsruhe, Alexander insisted on having his own way – and was ready to renounce the throne rather than yield.

By carrying this point against such a father as Nicholas I, the Tsarevich showed how obstinate he could be; but it was also characteristic that he allowed the situation to develop in a manner ill befitting the love life of a future Emperor. Not yet united to his princess, he sought to break off the engagement and marry a Polish woman, Olga Kalinowski. This led to a clash with a father rootedly opposed to Poles and inconstancy in any shape or form. Nicholas also complained at this time that the young Alexander resented his advice, played whist in the evenings while on military manœuvres and had taken up smoking. At one point the Tsar even spoke of serving his son as Peter the Great had served the Tsarevich Alexis[5] – a threat which often recurred over the years in moments of domestic tension among Romanovs. What concerned Nicholas was the prospect of Russia one day

falling into the hands of a man who was not master of himself,[6] and later developments bore out these forebodings to some extent. Though Alexander's marriage
to the future Empress Mary was fruitful and in many ways harmonious until her
death in 1880, his reputation continued to suffer from various amorous escapades.
Lacking his father's self-confidence and discretion, he could not carry off these
affairs with impunity, besides which the modern age was already casting its
shadow over the court of St Petersburg. No longer could even a Russian autocrat
behave just as he pleased – he must increasingly take public opinion into account.

Though Alexander was an unsatisfactory heir in his vagueness, occasional laziness and inability to carry off his erotic adventures with proper imperial panache,
he was nevertheless his father's son. He was a staunch conservative, fully accepting
the principles of government followed by Nicholas I; to some, indeed, he seemed
even more of a diehard. Nicholas came to trust his heir sufficiently to invest him
with such responsible offices as that of chairman of two of the secret committees
set up to study the serf problem and made him his own deputy during absences
from St Petersburg – in addition to various high military appointments.

Succeeding at the age of thirty-six, Alexander II was, in the words of a recent
English biographer, 'perhaps the best-prepared heir-apparent ever to ascend the
Russian throne'.[7] It was as well that he should be, for he inherited a situation
complex and intractable in the extreme.

Although Alexander had shown himself so convinced a supporter of his father's
reactionary system of government, his accession aroused widespread hopes for
change such as commonly follow the death of a despotic ruler. The new Tsar
satisfied some of these expectations at the time of his coronation in 1856 with
concessions in the areas of taxation and military recruitment, as with milder
policies towards national and religious minorities of his empire. He also eased
restrictions imposed under Nicholas on foreign travel. To some extent these
features repeat the pattern which had developed in 1801 after the accession of
Alexander's 'blessed' namesake and uncle. However, as already indicated, the
second Alexander was no copy of the first. Less addicted to high-minded declara-
tions, he was concerned to translate word into deed by enacting reforms which
should change the face of Russia.

Among these reforms the emancipation of the serfs has pride of place, being
the most significant single episode in Russian nineteenth-century history as a
whole – as also in Alexander's own public life. Once the new Emperor had decided
to abolish slavery, he showed typical stubbornness in pushing the plan through
against many obstacles and difficulties. In an address to members of the Moscow
gentry on 30 March 1856, probably the most momentous speech ever made by
any Tsar, he stated that: 'The existing condition of owning souls cannot remain

unchanged. It is better to abolish serfdom from above than to wait until it begins to abolish itself from below.'[8] Fear of peasant revolution was, accordingly, prominent among Alexander's motives for promoting a reform which also seemed essential in the interests of the empire's economic efficiency and international reputation, not to mention humanitarian considerations.

The Tsar's first practical measure was to establish a secret committee under his own chairmanship to study the problem of emancipation, a step which seemed to promise little to those who knew that Nicholas I had established many such secret committees in his time, but without finding any satisfactory solution to the problem. Moreover, Alexander's new committee was largely conservative in complexion, and at first appeared to adopt delaying tactics until the Tsar served notice of more serious intent by making his radical-minded brother, the Grand Duke Constantine, a member. In late 1857, Alexander took an especially important step when he publicly added to the principle already enunciated (that the serfs must be freed) the vital condition that they must also acquire land of their own. The guide-lines for emancipation were now clear and there could be no turning back, though countless details – particularly those concerning the amount of land which the peasants were to obtain and the conditions on which they were to hold it – continued to pose baffling problems. But the Tsar refused to regard them as insoluble. He converted his secret committee into the 'main committee for peasant affairs' and took a leading part in its deliberations. He set up editing commissions and local committees to study the complex details of the problem and toured the provinces extensively, making it clear to the provincial gentry that he had definitely decided to end serfdom. On 19 February 1861 he signed the emancipation statute, and was one of those who publicly read out the flowery emancipation manifesto from the pulpits when the matter became public.

The complicated statute of several hundred pages was beyond the understanding of most peasants, but as its implications grew clearer they began to feel that they had been cheated, and took to rioting – or waited for a second, 'real' emancipation which never materialized. Receiving too little land for their needs, and compelled to make excessive payment for it, they had ample grounds for discontent. Moreover, it was partly through Alexander's own interventions that they obtained so poor a bargain. He had not ceased to regard himself as a champion of the landowning gentry, and the elaborate negotiations preceding emancipation had often seen him siding with the owners against the serfs on points of detail, though he would not abandon the general principle of emancipation with land, so unwelcome to the majority of landlords. However, the Tsar's firm policy on emancipation made him the chief architect of the most important reform of the century, which – with all its defects – released many millions from bondage. He had not only freed his slaves, as Abraham Lincoln was to do later in the same decade, but had also avoided

Alexander II (ruled 1855–81). Son of Nicholas I
and sharing his father's conservative views,
he nevertheless emancipated the serfs.
He was assassinated by revolutionaries.

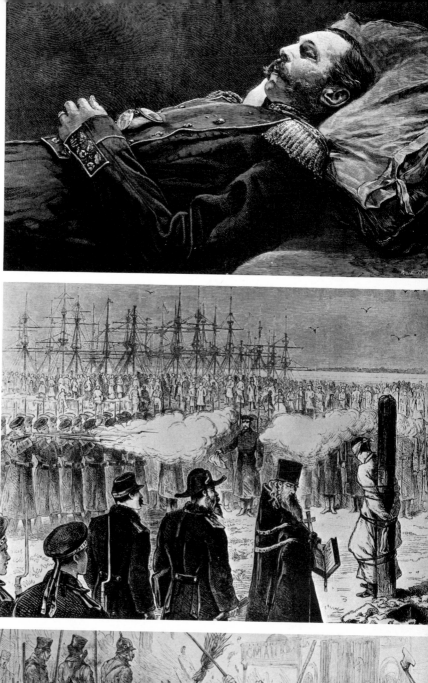

(*opposite*) The successful bomb attack by revolutionaries on Alexander II on the afternoon of 1 March 1881 on the Catherine Quay in St Petersburg.
This picture gives an artist's impression of the effect of the first bomb.

Alexander II after death.

Lieutenant Nicholas Sukhanov, nihilist and naval officer, executed by firing squad in Cronstadt in 1882 for complicity in the assassination of Alexander II.

(*opposite*) 1 March 1881. The explosion of the second bomb on the Catherine Quay, leading to the death of Alexander II.

A Jew is assaulted while soldiers fail to intervene: a scene from the Kiev pogrom of 1881. The new Tsar, Alexander III, held anti-semitic views and the imperial authorities, national and local, were often far from zealous in protecting the Jewish population.

Russian peasants in the second half
of the nineteenth century.

Alexander III as Tsarevich with his wife,
the former Princess of Denmark, and son.

Alexander III. (*opposite*) The Empress Mary, wife of Alexander III.

Constantine Pobedonostsev was Chief Procurator of the Holy Synod from 1880 to 1905.
A tutor to both Alexander III and Nicholas II,
this notorious reactionary became a considerable
power behind the throne.

civil war and secured land for the ex-slaves – achievements which both eluded the American president, as has been noted,[9] though he is generally judged the greater statesman of the two.

Emancipation was merely the first and most important in the long series of reforms presided over by Alexander II. Among these complex enactments reaching into almost every department of Russian life, the reorganization of the judicial system on European models was probably the most successful. By establishing trial by jury, judges independent of the administration, public proceedings and an independent bar, the legal reforms brought an important new element into Russian public life, as did the institution of elective local government by zemstvo (rural council) and town council. Other reforms liberalized the education system, and embraced finance, censorship and the armed forces. In particular, the reduction in the period of compulsory military service from the twenty-five years customary under Nicholas I to six years and the new provisions removing the element of class privilege from conscription did much to lighten an intolerable burden. Particularly influential in creating a more civilized tone in Russian life were the restrictions imposed on corporal punishment both for civilians and members of the forces. Though legalized beatings were not entirely abolished, the murderous judicial floggings of Alexander I and Nicholas I disappeared from the scene.

In these matters the Tsar took – and needed to take – less initiative than he had required to push through emancipation, but remained the moving spirit. The final decision was always his, so that he has been called his own prime minister,[10] as, indeed, were all the nineteenth-century Emperors. He thus earned his title of Tsar-liberator. Yet he always strove to remain an absolute monarch in the tradition of his father, and would brook no encroachment on the autocratic prerogative. When members of the provincial gentry ventured to argue the general principles of emancipation (instead of confining themselves to discussing the implementation of principles already enunciated from the throne), the Tsar became angry and forbade such indiscipline. He also prevented the press from considering the problems of emancipation after a brief period of open discussion. Always the autocrat, Alexander showed further displeasure when certain gentlemen in the province of Tver dared to make constitutional suggestions challenging the power of the central government. He exiled the local marshal of gentry, while thirteen liberal-minded trouble-makers were sent to the Peter and Paul Fortress for a time. Nor would the reforming autocrat heed the proposal – sometimes mooted by diehards as well as by radicals – that he should summon a national assembly such as had functioned in the sixteenth and seventeenth centuries and had since acquired the romantic aura of a traditional Russian democratic institution. Neither this nor any other diminution of his absolute power would he tolerate.

Alexander's reign witnessed intensive military and political activity on the borderlands of empire, where two far-flung areas – the peripheries of European and of Asiatic Russia – presented widely different problems.

On the marches of European Russia opportunities were more strictly limited by the greater interest of other major powers. The Tsar's prospects were not improved by the Crimean War, which Russia was in process of losing at the time of his accession, as the fall of Sevastopol emphasized in August 1855. The new Tsar visited the Crimean front, but shortly afterwards felt compelled to swallow his pride and accept the peace terms proposed by Austria, thereby taking the first significant policy decision of his reign. However, Crimean defeat proved a blessing in disguise to Russia, for the administrative inefficiency laid bare by the conduct of operations was so flagrant as to prompt even extreme conservatives to contemplate radical change. To this extent the battle for emancipation was won on the fields of Alma and Inkerman.

Having gained in some ways from her humiliation in the Crimea, Russia went on to defeat the Turks some twenty years later in the Russo-Turkish War of 1877–8 – no glorious victory, for the conduct of the war on the Russian side revealed continuing incompetence sadly reminiscent of the Crimean experience. The aftermath of war was no more encouraging, for the intervention of other European powers restricted Russian gains. Moreover, one major achievement of the war – the liberation of Bulgaria from Turkish oppression – only gave further cause for dissatisfaction since the Tsar's soldiers had apparently died to win for foreigners freedoms still denied to Russians.

Alexander's conduct of foreign affairs was hesitant, vague and weak – by contrast with his comparative steadfastness in handling domestic reform in the first half of the reign. This feebleness informed the Tsar's attitude to the Pan-Slav movement of the 1870s, when the feeling grew that Russia (as eldest brother in the Slav family) should protect junior brethren against foreign oppression. Although the Empress Mary and the Tsar's eldest son (the Tsarevich Alexander Aleksandrovich) supported the Pan-Slavs, the Tsar himself was hostile – yet seemed incapable of keeping the movement within bounds. The most striking instance of this collapse of authority was the departure, shortly before the outbreak of Russo-Turkish hostilities, of several thousand Russian volunteers to fight for the Serbs against the Turks in defiance of the Emperor's wishes – a challenge to the autocratic principle such as would have been unthinkable under Nicholas I.

Alexander showed similar vacillation on the sprawling frontiers of Asiatic Russia. Here the absence of serious military opposition from China or the peoples of central Asia encouraged the acquisition of enormous new areas which made this reign the great age of nineteenth-century Russian colonial expansion. By 1860 Russia had annexed two vast territories from the Chinese – the left bank

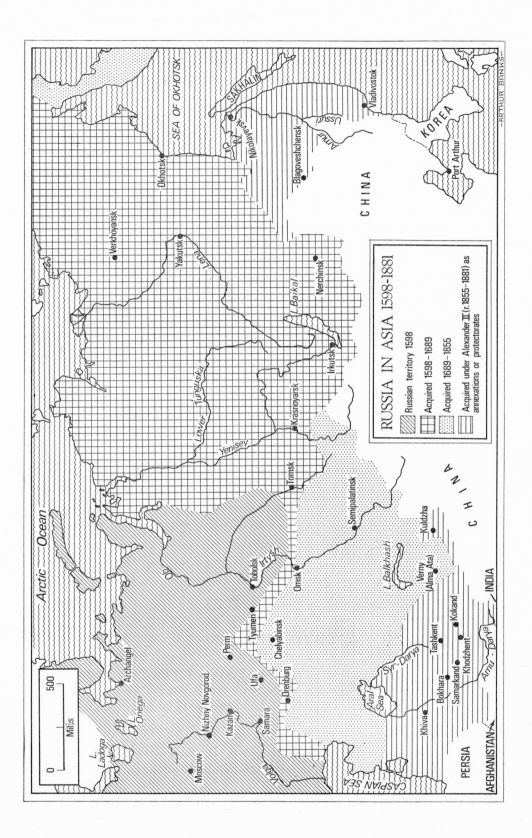

RUSSIA IN ASIA 1598-1881

Russian territory 1598
Acquired 1598 – 1689
Acquired 1689 – 1855
Acquired under Alexander II (r.1855–1881) as annexations or protectorates

Arctic Ocean

SEA OF OKHOTSK

SAKHALIN

KOREA

Port Arthur

Vladivostok

Ussuri

Amur

Blagoveshchensk

CHINA

Nikolaevsk

Okhotsk

Verkhoyansk

Yakutsk

Lena

L.Baikal

Nerchinsk

Lower Tunguska

Irkutsk

Yenisey

Krasnoyarsk

Tomsk

Semipalatinsk

Kuldzha

CHINA

L.Balkhash

Verny (Alma Ata)

Tashkent

Kokand

Khodzhent

Samarkand

Bokhara

Khiva

Aral Sea

Syr-Darya

Amu-Darya

AFGHANISTAN

PERSIA

INDIA

CASPIAN SEA

Volga

Samara

Orenburg

Ufa

Chelyabinsk

Tyumen

Tobolsk

Irtysh

Omsk

Ob

Perm

Kazan

Nizhny Novgorod

Moscow

Archangel

L.Onega

L.Ladoga

500

0

Miles

–ARTHUR BANKS–

of the River Amur and the Maritime Province on the Sea of Japan down to Vladivostok. In central Asia, Russian military activity continued throughout much of the reign, vastly extending the bounds of empire to approximately the present borders of the USSR with Persia, Afghanistan, India and China.

The Emperor's attitude to these activities was mixed. Himself a patriotic Russian – though one of German descent – he approved in principle of imperial expansion, a cause which he had already championed as Tsarevich. But he was also peacefully disposed, not wishing to antagonize an England increasingly concerned with the threat to India posed by Russian armies advancing in Asia. It thus happened again and again that the Tsar sponsored sincere assurances of his pacific intentions in St Petersburg, only to find his words belied two thousand miles away by Russian warlords who knew that they could act independently without being called to account. This created an impression of weakness and duplicity on the part of the Tsar – perhaps unfairly. He seems, rather, to have possessed a curious mental flaw whereby he could simultaneously entertain two mutually contradictory propositions. His ambivalence served Russian interests to the extent that peaceful diplomatic postures in St Petersburg helped to lull foreign suspicions while Russian generals were continuing to annex alien territories on a sub-continental scale beyond the Caspian. But by permitting distant proconsuls to flout his wishes and instructions with impunity, the Tsar did a greater disservice to the cause of autocracy than successful empire-building could counterbalance, since it is hard for absolute rule to flourish under a monarch known to permit open indiscipline.

One subject people, that of Poland, was unlikely to complain of any failure by Alexander to exercise his autocratic will. The Tsar began his reign – as King of Poland as well as Tsar of Russia – with concessions. He was prepared to govern Poland mildly provided always that she submitted fully to Russian domination and did not entertain the dreams of independence against which he issued warnings during a visit to Warsaw made in the second year of his reign. However, Russo-Polish relations remained a serious problem which the second Polish revolution of the century – that of 1863-4 – gravely aggravated. Alexander suppressed the rising with great severity and henceforward treated the Poles as a conquered nation, behaving towards them more as a Nicholas I than as a Tsar-liberator. With another subject people, the Finns, the Emperor remained relatively popular, no doubt because the citizens of Helsingfors appreciated the realities of power more nicely than did those of Warsaw.

Least welcome to the Tsar among the many innovations of his reign was a rising revolutionary movement such as had not previously existed in the empire or indeed anywhere else. When the revolutionaries first emerged – to be christened 'nihilists' by Turgenev in his novel *Fathers and Children* (1862) – they were long-haired, voluble, earnest, eccentrically garbed, bespectacled intellectuals of both sexes who seemed a curiosity rather than a danger. However, the movement gradually switched its emphasis from impassioned protest to violent deed. The late 1850s saw the first demonstrations of student unrest such as led to the closure of St Petersburg University in 1861–2. Alexander was inclined to meet these disturbances with conciliation, replacing his reactionary minister of education (a retired admiral) with a milder figure, and giving the key post of governor-general of St Petersburg to the easy-going and popular Prince Suvorov. But such concessions did little to allay the growing unrest of the period. In 1862 mysterious fires devastated St Petersburg and were widely attributed to revolutionary arsonists, while the outbreak of Polish rebellion in 1863 suggested that the periphery of the empire was as combustible as its capital. Illegal political manifestoes, some calling for the murder of the imperial family, began to appear in St Petersburg – on one occasion scattered along the Nevsky Prospekt by a galloping horseman. It was for his part in composing such material and smuggling it into Russia that the minor poet Michael Mikhaylov suffered arrest in 1861, and was taken to Siberia in fetters after undergoing the first political trial of the reign. Mikhaylov's arrest preceded that of two better-known spokesmen of nihilism in Chernyshevsky and Pisarev, while the Tsar's right to vary at whim the sentences of his courts made him seem responsible for each individual act of repression in the eyes of nihilists increasingly disposed to treat him as a personal enemy.

As the decade progressed, members of the revolutionary underground began to see as their ideal the assassin who would strike down the autocrat in an act of self-sacrificing people's vengeance. It was from a particularly virulent nihilist group called 'Hell' that the first serious potential regicide emerged in Dmitry Karakozov, who – typically of the period – combined religious with political mania. No less characteristic was his status as a former student . . . and one, moreover, who had been expelled from two universities. Exalted by his craving for martyrdom and armed with a revolver, Karakozov waylaid the sovereign in the Summer Garden in St Petersburg on 4 April 1866; but a loyal bystander deflected his aim at the last moment, and the Tsar escaped unhurt. Karakozov suffered arrest, trial and public hanging. But judicial revenge could not repair the damage done to Alexander's political attitude by the assassin's bullet, especially as another attempt occurred in 1867, when a Pole fired at the Tsar during a visit to Paris.

As a sign of his changed mood, Alexander entrusted the investigation of the Karakozov affair to 'Hangman' Muravyov, so called because of his savage repression of Polish rebellion. In the same spirit, Alexander appointed Count Peter Shuvalov head of the Third Section, and since he was a wholehearted delegator once he had found someone whom he trusted, this new chief of his security police became for several years virtual dictator of the country so far as internal affairs were concerned. Shuvalov persuaded the Tsar to abolish the post of governor-general of St Petersburg – which meant dismissing the easy-going Prince Suvorov – and to make General Trepov, scourge of nihilists, city prefect and thus master of the capital. Another counter-revolutionary move was the appointment of the notorious reactionary Count Dmitry Tolstoy as minister of education. A period of repression had begun, though the name 'white terror', sometimes given to it, is perhaps over-dramatic, and the Tsar himself – now almost a voluntary captive of the police – was in a sense his own chief victim.

In the 1870s nihilist forces cowed by the white terror gradually began to reassert themselves, first pacifically and later in an atmosphere of accelerating violence. The peasantry became the chief target for their efforts when large numbers of young nihilists took part in the 'pilgrimages to the people' of 1873–4 by going into the villages, sometimes in peasant disguise, and attempting to revolutionize these 'dark people' directly. But the peasants were too sunk in political ignorance – and too devoted to their Tsar – to recognize these earnest boys and girls as bearers of the light, and often reacted by handing them over to the police.

After this attempt to compass the political evangelization of rural Russia had ended in fiasco, many of the nihilists concerned figured in two mass trials and their movement as a whole seemed to have little future. However, they rallied their forces, abandoned the countryside, embraced the cities, established more centralized organizations and set themselves to develop the techniques of revolutionary terrorism. January 1878 saw the beginning of this new phase when a nihilist girl shot at and wounded the hated Trepov as revenge for the flogging of an imprisoned revolutionary who had refused to remove his cap in the general's presence. Other victims of nihilist bullets or daggers during the same year included the chief of the Third Section – one of Shuvalov's successors – who was stabbed to death on a main street of the capital. The following year saw a further attempt on the Tsar's life. On 2 April the nihilist Alexander Solovyov ambushed him as he came out for his morning walk in the grounds of the Winter Palace, firing five shots which the Emperor managed to avoid. The authorities tried and hanged Solovyov, as they did a score more nihilists during the last years of the reign, but these counter-measures achieved no more than a temporary halt in terrorism.

A crucial episode in the nihilist campaign was the formation in summer 1879 of People's Will, a ruthless association of political conspirators. On 26 August they met in a forest and formally pronounced sentence of death on Alexander Romanov. This was in many ways an irrational decision, for the conspirators realized that they had no prospect of assuming power even if the assassination should succeed; the most that they could hope was to replace the reactionary

Alexander II with the unknown quantity of Alexander III. However, reason was not always decisive in a movement increasingly powered by mystical exaltation and the yearning for personal martyrdom. Deciding to use explosives rather than revolvers, the nihilists of People's Will put no less than six such attempts under way in late 1879 and early 1880, aiming three of them at the imperial train in which Alexander returned to St Petersburg from his Crimean residence in Livadia. One mine proved useless because the Tsar did not follow the expected route, another because it did not explode at the crucial moment, while the third charge was successfully detonated under the railway line on the outskirts of Moscow – but struck the wrong train owing to a failure in nihilist intelligence. Most spectacular of the failures was the huge explosion set off in the Winter Palace itself at twenty minutes past six on the evening of 5 February 1880. The bomb was intended to destroy the Emperor in his dining-room; it failed to do so because he happened to be late for his meal, but killed or injured over fifty people – mostly soldiers of the palace guard.

A lull in terrorism followed this outrage, and the Tsar and his advisers took the opportunity to give more careful consideration to steps against the nihilists, who still seemed ill equipped to challenge an embattled empire – consisting as they did of only a few hundred students and hangers-on. Himself increasingly demoralized and apathetic, Alexander decided to put his trust in General Loris-Melikov, a proven exponent of counter-terrorism in the provinces, who now received dictatorial powers over the country. However, he had barely assumed his new role before he too became the target for nihilist bullets when an aspiring assassin fired at him. Despite this inauspicious beginning the new overlord clung to his policy of conciliating the discontented and winning public opinion over to the side of the authorities. Although he was not outstandingly successful in achieving either aim, one of his initiatives is of special interest. He persuaded the Tsar to approve the principle of admitting persons elected by the public or zemstvos to bodies entitled to advise the government on legislation. This measure could conceivably have marked a step – though a very tentative one indeed – along the road to constitutional government.

Meanwhile Alexander's position had suffered further erosion through the indiscretions of his love life – in particular, his liaison with Princess Catherine Dolgoruky. This association began when the sovereign was in his late forties and his paramour some thirty years younger – a difference in ages thought to render more shocking a clandestine intrigue which involved the princess in entering the Winter Palace through a back door to keep assignations with her lover. When the affair gave rise to talk, Alexander established her in a luxurious apartment in St Petersburg. But threats to his life by nihilists later persuaded him to install her in the palace itself – and this during the lifetime of the Empress Mary, whose declining days were enlivened by the sound of her husband's bastards playing in the room above her own. Although Nicholas I had enjoyed a similar arrangement with Barbara Nelidov, Alexander was ill equipped to carry off such a situation discreetly. Deeply attached to Catherine, he had long wished to marry her, and did so morganatically forty days after the Empress's death in June 1880. His bride now took the title of Princess Yuryevsky, but this by no means made an honest woman of her in the eyes of her more censorious critics, who included the heir to the throne.

After the bomb explosion in the Winter Palace, political terrorism went underground for a time, but the plotters of People's Will did not abandon their faith in shovel and dynamite. Stalking the monarch on the streets of his capital, they sought data about his movements which would enable them to choose a suitable ambush. These researches led them to rent basement premises in Maly Sadovy Street, where they drove a tunnel under the road and laid explosive at a spot over which the Emperor regularly passed on Sunday visits to the cavalry parade-ground situated not far from the Winter Palace. The leaders of People's Will fixed on Sunday 1 March as the date for the assassination attempt. Just before one p.m. on that day the Tsar left his palace for the parade-ground according to schedule – but happened to choose a route along the Catherine Quay which did not take him over the Maly Sadovy. However, Sophia Perovsky – the ex-schoolmistress who commanded the assassins – had a reserve plan to cover such an eventuality. As soon as it became clear that Alexander was likely to return to his palace by the route which he had already taken on his outward journey, she switched to the Catherine Quay her mobile strike-force of four young men, each armed with a cumbrous bomb hastily constructed during the previous night. Having posted them, she stood at a convenient vantage-point to give warning of the Emperor's immediate approach by signalling with her handkerchief.

The imperial cavalcade made a brave sight as it careered through the snow-covered streets on its homeward journey just after two o'clock in the afternoon. Alexander sat alone in his carriage. He was driven by a coachman in dazzling livery and escorted by Cossacks mounted on black horses and resplendent in scarlet coats and fur caps. Two sleighs followed, conveying the capital's chief of police and other officers in uniform as the glittering cortège sped down Engineer Street. As it was about to turn right at the T-junction with the Catherine Quay, Perovsky showed her handkerchief and about a hundred yards from the turning one of her men flung the first infernal device. It exploded under the back axle of the Tsar's carriage, but failed to put the vehicle out of action. Himself unhurt, the Tsar might have escaped had he driven on – instead of which he insisted on descending and walked back to the scene of the explosion. After speaking briefly to his assailant, who had been put under arrest, he had just turned towards his

Nicholas II as Tsarevich. As a young man he
was chiefly interested in hunting, dancing,
theatre-going and military manœuvres.

(*above*) The coronation procession of Nicholas II in the streets of Moscow.

Nicholas II as Tsarevich with his wife, the future Empress Alexandra.

(*opposite*) Tsar Nicholas II and the Tsaritsa Alexandra in their full coronation regalia. Their coronation was celebrated in May 1896.

The disaster of Khodynka Fields near Moscow when over twelve hundred people perished in a mass stampede which occurred during the celebrations of Nicholas II's coronation.
An artists' impression based on a photograph.

Gregory Rasputin, the Siberian peasant who gained ascendancy over the Empress Alexandra and Nicholas II through his ability to cure the symptoms of haemophilia in the Tsarevich Alexis by hynoptic means.

Peter Stolypin, President of the Council of Ministers, 1906–11. He was assassinated in the presence of Nicholas II at a gala performance in the Kiev opera house.

Nicholas II with his son, the Tsarevich Alexis,
who was heir to the throne and suffered from
the hereditary disease of
haemophilia.

Nicholas II arrives at the front during World War I. In August 1915 he assumed supreme command over the Russian armed forces.

(*opposite*) The deposed Tsar Nicholas II in the grounds of the imperial palace at Tsarskoye Selo where he was held with his wife and children after the February Revolution, 1917, before being sent to Tobolsk in Siberia in August.

The deposed Tsar Nicholas II with the Tsarevich Alexis and his second daughter, the Tsarevna Tatyana.

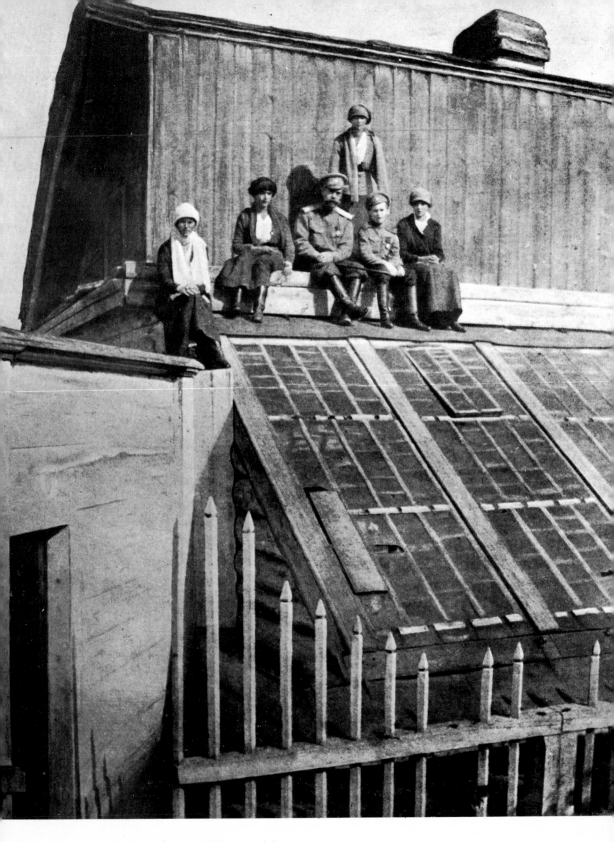

The deposed Tsar Nicholas II and the Empress
Alexandra with members of their family
under arrest at Tobolsk in western Siberia in
1918 shortly before their death at Yekaterinburg.

carriage when another nihilist, lurking unnoticed among the horrified onlookers, threw a second grenade, which exploded violently and hurled the Emperor against the railings of the quay in a flurry of blood and snow. His helmet and cloak blown off, his uniform torn to shreds, Alexander called weakly to be conveyed to the Winter Palace to die.

At three fifty-five in the afternoon the palace flag was lowered and the population of St Petersburg learnt that the reforming autocrat was no more. The general reaction was one of indifference.

With his powerful frame and large beard, Alexander III made a fine figure of a Tsar, and his bluff, 'folksy' manner supposedly commended him to the peasant masses. He was physically strong, and would entertain children by tying pokers into knots and tearing packs of cards in half with his bare hands. When involved on one celebrated occasion, in a train derailment in south Russia, he was able to hold up the roof of his carriage as it was about to collapse on members of his household. Such was the eldest surviving son of Alexander II who succeeded to the throne on his father's assassination. Popular imagination had wishfully painted the new monarch as a progressive. But in fact he was even less liberal-minded than his father and more resembled Nicholas I – in keeping with the tendency for stern, uncomplicated Romanov Tsars to alternate with those of gentler and more elusive temperament.

Born on 26 February 1845, the new Tsar had not been groomed for the throne in boyhood, for it was only in his twentieth year – when his elder brother Nicholas died – that he became heir presumptive. He had been trained for the army, and an urgent need arose to fill the many gaps in his general education. Among his tutors was the great historian of Russia, Sergey Solovyov, who inspired the Tsarevich Alexander with such an interest in his country's past that he helped to found the Imperial Russian Historical Society, and became its president. But the strongest formative influence was that of another tutor – Constantine Pobedonostsev, the intelligent and worldly but extremely reactionary statesman who was to dominate his pupil's reign and much of his successor's too. Under Pobedonostsev's eye the Tsarevich Alexander developed as a rigid conservative and nationalist. It is an irony of history that the nihilist assassins of the Catherine Quay should have given their lives to substitute for the slaughtered Tsar-liberator this unimaginative, phlegmatic, honest diehard who devoted the thirteen years of his reign to undoing much of his father's work.

The Tsarevich Alexander also disapproved of his father's liaison with the young mistress whom he had married with barely decent haste after the death of his Empress. Such impropriety much offended an heir who was himself a model family man as husband to Mary, Orthodox name of the former Princess Dagmar of Denmark. By contrast with his disreputable sire, the younger Alexander led a secluded life to which meetings of his Historical Society lent variety, as did musical soirées in which he himself took part, being a performer on the French horn and 'cello. Not that the Grand Duke Alexander was entirely a recluse. He gained some credit by his energetic measures to combat famine in the Smolensk Province in 1868, while war against the Turks in the following decade saw him commanding a formation of the Russian army. He also took part in meetings of the council of state and committee of ministers, and was by no means entirely unprepared for rule when the nihilist bomb attack precipitated him on to the throne on 1 March 1881.

After his father's assassination the new Emperor reputedly panicked, though there is no unanimity on the point, and it is hard to conceive the manly Alexander in the cringing posture which revolutionaries liked to imagine. In any case the Tsar's police and officials lost little time in arresting and putting on trial his father's assassins. The great novelist Leo Tolstoy wrote to the new Emperor pleading for the life of the condemned, but Pobedonostsev deliberately failed to pass his letter on to Alexander. On 3 April 1881 five young agents of People's Will were publicly hanged in the Semyonovsky Square in St Petersburg with the gross technical incompetence characteristic of imperial Russian executioners and in the presence of troops, crowds, officiating priests and foreign diplomats.

Besides the execution of the assassins, the first few weeks of the new reign also saw a struggle for influence over the Tsar between the forces of reform and those of reaction. The former included Loris-Melikov and the Grand Duke Constantine (the Emperor's radical uncle), while the chief reactionary remained Pobedonostsev. Despite the sovereign's conservative leanings, the result of this clash was no foregone conclusion, for the younger Alexander's opposition to his father had not excluded all filial piety and the new accession did not repeat the situation created on the death of Catherine II when the Emperor Paul had set himself to undo the work of a hated parent.

The crucial test of Alexander III's approach was his handling of Loris-Melikov's plan for limited elected representation on official bodies to be charged with advising the Tsar on legislation – a project approved by Alexander II on the morning of his death. However suspicious his heir might be that this modest proposal could prove a first step towards the constitution so dreaded by advocates of absolute rule, he did not disavow Loris-Melikov at the moment of mounting the throne, but called a series of ministerial conferences to discuss the proposals. Increasingly dominating these deliberations, Pobedonostsev scored a decisive triumph with the publication on 29 April of an accession proclamation signed by Alexander, but drafted by himself. Despite respectful references to the 'great reforms' of the previous reign, the most striking section of this manifesto was that in which the new Tsar expressed his firm resolve to uphold the autocratic principle: 'In our great grief God's voice bids us boldly take the helm of government, trusting in divine providence and believing in the strength and truth of the autocratic power which we are called upon to confirm and defend from all encroachments for the good of the people.'[11]

These words seemed like a deliberate affront to Loris-Melikov, especially as the proclamation appeared without his foreknowledge and approval. Realizing that his prospects were now hopeless, he resigned, as did some of his associates. From this point onwards Pobedonostsev's ascendancy was unchallenged. He held the post of chief procurator of the holy synod, but his influence extended beyond church affairs to policy in general, and he often had the deciding voice in determining ministerial appointments. After a short interval under another official, the ministry of the interior went to Count Dmitry Tolstoy – an indication that internal affairs would be conducted in the reactionary spirit which had informed the same minister's management of education under Alexander II. Pobedonostsev secured the appointment of another reactionary as minister of education, and the general principles of the new reign now seemed abundantly clear.

Shunning the dangers of St Petersburg, Alexander took to residing some thirty miles south of the capital at Gatchina, once the headquarters of the Tsarevich and future Emperor Paul. Here the latest Romanov Tsar lived with his family in seclusion and under heavy guard, making occasional sorties to the capital dictated by his more pressing duties. Meanwhile his police was mopping up the broken remnants of People's Will; many leading terrorists departed to voluntary exile in western Europe, and Vera Figner – the most notable nihilist still at large in Russia – was arrested in 1883. But although revolutionary terrorism had slumped, a small group of assassins was found plotting to kill the new Tsar. Home-made hand-grenades having proved so effective against Alexander II, these later terrorists decided to employ the same technique against his son, but added the refinement of priming their bombs with pellets of strychnine to make the assault doubly lethal. As the date for the attempt they chose 1 March 1887, sixth anniversary of the murder of Alexander II. However, their movements in the capital had already alerted the police, who arrested them before they could strike, the rest of their small organization being rounded up shortly afterwards. Among the five terrorists hanged for their part in this affair was Alexander Ulyanov. His brother Vladimir, later known as Lenin, was a mere youth at the time, but reputedly swore vengeance, which he exacted with interest by his role in events leading to the death of Tsar Alexander's son and successor in 1918.

Moulded by Pobedonostsev and sharing that great reactionary's devout, nationalist, ultra-conservative leanings, the Tsar brought his repressive policies to bear on many aspects of Russian life. To counter-terrorism he added a running revision of Alexander II's reforms in such a spirit that the new reign became known as the age of counter-reforms. These reached into many spheres, including judicial organization, local government and education. The emancipation of the serfs, main achievement of the previous reign, still stood; but the peasants came under the closer control of officials, while agriculture in general stagnated.

Besides many general measures designed to intensify bureaucratic domination over the whole population, other oppressive steps affected specific groups – the empire's numerous religious and national minorities. As defender of Orthodoxy, Alexander sympathized with measures taken by Pobedonostsev against the Old Believers and adherents of numerous religious sects, and also showed himself an apt pupil of his chief procurator by championing the cause of Russian nationalism at the expense of minority peoples of the empire. Other Romanov Tsars had been ardent Russian patriots, but Alexander III differed from these predecessors in his anti-German orientation – an attitude all the more surprising since his own ancestry was even more exclusively Teutonic than theirs. However, this consideration did not prevent him from 'russifying' his Baltic provinces with their German élite which had furnished the empire with so many generals and administrators since the time of Peter the Great. Alexander now imposed Russian as official language on this quarter of the realm, together with Russian educational and judicial procedures; and also had the German University of Dorpat reopened as the Russian University of Yuryev. Alexander's own dislike of Germans was well illustrated by the occasion on which a number of his officers were presented to him when he was Tsarevich. As their names, all of them obviously Teutonic – as was not unusual in the Russian army – were pronounced one after the other, Alexander showed marked impatience until at last a Slav name appeared, and evoked the curt comment: 'About time too.'[12]

Anti-semitic as well as anti-German, Alexander once annotated an official document with the words 'we must not forget that it was the Jews who crucified our Lord and spilled his precious blood'.[13] Such sentiments were frequently encountered in Russian government circles, and also among the common people – at least among those of them (Ukrainians, White Russians and others) who inhabited areas within the pale of settlement, that section of the south and west to which most Jews were legally confined. Anti-semitic agitators claimed that the murder of Alexander II was the work of the Jews (one of the condemned, Jessie Helfmann, being a Jewess), and pogroms broke out in 1881, inspired by racial and religious prejudice laced with loyalist sentiment. Although the government did not officially encourage these outrages, it tacitly permitted them until Count Dmitry Tolstoy, as minister of the interior, showed that he preferred law and order to anti-semitism, whereupon pogroms ceased to present a serious problem during the next two decades. However, Alexander proceeded to increase the legal disabilities of the Jews – imposing a quota for admission to educational institutions, banning Jewish lawyers from the Russian bar, introducing yet stricter residential restrictions and deporting Jews *en masse* from Moscow and Kiev.

Although Jews, Germans, revolutionaries, sectarians and other groups had good cause to detest Alexander III, he often received credit for an achievement which makes him unique among the Tsars – that of preserving peace throughout his reign, apart from some minor skirmishing in central Asia. This blessing earned him the title of peacemaker from his more grateful subjects. However, as the disasters of the following reign were to show, Alexander III's peace was but the calm before a sequence of appalling catastrophes.

31 Nicholas II   1894-1917

Nicholas II was born on 6 May 1868. From his tutor Pobedonostsev and his father Alexander III he acquired the political principles which he held all his life. He was convinced, like many earlier Tsars, that he owed his throne to God, and he had a keen sense of personal responsibility for preserving the autocracy intact. Believing that a sacred bond united Emperor and common people in a mystical union, he thought the intervention of elected politicians superfluous, and tended to dislike them – as he also did intellectuals in general. The assassination of his grandfather by members of the revolutionary intelligentsia helped to confirm the thirteen-year-old Tsarevich in his conservative views. But serious preoccupations were not dominant in Nicholas's childhood and youth – a time when thoughts of mystical intercourse with his people occupied him less than skating, tobogganing, theatre-going, dancing, gypsy entertainments, stag-hunting, military manœuvres and a romantic attachment to the ballerina Matilda Kshesinsky.

Having completed his formal education, the heir undertook a world tour in 1890-1, visiting Egypt, India and China. His stay in Japan was curtailed after a Japanese policeman, a Samurai, had tried to kill him with a sabre to avenge national honour affronted by the disrespectful behaviour of Nicholas and his travelling companion Prince George of Greece during visits to local temples. Saved by Prince George and his rickshaw-man from possible death, and slightly wounded in the head, the Tsarevich sailed on to Vladivostok and inaugurated the new Trans-Siberian Railway by shifting the first barrowful of soil on the Ussuri line. He returned home along the route of the projected railway, a journey which lasted two and a half months and was fêted all the way.

The young heir's unimaginative reactions to this expedition, as recorded in his diary, suggest that he was not built to the dimensions of his far-flung empire, being more of a kindly country squire by temperament than a global potentate. He had ranged the gorgeous east in the spirit of a child pottering about its backyard, and continued after his return to make an impression of immaturity such as often aroused comment. When, in 1892, the suggestion arose that Alexander III might appoint his son chairman of the Siberian railway committee, the Tsar protested that Nicholas (aged twenty-three at the time) was a mere boy whose infantile thought processes made him unsuitable. But the appointment was made, and the youthful chairman certainly showed himself quicker witted and more sensitive over the years than the ponderous father who had dismissed his claims. The Tsarevich also attended meetings of the council of state and committee of ministers, and during the famine of 1891 he headed a relief committee – one, however, which became notorious for its incompetence. Such passing brushes with affairs had done little to equip the heir for supreme rule when, on 20 October 1894, his father's death from nephritis suddenly brought him to the throne, a prospect which he had always dreaded.

Often judged a weakling, Nicholas had already shown himself able to enforce his will by insisting (like his grandfather) on marrying in defiance of his parents' wishes. His bride, Princess Alice of Hessen-Darmstadt, became the Empress Alexandra of Russia. She was deeply religious, and at first reluctant to abandon the Protestant faith of her childhood. Eventually, however, she embraced Orthodoxy, as also the autocratic principle, with such fervour that she too might have been indoctrinated from the cradle by Pobedonostsev rather than reared (as she actually was) by her grandmother Queen Victoria in Kensington Palace. Even before her marriage the beautiful and determined young bride tried to infuse her adoring 'Nicky' with a resolution alien to his nature. As Tsaritsa she became generally unpopular in court circles, being shy and excessively devoted to the society of a few favoured eccentrics. But these tendencies did not affect Nicholas's lifelong devotion to his wife.

The accession of a new Emperor raised hopes that he might relax the rigours of autocratic rule. However, in an address delivered at the beginning of his reign, Nicholas made it clear that he would do nothing of the sort. He dismissed suggestions of popular participation in government as 'insensate dreams', proclaiming his intention to maintain the autocratic principle in the tradition of his father. But he lacked the imposing physical stature and imperious manner of the born autocrat. Though far from ill-favoured in appearance, he had grown into a narrow-shouldered, dapper young man with lustrous grey eyes, delightfully courteous in manner and possessed of great charm. So strongly did he dislike disagreeable personal confrontations that an unsuspecting minister might leave an audience entranced by the Tsar's graciousness, only to find immediately afterwards that he had been dismissed from office by a decision which Nicholas was too delicate to communicate in person. But the Tsar was not deliberately deceitful, merely very polite. Nor was he vindictive towards his numerous enemies among Russian politicians, on whom he would bestow honours and pensions.[14]

Despite certain traits – including his prejudice against Jews and intellectuals – which show him less than angelic, Nicholas was in general a courtly, almost saintly sovereign who supposed that all would be for the best if he carried out what he believed to be God's will. This faith enabled him to bow his head to fate with an air of impassive resignation which sometimes incurred criticism – as after the shocking tragedy which marred the celebration of his coronation in Moscow in May 1896. A crowd of some half a million had gathered in the Khodynka Fields near the city to receive certain traditional presents from the Tsar, including mugs embellished with the imperial crest. Somehow a mass stampede occurred, and over twelve hundred people were trampled to death in about a quarter of an hour. Although the Tsar bore no responsibility for this calamity, his ill-advised attendance at a ball given by the French ambassador on the same evening wrongly branded him as indifferent to his subjects' fate.

Russia seemed generally docile at the beginning of Nicholas's reign. But behind the façade of loyalty and decorum many educated citizens of moderate political views had come to regard the Emperor and his court as an anachronism. On a more extreme level, secret revolutionary activity was gaining new momentum. The year 1898 saw the founding of the Russian Social Democratic Labour Party, forerunner of the Bolsheviks and Mensheviks; in rivalry to which Marxist organization another important revolutionary party, that of the Socialist Revolutionaries, seemed to pose a greater threat to the throne because of its appeal to the peasants who constituted some three-quarters of the population. Admittedly the peasants still appeared generally loyal to the Tsar whom they called their little father, but their ultimate potential was uncertain – hence the name 'dark people' commonly given to them. However, it was less the agitation of the dark people which brought the Socialist Revolutionaries into prominence than their revival of political assassination on a scale unprecedented in Russia. They greeted the twentieth century by shooting a minister of education, the first political murder of the reign, and their other early victims included two ministers of the interior within three years.

It was in this atmosphere of mounting tension that hostilities with Japan broke out in 1904, partly provoked by Nicholas's hesitations and willingness to accept irresponsible advice. To enthusiasts for the Russian autocracy the new war seemed to promise some relief, since a limited, victorious campaign in a distant theatre might divert attention from domestic discords. But the war proved neither victorious nor so limited in scope as expected. Although Russian patriots had calculated that a small upstart oriental nation could never match the military strength of the Slav colossus brought to the arena of conflict along the new Trans-Siberian railway, the Japanese proved too formidable an enemy. They inflicted a series of crushing defeats, including the capture of Port Arthur, and the destruction of a large Russian fleet in the Straits of Tsushima, until the Russians were glad to accept American mediation and make their peace with Japan in September 1905. This, the first modern victory of an Asiatic over a European power, seemed to prove the need for political change in St Petersburg.

The need for change was also emphasized by the first Russian revolution, that of 1905, which struck the autocracy a further blow.

The revolutionary year began with strikes and the episode of 'bloody Sunday' on 9 January when St Petersburg workers, numbering with their wives and children some two hundred thousand, began to converge on the Winter Palace to witness the presentation of a petition to the Tsar by the priest and trade-union leader Father Gapon. The demonstrators seemed loyal, since they bore icons and portraits of the Tsar while singing hymns and patriotic songs. Gapon's petition too was effusively loyalist in tone, yet called for a capitulation by the autocracy, since the main demand was for a constituent assembly – that is, for a body to draw up a constitution to replace the autocracy. But Gapon did not succeed in presenting his petition as planned. He had given the authorities advance notice of his demonstration, with the result that troops were posted to block the approaches to the Palace. Soldiers fired as the crowds tried to pass, and mounted Cossacks charged the people. Nevertheless, some demonstrators did penetrate the Palace Square, where the massacre continued – over a hundred people being killed in all, even according to official figures. The Tsar was not in residence, and it is impossible to hold him directly responsible; but the episode helped to earn him the nickname of Nicholas the Bloody – though he probably deserved the epithet less than any other Tsar.

Disorders followed in many parts of the country. Strikes spread until nearly half a million workers were out by the end of January, and the following month saw the assassination by a Socialist Revolutionary of the Tsar's uncle, the Grand Duke Sergey. Revolutionary unrest continued on an increasing scale in the summer with further strikes and many peasant riots. Persuaded to consider political concessions, Nicholas instructed his minister of the interior to draw up a plan for a State Duma – conceived as an elected consultative assembly to examine future legislation – but the plan turned out so modest in scope that it only inflamed public unrest. Further strikes and armed clashes between workers and police broke out in Moscow in September, and developed on such a scale that they seemed to threaten the imperial system. The entire railway network came to a standstill, and a general strike swept the empire. October also saw the establishment in St Petersburg of the Soviet of Workers' Deputies dominated by Trotsky, which was eventually to give a name to a new Russian political system. In this atmosphere of revolutionary upheaval the Tsar agreed to proclaim widespread political concessions, and signed on 17 October a manifesto promising the country extensive civil rights. They included inviolability of the person, freedom of speech, conscience, assembly and association, and a considerable extension of the powers of the projected State Duma, which was to sanction all future legislation and to be elected on a democratic franchise.

Strictly speaking, the Russian autocracy ceased to exist with the publication of the manifesto of 17 October 1905.[15] But when the time came to redeem the pledges of October, revolutionary pressure had subsided. The Tsar and government therefore felt able to reduce their concessions, as they did by the fundamental laws issued in April 1906 and other enactments. A State Duma was indeed set up, and did indeed receive legislative powers, being entitled to revise and repeal existing laws, and also to propose and sanction new measures. But these rights would have been more impressive had not the Duma's decisions been made subject to veto by the sovereign, who was also free to dissolve it at will. Nor could the Duma bring down the government, for though it had the right to interrogate and censure ministers, it had no control over them whatever. The Tsar continued, as before, to appoint and dismiss them, including the prime minister – that is, the president of the council of ministers, a co-ordinating body now set up to function as the government. But though he now had a kind of prime minister, a kind of cabinet and a kind of parliament, it is significant that Nicholas officially retained the title of autocrat and most of an autocrat's powers, though he had also become, to however limited a degree, a constitutional monarch. As for the complex system by which the Duma members were elected, this was never fully democratic, and it became less so in course of time. But despite restrictions on their work, Duma members did use their legislative powers to some effect in the spheres of education, peasant affairs, local government, labour conditions and defence. Not being subject to censorship, their criticism of the government was outspoken, and received wide publicity. The Duma thereby exercised a certain influence on policy too, despised though it has understandably been as a home of idle chatter.

From 1906 to 1911 the office of prime minister was held by Stolypin, most influential politician to occupy that position during the twelve years of the Dumas' existence. He combined a reforming policy with ruthless efforts to strengthen the monarchic power, as seemed particularly necessary in a situation of continuing violence. So common had political assassination now become that during the years 1906–07 over four thousand persons, chiefly imperial officials, were murdered by terrorists.[16] Stolypin retaliated by setting up courts martial empowered to dispense summary justice, with the result that nearly seven hundred persons were executed in eight months. To governmental and left-wing violence were added hundreds of pogroms and various other outrages perpetrated by the Black Hundreds and other disreputable monarchist organizations of the extreme right.

Determined to ensure the election of a more docile Duma in 1907, Stolypin contravened the fundamental laws by imposing new electoral arrangements – a high-handed measure equivalent to a *coup d'état*. As the result of this intervention, the Third and Fourth Dumas, covering the period 1907 to 1917, were more conservative in composition than the first two. Even so they were far from servile or silent, and continued to act as a sounding-board for political dissidence while cut off from real political power. The Duma also formed a particularly suitable stage for the development of the *skandal* – as when the flamboyant Purishkevich, a deputy of the far right, once appeared sporting a red carnation in his flies.[17]

Meanwhile revolutionary fervour had subsided, and the country lapsed into comparative political apathy. But despite numerous continuing restrictions, a greater measure of freedom existed in Russia in the last decade of Nicholas's reign than at any other time under the Tsars – and this despite the common practice of describing the period as one of reaction triumphant. Russia also progressed economically in the aftermath of 1905. If increasing personal freedom and individual prosperity are criteria of good government, Nicholas II's post-1905 administration deserves more credit than it has generally received, even if it is impossible to rate the autocrat's own contribution very high. Nor is it easy to judge how much Russia did or did not owe to Stolypin, whom in 1911 a certain Dmitry Bogrov – agent both of the police and of a revolutionary party – assassinated in the Tsar's presence at a gala performance in the Kiev opera house. It is typical of this period of *agents provocateurs*, and of the intensive penetration of police by revolutionaries and of revolutionary parties by police informers, that the killer's affiliations are still obscure, and were possibly not clear even to the man himself.

The outbreak of war with Germany in the summer of 1914 rallied public opinion round the autocracy. St Petersburg was now renamed in native style, becoming Petrograd. The Tsar himself felt more in his element and busied himself with military duties, visiting the fronts and inspecting the troops. But encouragement by the monarch could not compensate for inferior equipment, training, command and supply, and the first year of the war brought heavy defeats together with the loss of strategic areas on the Russian western front. In August 1915, at a particularly low point in Russia's military fortunes, Nicholas aroused severe criticism by assuming supreme command over the armed forces – a hazardous move for the autocracy, since from now onwards the autocrat's own person would be identified with any further disasters. But the Tsar insisted, while leaving the actual conduct of military operations to his experienced chief of staff.

Russian military fortunes improved under the new supreme commander, but the domestic position of the autocracy deteriorated. By now Nicholas's devotion to his wife was proving an ever graver handicap. As a former German princess, she was an enemy alien by origin, while her increasing capricious interference in Russian governmental appointments and high policy became a public scandal – even if the exact extent of her influence remains a matter of dispute. She caused further scandal by her continued close association with Gregory Rasputin, most notorious among the picturesque charlatans and religious cranks whom she had long encouraged. This unsavoury and dissolute peasant, the consort of prostitutes and society ladies, professed the doctrine that sexual intercourse offers a short cut to sanctity, and practised his own teachings on so impressive a scale that rumour began to whisper, however absurdly, of improper relations between him and the Empress herself. But Rasputin's real hold over that pious gentlewoman came through her son, the Tsarevich Alexis, who had inherited through her the disease of haemophilia. Since the slightest scratch or bruise might prove fatal to the boy, Rasputin's ability to stop his bleeding through hypnosis appeared to give this most bizarre of all imperial favourites unlimited power over an entire empire. There was talk of a 'Rasputin circle' or 'black bloc' of 'dark forces' surrounding the Empress, and she was also believed to be negotiating with her German relatives a separate peace disastrous to Russian interests.

This tissue of gossip gained wide belief in political circles of the capital, and also reached the masses, who added 'Down with the German woman' to the numerous slogans of the period. Alexandra was not in fact conspiring with the enemy, nor was there any black bloc or Rasputin circle, while the political influence of the nefarious homespun seer was generally overestimated. Nevertheless, the odour of unholiness emanating from Rasputin remained a powerful factor in discrediting the autocracy – so much so that it was among monarchists of a sort that the plot to assassinate him arose in December 1916. Rasputin took an unconscionable deal of killing – and only succumbed after Prince Felix Yusupov had fed him poisoned cakes and wine, shot him with a revolver and finally helped to push him under the ice of the Neva. But the monster's death seemed to leave the political situation little changed.

Although revolutionary extremists were active to some extent during this period, an impressive subversive role also fell to certain liberals of the Duma. They felt understandably frustrated, being denied influence on the conduct of the war by a government which enjoyed little repute. The sheer quantity of sudden dismissals and new appointments to the ministries in 1916 was alone enough to suggest that the Tsar was leading Russia into chaos and military defeat. Moreover, some of the ministers concerned were demonstrably incompetent or even deranged, though it is by no means certain that their critics in the Duma were themselves on average better fitted for the conduct of affairs. Criticism of the autocracy in the Duma reached its peak with the scandalous speech delivered on 1 November 1916 by the liberal leader Paul Milyukov, who quoted in German words from an Austrian newspaper calculated to suggest that the Empress Alexandra was guilty of treason, as had long been falsely rumoured. This speech was distributed in thousands of copies, and contributed to general disillusionment with the monarchy on the eve of its downfall.

The fall of the house of Romanov occurred suddenly in the course of the nine-day revolution of 23 February to 3 March 1917. Not a *coup d'état* staged by Bolshevik or other conspirators, the February Revolution came about more through the collapse of imperial authority than through any co-ordinated plan by revolutionaries to overthrow the Tsars at this particular moment in time. The upheaval involved a confused interplay of events between the main area, Petrograd, the army supreme headquarters in Mogilyov, where the Tsar began the nine-day crisis, and the northern headquarters where he ended it.

On 23 February, civil disturbances broke out in Petrograd with riots provoked by local bread shortages. Angry citizens demanded bread and shouted 'Down with the autocracy', their ranks swelled by strikers and workers locked out of the large Putilov works after an industrial dispute. The strike movement in the capital grew rapidly until, on 25 February, there was a general stoppage of work and many of the strikers were out on the streets and squares among those shouting slogans, and displaying placards and red banners. But though these disturbances grew rowdier and there was some throwing of stones and chunks of ice, troops and Cossacks did not attack the crowds, and the situation still seemed under control. Such episodes had occurred in Petrograd before.

It was on 26 February that a new and far more dangerous phase began with the more active involvement of the military in the continuing street disorders. On the previous evening the Tsar had telegraphed from Mogilyov to the commander of the Petrograd Military District, ordering him to suppress the riots as inadmissible in time of war. Some soldiers did now obey orders, firing on the rioters and killing a number of people. But others fraternized with the crowds or openly mutinied, shooting several officers. Mobs with strikers and army deserters among them broke into the arsenals and the Peter and Paul Fortress, most celebrated bastion of Tsarism.

As the Emperor was just about to leave Mogilyov for the capital, the imperial government – that is, the council of ministers – collapsed. It held its last meeting on the night of 27–8 February, after which it dispersed, never to meet again. Members of the State Duma now defied a prorogation order issued in the Tsar's absence, and set up in the Tauris Palace a provisional committee – the origin of the provisional government which was to rule Russia until the Bolshevik seizure of power in October of the same year. On the same day, 28 February, the nucleus of a Soviet (later to be called the Soviet of Workers' and Soldiers' Deputies) was established, also in the Tauris Palace, and was to coexist in uneasy rivalry with the provisional government for the next eight months. It was not clear exactly who now held power in Russia, but it was abundantly clear that sovereignty in the seething capital city no longer rested with the Tsar – though it must be added that serious disturbances were confined to Petrograd and Moscow, the rest of the country remaining quiet.

By no means fully aware of the march of events, the Emperor had left Mogilyov by train in the small hours of 28 February to return to his palace at Tsarskoye Selo near Petrograd, where his children were suffering from measles. It thus came about that while the monarchy was slipping to its doom, the monarch himself was on the move, imperfectly informed of developments in his capital over the railway telegraph system. Forced to approach Petrograd by a lengthy detour, he reached a point about a hundred miles to the south-east early on 1 March, only to learn that the line ahead of him was in revolutionary hands. He therefore decided to turn back and make for Pskov, about a hundred and fifty miles south-west of Petrograd – seemingly a safe haven, since it was the northern headquarters of the Russian army.

By this time, however, some of Nicholas's own generals felt that the Tsar must make immediate sweeping political concessions. After a long discussion in Pskov with General Ruzsky, commander-in-chief of the northern front, Nicholas gave way and telegraphed his permission for the president of the Duma to form a government – that is, to appoint ministers, which had hitherto been the Tsar's exclusive prerogative. This arrangement did not envisage abdication. But the time for such a drastic concession seemed to have come when messages reached Pskov on 2 March from certain senior generals who politely indicated that they wished the Tsar to renounce his throne immediately in favour of the Tsarevich Alexis with the Grand Duke Michael (Nicholas's brother) as regent. These expressions of opinion probably provided the last impulse which broke Nicholas's resistance to the idea of abdication. He was in any case so dedicated to the concept of absolutism that he felt happier to renounce his throne entirely than to function as a mere figurehead – powerless, but still (as he believed) responsible to God for the mistakes of others.

On the afternoon of 2 March, and in the imperial train now standing on a siding in Pskov, the last Tsar took the momentous decision to relinquish his throne. Consulting his doctor, who confirmed that there was no hope of a cure for the Tsarevich Alexis, Nicholas decided not to burden the ailing boy with the succession. The crown should go direct to the Grand Duke Michael instead, and it was an instrument of abdication drawn up in this sense that Nicholas signed in the presence of two Duma emissaries newly arrived from Petrograd. However, the grand duke declined the dangerous office of Tsar, a decision which brought the end of the Romanovs as a ruling dynasty on 3 March 1917. It also put an end to the ancient Russian monarchy founded according to official doctrine by Ryurik more than a thousand years previously.

On the day of his abdication, Nicholas bore himself with his usual imperturbable self-control, and some observers therefore judged him unfeeling and insensitive – which was far from the case.[18] After signing his empire away, the ex-Tsar paid a last visit to supreme headquarters in Mogilyov to take farewell of his army. Citizen Nicholas Romanov was then removed in custody to his palace at Tsarskoye Selo, there to await the further dispositions of the provisional government which was to exercise imperfect control over Russia until overthrown by the Bolsheviks.

Confined to their own palace at Tsarskoye Selo, the ex-Tsar and his family at first enjoyed fairly favourable conditions marred by the occasional rudeness of their more revolutionary-minded custodians. It was a severe blow – and an evil omen for their future – when they learnt that the British government had decided to withdraw a promise previously made of political asylum. As is now known, Nicholas's cousin King George v himself initiated the move to deny refuge in England to the imperial Russian family.[19] Meanwhile it was becoming impossible for the Romanovs to remain indefinitely only fifteen miles from the disturbed capital of revolutionary Russia; such at any rate was the view of Alexander Kerensky, prime minister in the provisional government, who decided to send them to the governor's mansion at Tobolsk in western Siberia.[20] They left Tsarskoye Selo secretly by train in August.

The ex-Tsar and his family bore their imprisonment calmly. Always a devoted husband and father, Nicholas may even have been happier after his abdication than before; cutting firewood and reading to his children, he seemed to have found a truer vocation than the throne. But the captives' lot grew worse, particularly after news of the October Bolshevik Revolution reached Tobolsk in November 1917. The Romanovs were put on soldiers' rations and housed in growing discomfort, and their guards began to treat them with less ceremony than ever. Matters took a further turn for the worse after the imperial family had been conveyed from Tobolsk to Yekaterinburg (now Sverdlovsk) in the Urals. They were held in a dwelling ominously renamed 'the house of special purpose', and subjected to irksome confinement. The Tsar's daughters had to sleep on the floor, and their guards showed their revolutionary zeal by accompanying the young girls to the lavatory and making obscene remarks, as if anxious to leave no doubt that the century of the common man had indeed arrived.

By now civil war had broken out between Reds and Whites, and advancing anti-Bolshevik forces were threatening to capture Yekaterinburg. Few Whites wanted to restore the monarchy, but the disadvantages of allowing the enemy to free Nicholas and his son were evident to the Bolshevik leaders, who planned accordingly. Although it once seemed that the decision to liquidate Nicholas and his entire family was taken locally, the claim is made in Trotsky's recently published diary that it was Lenin himself who ordered the massacre from Moscow. Lenin believed (according to the leading Bolshevik Sverdlov, as reported by Trotsky) that 'we should not leave the Whites a live banner to rally round'.[21]

The vault in the Cathedral of St Peter and St Paul in Leningrad (St Petersburg), where all Emperors and Empresses of the House of Romanov are buried, from Peter the Great onwards, except Peter ii, together with their consorts and children.

The chief role in the physical elimination of the Romanovs went to a minor Siberian Communist, Yurovsky, who was aided by a small squad of Latvian and other Bolshevik political police. At midnight on 16–17 July 1918, they roused the ex-Tsar and his family and ordered them downstairs. Nicholas himself carried his sick son, accompanied by his wife Alexandra, their four daughters, their doctor and three servants. The eleven victims seemed calm and unsuspicious as Yurovsky began to mumble his intention of executing them . . . then suddenly shot his former Emperor at point blank range. Alexis fell with him. Guards fired their revolvers at the other members of the household and finished them off with bayonets. The Tsaritsa's maid frantically tried to defend herself with a cushion, and the room flowed with blood and echoed with shrieks.

Yurovsky took the corpses by truck to a disused mine about thirteen miles away where his assistants hacked them to pieces, partially destroyed them with vast quantities of acid and burnt them with petrol. They threw such remains as survived this treatment down a mine shaft, from which some grim relics were recovered after White forces had captured Yekaterinburg on 25 July and begun to investigate the massacre of the last Russian Emperor and his family.

Such was the brutal and sordid finale to three centuries and seven decades of rule – itself often brutal and sordid in its details – by the Tsars who had begun their history with lavish ritual splendour when, in 1547, Ivan the Terrible was crowned in the Uspensky Cathedral in Moscow.

Notes

For fuller details of works to which reference is made, see Bibliography.

PART 1 [pages 23–80]

1 Kurbsky-Ivan *Correspondence*, p. 74.
2 Kurbsky, *History of Ivan IV*, p. 10.
3 Cited in Zimin, *Reformy Ivana Groznogo*, p. 267.
4 Kurbsky-Ivan *Correspondence*, p. 81.
5 Karamzin, vol. viii, pp. 95–6.
6 Barbour, pp. 307–09.
7 Cited in Brewster, pp. 13–14.
8 Zimin, *Reformy Ivana Groznogo*, p. 65.
9 Solovyov, vol. iii, p. 435.
10 Kurbsky, *History of Ivan IV*, p. 16.
11 Kurbsky-Ivan *Correspondence*, p. 25, footnote.
12 Zimin, *Reformy Ivana Groznogo*, p. 316.
13 Kurbsky, *History of Ivan IV*, p. 18.
14 Skrynnikov, p. 96.
15 Stökl, p. 242.
16 Riasanovsky, *History of Russia*, p. 157.
17 Karamzin, vol. ix, p. 22.
18 Kurbsky, *History of Ivan IV*, p. 180, footnote.
19 Ibid., p. 180.
20 Ivan, *Poslaniya*, p. 213.
21 Ibid., p. 142.
22 Karamzin, vol. ix, p. 78.
23 Zimin, *Oprichnina Ivana Groznogo*, p. 304.
24 Karamzin, vol. ix, pp. 156–7.
25 Zimin, *Oprichnina Ivana Groznogo*, pp. 438–9.
26 Kurbsky, *History of Ivan IV*, p. 289.
27 Veselovsky, p. 25.
28 Fletcher, ed. Schmidt, p. 91.
29 Solovyov, vol. iii, pp. 620–1.
30 Hakluyt, vol. i, p. 256.
31 Graham, *Ivan the Terrible*, p. 231.
32 Solovyov, vol. iii, p. 592.
33 Kurbsky-Ivan *Correspondence*, pp. 245–6, footnote.
34 Yevreinov, pp. 46–7.
35 Kurbsky, *History of Ivan IV*, p. 198.
36 Karamzin, vol. ix, p. 351.
37 Waliszewski, *Ivan the Terrible*, pp. 263 ff.
38 Klyuchevsky, vol. ii, p. 190.
39 Fletcher (Cambridge, Mass. edition), p. 110.
40 Zabelin, vol. ii, p. 465.
41 Rimscha, p. 201.
42 Solovyov, vol. iv, p. 352.
43 Platonov, *Ocherki po istorii smuty v Moskovskom gosudarstve XVI–XVII vv.*, p. 172.
44 Barbour, pp. 321–7.
45 Barbour, p. 358.

PART 2 [pages 81–106]

1 Solovyov, vol. v, p. 9.
2 Platonov, *Lektsii po russkoy istorii*, p. 320.
3 Ibid., p. 335.
4 Neubauer, p. 47.
5 Zabelin, vol. ii, p. 239.
6 Solovyov, vol. v, p. 128.
7 Collins, pp. 44–5.
8 Ibid., p. 110.
9 Klyuchevsky, vol. iii, pp. 323–4.
10 Kotoshikhin, quoted in Zabelin, vol. i, p. 317.
11 Zabelin, vol. ii, p. 450.
12 Collins, p. 63.
13 Zabelin, vol. ii, p. 259.
14 Solovyov, vol. v, p. 483.
15 Platonov, *Lektsii po russkoy istorii*, p. 404.
16 Florinsky, *Russia: a History and an Interpretation*, vol. i, pp. 277 and 283.
17 Neubauer, p. 152.
18 Ibid., p. 170.
19 Zabelin, vol. i, p. 230.
20 Barbour, p. 142.
21 Zabelin, vol. i, p. 319.

22 Solovyov, vol. vii, p. 250.
23 Waliszewski, *Le Berceau d'une dynastie: les premiers Romanov*, p. 532.

PART 3 [pages 115–160]

1 Solovyov, vol. vii, pp. 567.
2 Wittram, vol. i, pp. 177–8.
3 Ibid., pp. 105 and 270.
4 Waliszewski, *Peter the Great*, p. 106.
5 Klyuchevsky, vol. iv, pp. 37–8.
6 Waliszewski, *Peter the Great*, p. 153.
7 Solovyov, vol. ix, p. 141.
8 Ibid., pp. 157–60.
9 Solovyov, vol. ix, p. 128.
10 Yevreinov, p. 48.
11 Golikova, pp. 14–15.
12 Wittram, vol. ii, p. 501.

PART 4 [pages 161–213]

1 Rimscha, p. 311.
2 Florinsky, *Russia: a History and an Interpretation*, vol. i, p. 452.
3 Waliszewski, *L'Héritage de Pierre le Grand*, p. 335.
4 Bilbasov, vol. ii, p. 335.
5 Solovyov, vol. xi, p. 140.
6 Waliszewski, *La dernière des Romanov*, p. 16.
7 Solovyov, vol. xi, p. 124.
8 Waliszewski, *La dernière des Romanov*, p. 72.
9 Ibid., p. 94.
10 Catherine II, *Mémoires*, p. 95.
11 Catherine II's *Mémoires*, cited in Grey, *Catherine the Great*, p. 48.
12 Grey, *Catherine the Great*, pp. 108–09.
13 Rimscha, p. 333.
14 Bilbasov, vol. ii, p. 94.
15 Ibid., vol. ii, p. 394.
16 Olga Wormser-Migot in Gaxotte, p. 204.
17 Rimscha, p. 349.
18 Grey, *Catherine the Great*, p. 150.
19 Waliszewski, *Autour d'un Trône*, p. 153.
20 Ibid., p. 429.
21 Grey, *Catherine the Great*, p. 196.

PART 5 [pages 214–258]

1 Schiemann, *Geschichte Russlands unter Kaiser Nikolaus I*, vol. i, p. 13.
2 Ibid., p. 38.
3 Waliszewski, *Paul the First of Russia: the son of Catherine the Great*, p. 106.
4 Ibid., p. 115; see also Yevreinov, pp. 87–9.
5 Schiemann, *Geschichte Russlands unter Kaiser Nikolaus I*, vol. i, p. 15.
6 For various versions of the incident, see Schiemann, *Die Ermordung Pauls und die Thronbesteigung Nikolaus I*.
7 Raeff, p. 43.
8 Waliszewski, *Le Règne d'Alexandre I-er*, vol. i, p. 175.
9 Ibid., pp. 225–6.
10 Nicholas, Grand Duke, vol. i, pp. 97–8.
11 Ibid., p. 128.
12 Nicolson, *The Congress of Vienna*, p. 250.
13 Waliszewski, *Le Règne d'Alexandre I-er*, vol. ii, p. 360.
14 Schiemann, *Geschichte Russlands unter Kaiser Nikolaus I*, vol. i, p. 498.
15 Nicholas, Grand Duke, vol. i, p. 233.
16 Raeff, p. 37.
17 Ibid., pp. 190–1.
18 Kizevetter, p. 319.
19 Vasilich, *Imperator Aleksandr I i starets Feodor Kuzmich*, p. 12.
20 Nicholas, Grand Duke, vol. i, p. 251.
21 Ibid., p. 179.
22 Shilder, *Imperator Nikolay I*, vol. i, p. 288.
23 Ibid., p. 287.
24 Gernet, vol. ii, p. 156.
25 Schiemann, *Geschichte Russlands unter Kaiser Nikolaus I*, vol. iv, p. 48.
26 Herzen, vol. i, pp. 41–2.
27 Riasanovsky, *Nicholas I and Official Nationality in Russia*, p. 20.
28 Gershenzon, p. 18.
29 Riasanovsky, *Nicholas I and Official Nationality in Russia*, p. 195.
30 Pushkin, ed. Nabokov, vol. iii, p. 112.
31 Riasanovsky, *Nicholas I and Official Nationality in Russia*, p. 202.

32 Schiemann, *Geschichte Russlands unter Kaiser Nikolaus I*, vol. ii, p. 209.

33 Custine, p. 237.

34 Schiemann, *Geschichte Russlands unter Kaiser Nikolaus I*, vol. iii, p. 146.

35 Westwood, p. 30.

36 Schiemann, *Geschichte Russlands unter Kaiser Nikolaus I*, vol. i, p. 223.

37 Shilder, *Imperator Nikolay I*, vol. ii, p. 487.

38 Ibid.

39 Yevstafyev, p. 208.

40 Riasanovsky, *Nicholas I and Official Nationality in Russia*, p. 210.

41 Gershenzon, p. 59.

42 Schiemann, *Geschichte Russlands unter Kaiser Nikolaus I*, vol. ii, p. 209.

43 Gernet, vol. ii, pp. 225–31.

44 Brodsky, p. 414.

45 Riasanovsky, *Nicholas I and Official Nationality in Russia*, p. 223.

46 P. S. Squire, 'Nicholas I and the Problems of Internal Security in Russia in 1826', Harcave, p. 338.

PART 6 [pages 259–305]

1 Mosse, p. 37.

2 Tatishchev, *Imperator Aleksandr II*, vol. i, p. 53.

3 Mosse, p. 31.

4 Herzen, vol. i, p. 206.

5 Schiemann, *Geschichte Russlands unter Kaiser Nikolaus I*, vol. iii, p. 376.

6 Ibid., p. 372.

7 Mosse, p. 36.

8 Cited in Kornilov, vol. ii, p. 137.

9 Seton-Watson, *The Russian Empire*, pp. 347–8.

10 Mosse, p. 84.

11 Cited in Kornilov, vol. iii, p. 271.

12 Daudet, pp. 3–4.

13 Florinsky, *Russia: a History and an Interpretation*, vol. ii, p. 1119.

14 Oldenburg, vol. i, pp. 39–40.

15 Karpovich, p. 74.

16 Florinsky, *Russia: a History and an Interpretation*, vol. ii, p. 1195.

17 Katkov, p. 202, footnote.

18 Ibid., p. 343.

19 Nicolson, *King George V: his Life and Reign*, pp. 299–302.

20 Kerensky, p. 336.

21 Trotsky, p. 81.

Bibliography

ALEXANDRA, Empress, *Pisma imperatritsy Aleksandry Fyodorovny k imperatoru Nikolayu II*, trans. from the English by V. D. Nabokov, 2 vols (Berlin, 1922)

ALEXIS, Tsar, *Sobraniye pisem tsarya Alekseya Mikhaylovicha*, ed. P. Bartenyev (Moscow, 1856)

BARBOUR, Philip L., *Dimitry Called the Pretender: Tsar and Great Prince of All Russia, 1605–06* (London, 1967)

BERKH, V., *Tsarstvovaniye tsarya Mikhaila Fyodorovicha i vzglyad na mezhdutsarstviye*, 2 parts (St Petersburg, 1832)

—— —— *Tsarstvovaniye tsarya Alekseya Mikhaylovicha*, 2 parts (St Petersburg, 1831)

—— —— *Tsarstvovaniye tsarya Fyodora Alekseyevicha i istoriya pervogo streletskogo bunta*, 2 parts (St Petersburg, 1834)

BILBASOV, V. A., *Istoriya Yekateriny vtoroy*, 2 vols (Berlin, 1900)

BILLINGTON, James H., *The Icon and the Axe: an Interpretative History of Russian Culture* (London, 1966)

BLUM, Jerome, *Lord and Peasant in Russia: from the Ninth to the Nineteenth Century* (New York, 1964)

BOGOSLOVSKY, M. M., *Pyotr I: materialy dlya biografii*, 5 vols (Moscow, 1940–8)

BREWSTER, Dorothy, *East-West Passage: a Study in Literary Relationships* (London, 1954)

BRODSKY, N. L., *A. S. Pushkin: biografiya* (Moscow, 1937)

BULYGIN, Paul, *The Murder of the Romanovs: the Authentic Account* (London, 1935)

BYKOV, P. M., *The Last Days of Tsardom*, trans. with preface by Andrew Rothstein (London, n.d.)

CATHERINE II, *Mémoires de Catherine II: écrits par elle-même*, with introduction by Pierre Audiat (Paris, 1953)

CHAMBERLIN, William Henry, *The Russian Revolution, 1917–21*, 2 vols (New York, 1935)

CHARQUES, Richard, *A Short History of Russia* (London, 1956)

—— —— *The Twilight of Imperial Russia* (London, 1958)

CHERNIAVSKY, Michael, *Tsar and People: Studies in Russian Myths* (New Haven, 1961)

CLARKSON, Jesse D., *A History of Russia from the Ninth Century* (London, 1962)

COLLINS, Samuel, *The Present State of Russia in a Letter to a Friend at London* (London, 1671)

CUSTINE, Marquis de, *Russia*, abridged from the French (London, 1855)

DASHKOV, Princess E. R., *Memoirs*, trans. and ed. Kyril Fitzlyon (London, 1958)

DAUDET, Ernest, *L'avant-dernier Romanoff: Alexandre III* (Paris, 1920)

DRUZHININ, N. M. and others, ed., *Absolyutizm v Rossii (XVII-XVIII vv.)* (Moscow, 1964)

FENNELL, J. L. I., *Ivan the Great of Moscow* (London, 1963)

FIGNER, Vera, *Zapechatlyonny trud* (Moscow, 1964)

FLETCHER, Giles, *Of the Rus Commonwealth*, ed. Albert J. Schmidt (Ithaca, 1966). Also published as *Of the Russe Commonwealth*, facsimile edition with variants, with an introduction by Richard Pipes (Cambridge, Mass., 1966)

FLORINSKY, Michael T., *Russia: a History and an Interpretation*, 2 vols (New York, 1947)

—— —— *The End of the Russian Empire* (New York, 1961)

FOOTMAN, David, *Red Prelude: a Life of A. I. Zhelyabov* (London, 1944)

FRANKLAND, Noble, *Crown of Tragedy: Nicholas II* (London, 1960)

FREEBORN, Richard, *A Short History of Modern Russia* (London, 1966)

GAXOTTE, Pierre and others, *Catherine de Russie* (Paris, 1966)

GERHARDI, William, *The Romanovs: Evocation of the Past as a Mirror for the Present* (London, 1940)

GERNET, M. N., *Istoriya tsarskoy tyurmy*, third edition, 5 vols (Moscow, 1960–3)

GERSHENZON, M. O., ed., *Epokha Nikolaya I* (Moscow, 1910)

GOLIKOVA, N. B., *Politicheskiye protsessy pri Petre I: po materialam Preobrazhenskogo prikaza* (Moscow, 1957)

GOLOVINE, Countess Barbara, *A Lady at the Court of Catherine II*, trans. from the French by G. M. Fox-Davies (London, 1910)

GOOCH, G. P., *Catherine the Great and Other Studies* (London, 1954)

GRAHAM, Stephen, *Ivan the Terrible: Life of Ivan IV of Russia Called the Terrible* (London, 1932)

—— —— *Boris Godunof* (London, 1933)

—— —— *Tsar of Freedom: the Life and Reign of Alexander II* (New Haven, 1935)

GREY, Ian, *Ivan the Terrible* (London, 1964)

—— —— *Peter the Great* (London, 1962)

—— —— *Catherine the Great: Autocrat and Empress of All Russia* (London, 1961)

—— —— *The First Fifty Years: Soviet Russia, 1917–67* (London, 1967)

GURKO, V. I., *Features and Figures of the Past: Government and Opinion in the Reign of Nicholas II* (Stanford, 1939)

HAKLUYT, Richard, *The Principal Navigations, Voyages, Traffiques and Discoveries of the English Nation*, 8 vols (London, 1939)

HARCAVE, Sidney, *Readings in Russian History, vol. i: from Ancient Times to the Abolition of Serfdom* (New York, 1962)

HERBERSTEIN, Sigismund von, *Notes upon Russia*, trans. and ed. R. H. Major, 2 vols (London, 1851–2)

HERZEN, A. I., *Byloye i dumy*, 2 vols (Minsk, 1957)

HINGLEY, Ronald, *Nihilists* (London, 1967)

IVAN IV, Tsar, *Poslaniya Ivana Groznogo*, ed. V. P. Adrianova-Peretts (Moscow-Leningrad, 1951)

KARAMZIN, N. M., *Istoriya gosudarstva Rossyskago*, 12 vols (St Petersburg, 1852–3)

KARPOVICH, Michael, *Imperial Russia, 1801–1917* (New York, 1932)

KATKOV, George, *Russia 1917: the February Revolution* (London, 1967)

KERENSKY, Alexander, *The Kerensky Memoirs: Russia and History's Turning Point* (London, 1966)

KIZEVETTER, A. A., 'Imperator Aleksandr I i Arakcheyev', *Istoricheskiye ocherki* (Moscow, 1912)

KLYUCHEVSKY, V. O., *Sochineniya*, 8 vols (Moscow, 1956–9)

KOCHAN, Lionel, *The Making of Modern Russia* (London, 1962)

—— —— *Russia in Revolution, 1890–1918* (London, 1966)

KORFF, Baron von, *Die Thronbesteigung des Kaisers Nicolaus I* (Frankfurt a. M., 1857)

KORNILOV, A., *Kurs istorii Rossii XIX veka*, 3 vols (Moscow, 1918)

KOSLOW, Jules, *Ivan the Terrible* (London, 1961)

KOSTOMAROV, N. I., *Russkaya istoriya v zhizneopisaniyakh yeya glavneyshikh deyateley*, 3 vols (St Petersburg, n.d.)

KOTOSHIKHIN, G., *O Rossii v tsarstvovaniye Alekseya Mikhaylovicha* (St Petersburg, 1884)

KURBSKY, A. M., *Prince A. M. Kurbsky's History of Ivan IV*, ed. with a translation and notes by J. L. I. Fennell (Cambridge, 1965)

KURBSKY, A. M. and IVAN IV, Tsar, *The Correspondence between Prince A. M. Kurbsky and Tsar Ivan IV of Russia, 1564–79*, ed. with a translation and notes by J. L. I. Fennell (Cambridge, 1955)

LEROY-BEAULIEU, A., *L'Empire des Tsars et les Russes*, 3 vols (Paris, 1881–9)

MACKENZIE WALLACE, D., *Russia*, third edition (London, 1877)

MAZOUR, Anatole G., *The First Russian Revolution, 1825: the Decembrist Movement* (Stanford, 1961)

MELGUNOV, S., *Sudba imperatora Nikolaya II posle otrecheniya: istoriko-kriticheskiye ocherki* (Paris, 1951)

MILIOUKOV, Paul, SEIGNOBOS, C. and EISENMANN, L., *Histoire de Russie*, 3 vols (Paris, 1932–3)

MONAS, Sidney, *The Third Section: Police and Society in Russia under Nicholas I* (Cambridge, Mass., 1961)

MOSSE, W. E., *Alexander II and the Modernization of Russia* (London, 1958)

NEUBAUER, Helmut, *Car und Selbstherrscher: Beiträge zur Geschichte der Autokratie in Russland* (Wiesbaden, 1964)

NICHOLAS II, Tsar, *Journal intime de Nicholas II, 1890–1917* (extracts), trans. into French by A. Pierre (Paris, 1925)

—— —— *The Letters of the Tsar to the Tsaritsa, 1914–17*, trans. A. L. Hynes (London, 1929)

—— —— *The Letters of Tsar Nicholas and Empress Marie*, ed. Edward J. Bing (London, 1937)

NICHOLAS, Grand Duke, *Imperator Aleksandr I: opyt istoricheskogo issledovaniya*, 2 vols (St Petersburg, 1912)

NICOLSON, Harold, *The Congress of Vienna: a Study in Allied Unity, 1812–22* (London, 1946)

—— —— *King George V: his Life and Reign* (New York, 1953)

NISBET BAIN, R., *The Pupils of Peter the Great* (London, 1897)

—— —— *The Daughter of Peter the Great* (London, 1899)

—— —— *Peter III: Emperor of Russia* (London, 1902)

OLDENBOURG, Zoé, *Catherine the Great*, trans. Anne Carter (London, 1965)

OLDENBURG, S. S., *Tsarstvovaniye imperatora Nikolaya II*, 2 vols (Belgrade, 1939)

PALÉOLOGUE, Maurice, *The Enigmatic Czar: Alexander I of Russia*, trans. Edwin and Willa Muir (London, 1938)

—— —— *Aleksandr II i knyaginya Yuryevskaya* (Petrograd, 1924)

—— —— *La Russie des tsars pendant la guerre*, 3 vols (Paris, 1921–3)

PALMER, W., *The Patriarch and the Tsar*, 6 vols (London, 1871–6)

PARES, B., *A History of Russia*, revised edition (London, 1955)

—— —— *The Fall of the Russian Monarchy* (New York, 1939)

PLATONOV, S. F., *Ocherki po istorii smuty v Moskovskom gosudarstve XVI–XVII vv.* (Moscow, 1937)

—— —— *Lektsii po russkoy istorii* (Petrograd, 1917)

—— —— *History of Russia*, trans. E. Aronsberg (London, 1925)

POLIYEVKTOV, M., *Nikolay I: biografiya i obzor tsarstvovaniya* (Moscow, 1918)

PRESNYAKOV, A. Ye., *Apogey samoderzhaviya: Nikolay I* (Leningrad, 1925)

PUSHKIN, A. S., *Eugene Onegin: a Novel in Verse*, ed. V. Nabokov, 4 vols (New York, 1964)

RAEFF, Marc, *Michael Speransky: Statesman of Imperial Russia, 1772–1839* (The Hague, 1957)

RAPPOPORT, A. S., *The Curse of the Romanovs: a Study of the Lives and the Reigns of Two Tsars, Paul I and Alexander I of Russia, 1754–1825* (London, 1907)

RIASANOVSKY, Nicholas V., *Nicholas I and Official Nationality in Russia, 1825–55* (Berkeley, 1959)

—— —— *A History of Russia* (New York, 1963)

RIMSCHA, Hans von, *Geschichte Russlands* (Wiesbaden, n.d.)

ROBINSON, Geroid T., *Rural Russia under the Old Régime* (New York, 1949)

SCHIEMANN, Theodor, *Die Ermordung Pauls und die Thronbesteigung Nikolaus I* (Berlin, 1902)

—— —— *Geschichte Russlands unter Kaiser Nikolaus I*, 4 vols (Berlin, 1904–19)

SCHWARZ, Solomon M., *The Russian Revolution of 1905: the Workers' Movement and the Formation of Bolshevism and Menshevism* (Chicago, 1967)

SEMYONOV, Yuri, *Siberia: its Conquest and Development*, trans. from the German by J. R. Foster (London, 1963)

SETON-WATSON, Hugh, *The Decline of Imperial Russia, 1855–1914* (London, 1952)

—— —— *The Russian Empire, 1801–1917* (Oxford, 1967)

SHCHOGOLEV, P. Ye., *Duel i smert Pushkina: issledovaniye i materialy* (Moscow-Leningrad, 1928)

—— —— (compiler) *Petrashevtsy v vospominaniyakh sovremennikov: sbornik materialov* (Moscow-Leningrad, 1926)

SHILDER, N. K., *Imperator Pavel I* (St Petersburg, 1901)

—— —— *Imperator Aleksandr I: yego zhizn i tsarstvovaniye*, 4 vols (St Petersburg, 1904–05)

—— —— *Imperator Nikolay I: yego zhizn i tsarstvovaniye*, 2 vols (St Petersburg, 1903)

SHUKMAN, Harold, *Lenin and the Russian Revolution* (London, 1966)

SHUMIGORSKY, Ye. S., *Imperator Pavel I: zhizn i tsarstvovaniye* (St Petersburg, 1907)

SKRYNNIKOV, R. G., *Nachalo oprichniny* (Leningrad, 1966)

SMIRNOV, I. I., *Ocherki politicheskoy istorii russkogo gosudarstva 30–50 kh godov XVI veka* (Moscow-Leningrad, 1958)

SOKOLOV, N., *Ubystvo tsarskoy semyi* (Berlin, 1925)

SOLOVYOV, S. M., *Istoriya Rossii s drevneyshikh vremyon*, 15 vols (Moscow, 1959–66)

SPIRIDOVITCH, Alexandre, *Les Dernières Années de la cour de Tzarskoïe Selo, 1910–14*, trans. from the Russian by M. Jeanson (Paris, 1928–9)

STADEN, Heinrich von, *Aufzeichnungen über den Moskauer Staat*, ed. F. Epstein (Hamburg, 1930)

STÄHLIN, Karl, *Geschichte Russlands: von den Anfängen bis zur Gegenwart*, 4 vols (Berlin, 1923–39)

STÖKL, Günther, *Russische Geschichte: von den Anfängen bis zur Gegenwart* (Stuttgart, 1965)

SUMNER, B. H., *Survey of Russian History* (London, 1944)

—— —— *Peter the Great and the Emergence of Russia* (London, 1951)

TATISHCHEV, S. S., *Imperator Nikolay I i inostrannyye dvory* (St Petersburg, 1899)

—— —— *Imperator Aleksandr II: yego zhizn i tsarstvovaniye*, 2 vols (St Petersburg, 1903)

TROTSKY, L. D., *Trotsky's Diary in Exile, 1935* (Cambridge, Mass., 1953)

TUPPER, Harmon, *To the Great Ocean: Siberia and the Trans-Siberian Railway* (London, 1965)

TYUTCHEVA, A. F., *Pri dvore dvukh imperatorov*, ed. S. V. Bakhrushin and Ye. V. Gerye (Moscow, 1929)

ULAM, Adam B., *Lenin and the Bolsheviks: the Intellectual and Political History of the Triumph of Communism in Russia* (London, 1966)

UTECHIN, S. V., *Everyman's Concise Encyclopaedia of Russia* (London, 1961)

—— —— *Russian Political Thought: a Concise History* (New York, 1964)

VASILICH, G., *Imperator Aleksandr I i starets Feodor Kuzmich: po vospominaniyam sovremennikov i dokumentam* (Moscow, n.d.)

—— —— *Vosshestviye na prestol imperatora Nikolaya I*, 2 parts (Moscow, 1909)

VENTURI, Franco, *Roots of Revolution: a History of the Populist and Socialist Movements in Nineteenth-century Russia*, trans. from the Italian by Francis Haskell (London, 1960)

VERNADSKY, George, *A History of Russia*, latest revised edition (New Haven, 1961)

Veselovsky, S. B., *Issledovaniya po istorii oprichniny* (Moscow, 1963)

Vipper, R. Yu., *Ivan Grozny* (Moscow, 1922)

Viroubova, Anna, *Journal secret d'Anna Viroubova, 1909–17*, trans. from the Russian by M. Vaneix (Paris, 1928)

Voyeykov, V. N., *S tsaryom i bez tsarya* (Helsingfors, 1936)

Waliszewski, K., *Ivan le Terrible* (Paris, 1904); trans. by Lady Mary Loyd as *Ivan the Terrible* (Hamden, Conn., 1966)

—— —— *La Crise révolutionnaire, 1584–1614*, 2 vols (Paris, 1906)

—— —— *Le Berceau d'une dynastie: les premiers Romanov, 1613–1682* (Paris, 1909)

—— —— *Pierre le Grand: l'éducation, l'homme, l'œuvre* (Paris, 1914); trans. from the French by Lady Mary Loyd as *Peter the Great* (1898)

—— —— *L'Héritage de Pierre le Grand: règne des femmes, gouvernement des favoris, 1725–41* (Paris, 1900)

—— —— *La dernière des Romanov: Elizabeth I-re, Impératrice de Russie, 1741–61* (Paris, 1902)

—— —— *La Russie du temps d'Elisabeth I-re, dernière des Romanov* (Paris, 1933)

—— —— *Autour d'un Trône : Catherine II de Russie* (Paris, 1913)

—— —— *Le Roman d'une Impératrice: Catherine II de Russie* (Paris, 1893)

—— —— *Syn velikoy Yekateriny: imperator Pavel I* (St Petersburg, 1914); English version, *Paul the First of Russia: the Son of Catherine the Great* (London, 1913)

—— —— *Le Règne d'Alexandre I-er*, 3 vols (Paris, 1923–5)

Westwood, J. N., *A History of Russian Railways* (London, 1964)

Willan, T. S., *The Early History of the Muscovy Company, 1553–1603* (Manchester, 1956)

Wittram, Reinhard, *Peter I: Czar und Kaiser: zur Geschichte Peters des Groszen in seiner Zeit*, 2 vols (Göttingen, 1964)

Woolfe, Bertram D., *Three who made a Revolution: a Biographical History* (London, 1956)

Yarmolinsky, Avrahm, *Road to Revolution: a Century of Russian Radicalism* (London, 1957)

Yevreinov, N., *Istoriya telesnykh nakazany v Rossii* (St Petersburg, n.d.)

Yevstafyev, P. P., *Vosstaniye voyennykh poselyan Novgorodskoy gubernii v 1831 g.* (Moscow, 1934)

Zabelin, I. Ye., *Domashny byt russkogo naroda*, 2 vols (Moscow, 1872)

Zaozersky, A. I., *Tsar Aleksey Mikhaylovich v svoyom khozyaystve* (Petrograd, 1917)

Zayonchkovsky, P. A., *Krizis samoderzhaviya na rubezhe 1870–1880-kh godov* (Moscow, 1964)

Zimin, A. A., *Reformy Ivana Groznogo* (Moscow, 1960)

—— —— *Oprichnina Ivana Groznogo* (Moscow, 1964)

Index

The main reference to each Tsar is shown in italic figures

315